Distributive Justice and the New Medicine

To Judge Guido Calabresi, Eric A. Dubelier, Esquire, Dean Veryl V. Miles, Nancy J.M. Palermo, Esquire, Judge Richard A. Posner, Victor P. Smith, Esquire, Justice Frank Sullivan, Jr., and Professor Sir David G.T. Williams and Lady Williams, with enduring gratitude for their unwavering friendship, inspiration, and support during my pilgrimage

Distributive Justice and the New Medicine

George P. Smith, II

Professor of Law, The Catholic University of America Law School, Washington, D.C., USA

Edward Elgar

Cheltenham, UK • Northampton, MA, USA

Published by
Edward Elgar Publishing Limited
Glensanda House
Montpellier Parade
Cheltenham
Glos GL50 1UA
UK

Edward Elgar Publishing, Inc.
William Pratt House
9 Dewey Court
Northampton
Massachusetts 01060
USA

A catalogue record for this book
is available from the British Library

Library of Congress Control Number: 2008926580

ISBN 978 1 84720 757 9

Printed and bound in Great Britain by MPG Books Ltd, Bodmin, Cornwall

Contents

About the author

George P. Smith, II, is a Professor of Law at The Catholic University of America Law School in Washington, D.C. He began his law teaching career in 1964 at Indiana University, where he graduated with a B.S. in Business Economics and Public Policy in 1961 and a J.D. in 1964 and received an LL.D. degree, *honoris causa*, as well in 1998. He enjoys both a national and an international reputation as a lecturer and widely published scholar in the fields of Law, Science, and Medicine and Health Law. His postgraduate studies were completed at Columbia University Law School where he received an LL.M. degree in 1975 and at the Yale Law School's Commonwealth Program in Law, Science and Medicine in 1976–77 where he was a Senior Fellow. He received an Australian-American Fulbright Foundation Award to the University of New South Wales, Australia, in 1984, and was the Parsons Visiting Professor of Law at The University of Sydney in 1998 and 2003 and served as Distinguished Visiting Professor of Law at Macquarie University, Australia, in 2005.

Among his academic affiliations which contributed to the preparation of this book are those at: The American Medical Association, Institute of Ethics, Chicago, Illinois; Australian Institute of Ethics and the Professions, University of Queensland, Australia; Center for Ethics in Culture and The Reilly Center for Science, Technology and Values, Notre Dame University, Indiana; Centre for Medico-Legal Studies, Cardiff University Law School, Wales; Center for Socio-Legal Studies, Wolfson College, University of Oxford, England; Centre for the Study of Religion and Politics, University of St. Andrews, Scotland; Emory University Law School Center for the interdisciplinary Study of Religion, Georgia; George Washington University Institute for Spirituality and Health, Washington, D.C.; The Hastings Center, Institute of Society, Ethics and the Life Sciences, New York; The Hoover Institution, Stanford University; Institute for Health Law, Loyola University Law School, Chicago, Illinois; The Max Planck Institute, Heidelberg, Germany; University of Oxford, Rothermere American Institute, England; Emmanuel College and Wolfson College, University of Cambridge, England.

Professor Smith's other related books in the field include: *The Christian Religion and Biotechnology: a Search for Principled Decision-Making* (2005); *Human Rights and Biomedicine* (2000); *Family Values and the New*

Society (1998); *Legal and Healthcare Ethics for the Elderly* (1996); *Bioethics and the Law* (1993); *The New Biology* (1989); *Final Choices* (1989); *Medical-Legal Aspects of Cryonics* (1983); *Ethical, Legal and Social Challenges to a Brave New World* (1982) *and Genetics, Ethics and the Law* (1981).

Abbreviations

AATB	American Association of Tissue Banks
ADA	adenosine deaminase
ADA	Americans with Disabilities Act
CBER	Center for Biologics Evaluation and Research
COP	Conditions of Participation
DALE	disability-adjusted life expectancy
DALYs	disability-adjusted life-years
DHEW	Department of Health, Education, and Welfare
DNA	deoxyribonucleic acid
DOE	Department of Energy
EGE	enhancement genetic engineering
EPA	Environmental Protection Agency
ESCRO	embryonic stem cell research oversight
FDA	Food and Drug Administration
GLGT	germ-line gene therapy
GTP	good tissue practice
HBCD	heart-beating cadaver donor
HCT/Ps	human cellular and tissue-based products
HES	human embryonic stem
HEW	(Department of) Health, Education, and Welfare
HMOs	health maintenance organizations
HUGO	Human Genome Organization
IRB	institutional review board
IVF	*in vitro* fertilization
JCAHO	Joint Commission on Accreditation of Healthcare Organizations
NHBCD	non-heart-beating cadaver donor
NIH	National Institutes of Health
NOTA	National Organ Transplant Act
OHRP	Office of Human Research Protections
OMB	Office of Management and Budget
OPO	organ procurement organization
OPTN	Organ Procurement and Transplant Network
PGD	preimplantation genetic diagnosis
PKU	phenylketonuria

QALY	quality of adjusted life year
RCT	randomized clinical trial
SCGT	somatic cell gene therapy
UAGA	Uniform Anatomical Gift Act
UNOS	United Network for Organ Sharing
VSLY	value of statistical life year

1. Introduction

Reports from the Centers for Medicare and Medicaid Services and the Agency for Health Care Research and Quality released in 2006 showed—conclusively—that rising health care costs consume 16 percent of the nation's economic output. In 1997, health care accounted for 13.6 percent of the gross domestic product. Health care costs are growing substantially faster than inflation and wages—increasing by almost 8 percent in 2004. Indeed, in 2004, the nation spent almost $140 billion more for health care than the year before. And, by 2016, it is expected that an annual increase of 5.3 percent will translate into a national expenditure of one dollar of every five dollars for health care, bringing the overall total close to $4 trillion in overall budget costs just for health maintenance.[1] Sadly, as these costs escalate, many Americans—especially minorities and the poor—do not receive high quality of care.[2] Medical providers, acting under constant pressure from insurance companies, who in turn are pressured from employers, are battling daily to find ways by which health care costs can be cut.[3]

The unraveling of health care services is driven by advances in medical technology which, in turn, have the effect of allowing physicians the luxury of simply spending more on patient care. This creates a domino effect because it leads to higher insurance costs which in turn push employers to cease providing coverage. The net result, then, is that significant numbers of citizens become uninsured and thus encounter difficulties in getting basic care. In a direct sense, "Peter" is robbed, proverbially, of basic care in order to provide "Paul" with state-of-the-art care and treatment.[4]

Essentially, all efforts to achieve justice in the distribution of health care resources are utilitarian in character and definition.[5] Since these resources are not infinite, they cannot be offered to or used by everyone. This, of necessity, then forces choices between those individuals and among groups seeking their use. Allowing improper distribution of these scarce resources is not only inefficient, it is wasteful.[6]

For utilitarians, the general good is seen as superior to personal goal satisfaction.[7] Because of the difficulty in calculating the net good deriving from a utilitarian approach to decision making,[8] some have argued that this approach to health care decision making is not only unjust—but unfair.[9] Not only is utilitarianism viewed as cold and calculating, it is seen as denying the individual of what is his due.[10] The needs of those who are worse off are either ignored or neglected.[11]

QALYs

Drawing upon the progenitor of utilitarianism, Jeremy Bentham, who asserted all legislative enactments and public policies deriving therefrom should have as their goal the attainment of the greatest happiness for the greatest number of citizens,[12] proponents of finding an indicator for this level of contentment brought forward the notion that a "net good" could be determined by evaluating or ranking competing preferences or approaches to health care justice. Thus, it was (and is) believed today that "counting utilities provides a bridge to the quantification of the quality of human life."[13] In the 1970s, then, the quality of adjusted life year (QALY) came into its own and was advanced as not only a principle to account for an intuitive belief that most prefer, typically, ability to disability and contentment to distress,[14] but as a construct to measure both the quantity and the quality of life with or without medical care.[15]

Essentially, the QALY is a measuring tool which equals one life year for good health—without either disability or distress.[16] Accordingly, for a patient expecting five years of additional life after major surgery, the value of this health intervention is determined to be five. If however, this treatment leaves the patient in a state of distress or disabled for an additional five years, the value is diminished.[17] The ratio of the reduction is set by using a matrix based upon policy determinations derived from interviews with physicians, health care administrators and patients themselves.[18] Patient preferences are central to any effort to assess the quality of life gained from each medical benefit conferred or health improvement developed.

Once the QALY is set, it has been suggested that a higher level of "rational rationing" can be achieved by making a calculation of the costs of each health service as well as the cost offset by future savings through actual prevention.[19] With this informational base, a ranking of the various health services can then be undertaken—all according to the extent and nature of the benefit they offer per dollar expended (or, in other words, value for money). Within any given health plan, "services would be provided starting from the top of the list, down to the point where the insurance company's or Medicare money runs out."[20] Thus, those services offering the most health value would—in turn—get the highest priority for coverage. Physicians, as traditional gatekeepers, would be entrusted, accordingly, with judging that value based on not only patient preferences, but the efficacy of scientific evidence.[21]

A variant of this rational rationing approach was put in place in Oregon in the late 1980s. A state-wide rationing plan was designed as such to allocate scarce medical resources to treatments and establish policies which were seen as the most effective in terms of the quality and quantity of continued human life.[22] Although relied upon, initially, by Oregon in determining what treatments to be covered by Medicaid, QALYs were subsequently abolished.[23]

As will be seen in Chapter 2, QALYs are regarded by some as not only unjust and inevitably discriminatory—especially when applied to comparing the old with the young—but unfair because they force a decision to be made that one person's better life, with medical care, is valued over a poorer life. Perhaps, in very large measure, this inequity explains why QALYs are regarded presently as primarily an academic tool—with marginal use being made of them by U.S. governmental bodies, except the Food and Drug Administration in its rulemaking.[24] QALYs are used generally in cost-effectiveness studies,[25] by physicians, hospitals, HMOs, insurers, health economists, scholars in public health and others undertaking research in health care economics.[26] In cost-effectiveness studies, the health and the non-health impacts of differing choices affecting health are charted. In this regard, QALYs are beginning to compete with other metrics, such as the VSLY or value of statistical life year, for measuring health and longevity as a tool for monetizing mortality.[27]

While dollars are used to measure non-health impacts, health impacts are measured by use of a nonmonetary scale—either a disease-specific scale, in cases where the health effects of the particular choices are confined to a single disease or, alternatively, a QALY scale.[28] In order to determine which choice should be selected, cost-effectiveness ratios are then used.[29] "Alternatively, the choice which maximizes health given a fixed budget for non-health costs is selected."[30]

THE AMERICAN IDEAL

There is a strong, lingering sense that the new powers of medical technology may narrow if not blunt the very meaning of the American ideal which promotes the right to live in a free society and to pursue happiness.[31] The fundamental concern, then, becomes what degree of usefulness there is in pursuing goals beyond therapy towards genetic enhancement.[32] Are there, in other words, limits to the right of scientific investigation?[33] And, if there are, what are they?[34] Finally, is there a standard of "genetic responsibility"[35] which should be either self-imposed or set by society upon those working in the field—this, even though such a responsibility may very well be viewed as an unnecessary burden on the freedom of scientific inquiry? These issues will be analysed in Chapters 2 and 3.

Medical technology is so uniquely powerful that its impact is felt not only in daily life but in the way life is viewed. For example, the technology of mechanical ventilators, combined with heart transplantation, brought a societal re-examination of how death should be defined and led to the conclusion that the death of the entire brain is equivalent to, for all purposes, death of the whole person. This new definition, in turn, allowed the "harvesting" of hearts and other vital organs from individuals who—although dead under a brain death criterion—continued to have both circulation and respiration maintained artificially by medical ventilation.[36]

While Americans might decide to limit "halfway" or exotic, science-fiction inspired technologies, such as artificial hearts or brain transfers into robot bodies, it would appear unlikely they would ever approve limitations on medical research whose focus is to discover technologies, drugs and scientific techniques which not only maintain qualitative existence but extend life.[37] The reason for this position is simple and direct: "there is no coherent argument for arbitrarily ending a life that could be prolonged with reasonable quality at a reasonable price."[38]

Since the end of the twentieth century, the public has been almost overwhelmed with scientific information regarding the genome and the complexities of gene therapy and stem cell research.[39] Yet to come will be efforts to grow certain tissues for grafting—including skin, bladder and cartilage. Reportedly, cultured cells have been used successfully in an experimental setting to treat stroke victims; and in 2006 it was reported that seven children and teenagers had new implanted bladders grown from their own muscle and bladder cells.[40]

It is expected that the use of similar cells can be used to treat other disabling brain diseases. Genomics-derived drugs hold the potential to expand greatly the range of treatments achievable with human cells—this, because of their ability to control the cells as they grow and specialize.[41] Even more opportunities for regenerative medicine will be charted when the insights from the clonal experiment with Dolly the sheep are realized first with a re-set of the genetic clock inside a cell and, subsequently, without the need for egg cells.[42]

SCIENCE AND POLITICS

The issues of science become, inevitably, political issues because of one fact: namely, they raise to the surface the extent to which the government can restrict private medical research undertakings—in the name of either (generational) safety, morality (for example, non-coital reproduction) or the public good (for example, stem cell research).

As will be analysed in Chapter 3, a significant part of contemporary bioethics, under which the complex ethical, philosophical, socio-legal and medical issues of the new medicine are presented, is seen by some as "biopolitic" in that it has become "embryocentric"[43]—this, because of limitations on federal funding for human embryonic stem cell research.[44] These critics advocate a vision of global bioethics tied, inextricably, to fundamental principles of human rights. They would, in turn, tackle issues from a less restrictive present national "political agenda" designed to limit embryonic research to pre-existing stem cell lines and instead, for example, advance liberal health care for the present millions of uninsured Americans and one which thereby works to achieve respect and human dignity for all people, not just embryos.[45]

In January 2007 the director of the National Institutes of Health charged with implementation of President Bush's restrictive embryonic stem cell research policy suggested that this program is impeding medical research designed to seek medical cures for a variety of diseases. Indeed, the prohibition of research on newly derived stem cell colonies is precluding scientists from pursuing research to the fullest extent that could and should be done.[46]

If the successful process of coaxing ordinary mouse skin cells to become what are essentially embryonic stem cells without first creating and then destroying embryos is replicated with human cells—as is expected over time—the current embryonic debate would be recast. This scientific achievement would mean that an individual's own skin cells could be converted directly into stem cells without having to either collect healthy human eggs or destroy human embryos.[47]

Another approach to stem cell research science designed to avoid the ethical pitfalls of human embryo experimentation was brought forward in 2007 by Dr. Donald Landry of Columbia University. Under this proposal, stem cells would be extracted from "dead" frozen embryos left over from other laboratory procedures and not viable for implantation rather than live ones.[48] Instead of being disposed of, these moribund embryos could serve a useful scientific purpose. For Dr. Landry, a Catholic, an embryo is considered to be "dead" in those cases where "most of its cells have naturally and irreversibly stopped dividing."[49]

Legislative approaches in Congress—in both the House and the Senate—continue to be brought forward, all designed as such to loosen present restrictions on embryonic stem cell research[50] with one in fact incorporating the Landry proposal.[51] Indeed, in an attempt to accommodate those who wish to promote more stem cell research and—at the same time—

those who object to research of this nature which would harm embryos, in June 2007, President Bush issued Executive Order 13435 requiring the Department of Health and Human Services to develop guidelines for funding alternative approaches to embryonic research.[52] This White House initiative is an effort to blunt criticism of his veto of proposed legislation which would have loosened present restrictions on the federal funding of such research.[53]

Even with this conciliatory movement by the White House to expand research opportunities for creating new methods for creating embryonic stem cells without having to destroy human embryos, such action may be impeded by the federal policy of 2001 which forbids federal funds from being used to study embryonic stem cells created after 9 August 2001.[54] While prospective changes in NIH funding of stem cell research may ease, eventually, research concerns, yet another hurdle to wider rights of experimentation looms: namely, the degree of harm which may come to embryos from such laboratory procedures.[55]

While some new technologies promise not to destroy embryos for necessary investigations, there is a real concern, for some, that they will come under congressional scrutiny and—indeed—run afoul of legislative restraints imposed on studies which cause "harm" to human embryos.[56]

One new scientific approach, pioneered by a corporation in Worcester, Massachusetts, Advanced Cell Technology, is drawing particular attention. Under this method of investigation, stem cells are obtained from human embryos while leaving the actual host embryos functionally intact. Termed "blastomere biopsies," a single cell, or blastomere, is first removed from an eight-cell human embryo and coaxed, subsequently, to multiply into a colony of stem cells in a petri dish.[57]

The crux of the ethical issue here is whether this type of research subjects an embryo to more than an acceptable level of minimal risk and—if so— whether federal monies can be expended for the research. If such a level of research will benefit the embryo in question, greater risk is allowed. But, if the test embryo is subjected to more than "minimal risk," then some argue no federal monies may be used for experiments of this nature.[58] In the final analysis, perhaps the degree of harm to embryos utilized in this scientific research is truly in "the eye of the beholder" and, as such, subject to "interpretative discretion."[59]

In a very real sense, the scope of the new medicine is tied—inextricably— to issues of fecundity[60] and immortality.[61] In turn, these areas impact dramatically on the bulwark of American society—the family[62]—and what many consider to be its glue: namely, religion.[63] The promises of biomedical research are tantalizing in their anticipated translation into clinical applications which forestall death as well as alleviate pain and prevent disability.[64]

Indeed, termed "translational, or bench to bedside medicine,"[65] this research could serve easily as a foundation for enhancing a wide variety of human traits[66] which would validate what could well be seen as a return to positive eugenics. While some perceive this eugenic drift as morphing, rather insidiously, into the field of genetics and, thus, becoming a "new genetics" as it promotes a move toward a program of social engineering,[67] others see this research as both innovative and humane, designed as such to minimize human suffering and promote better genetic health.[68]

A bold step taken recently by the American College of Obstetricians and Gynecologists could well be viewed as an effort to advance eugenics—this, as a consequence of its decisions to offer screening for Down syndrome to all pregnant women regardless of age. Previously, screening for this chromosome abnormality was recommended only for women 35 years or older.[69] But, given the fact women are having babies later in life—with an astonishing 4.1 million babies being born to women ages 30 to 54 in 2005—perhaps the more enlightened view is to regard this policy as quite sound for improving genetic health.[70] Indeed, coupled with the fact that more women are choosing to remain single during and after pregnancy, such a policy is both wise and judicious.[71]

Social demographics show conclusively that, since the 1950s, more and more women are becoming less dependent upon men or the institution of marriage.[72] For some, surrogate motherhood and artificial insemination present attractive alternatives.[73] Assisted reproductive technologies offer countless opportunities for creativity in designing babies.[74] In the final analysis, "whatever turns out to be possible, will be wanted."[75]

Chapter 3 analyses at two levels the costs and the opportunities to the social, legal, ethical and medical communities within contemporary society of pursuing the development and the use of the new medicine. The second level of analysis tests, more specifically, the extent to which the freedom of scientific inquiry and investigation and the countervailing right of privacy both advance and confound the mandate of the new medicine to improve, through genetic diagnostics, the overall genetic health of society. More and more, the great promise of do-it-yourself genetic tests will become popularized—thereby allowing individuals to be apprised of the risks of coming down with disease before the actual syndromes are manifested.[76] Already, preimplantation genetic diagnosis (PGD)—designed to allow couples to test embryos that have been created *in vitro* when they are roughly three days old for serious genetic disease (for example, Down syndrome, Tay Sachs)—is seen by some as a potential means to expand a program to advance positive eugenics. As such, PGD could be used to test for milder risks or predispositions and then screen them out altogether from the reproductive cycle.[77]

The study of the epigenome—or, the suite of biochemical or molecular sequences and signals that determine which genes in an individual's DNA can be turned on or off—holds the awesome power to re-write, if and when mastered through clinical applications in epigenetics, the rules of disease, heredity and even identity.[78] This new science is illustrative of both the opportunity and the peril of scientific research which, in turn, advances change and forces revisionism. So significant is this field of research that researchers in Japan, Europe and the United States have begun pilot studies designed to assess the difficulty of undertaking a human epigenome project designed, as such, to map man's entire epigenome.[79] The challenge here is that each individual does not have but one epigenome, but rather a multitude of them.[80]

Information transfers across generations are inherited from one's parents in the form of DNA. The chromosomes inherited from parents account, however, for only 50 percent of the DNA. The other 50 percent is composed of protein molecules—with these proteins carrying, in turn, the epigenetic marks and information.[81] Research is showing that adaptive responses are neither innate nor passively emerging from the genome. Rather, they are "molded by the environment."[82]

The impact on public health responses to present and future generations of epigenetic research on the current epidemic of obesity is illustrative of the magnitude and far-reaching significance of this research.[83] Some scientists have speculated whether the obesity epidemic, blamed commonly "on the excesses of the current generation, may partially reflect life-styles adopted by our forebears two or more generations back."[84] Continued study of epigenetics will impact dramatically on how contemporary society understands history, sociology, political science, sociobiology and, as seen, public health.[85] For, if the environment is shown to have a decisive role in changing one's genome, the great gap between social processes and biological processes will have been bridged. This, in turn, will change demonstrably the frame of reference used for explaining all human and social responses.[86]

Cloning, designer pathogens, *in vitro* fertilization and other forms of assisted reproduction, organ transplantation and face and womb transplants, cryogenic preservation *pre* or *post mortem*, genetic enhancement through eugenic experimentation, stem cell research and even genetically modified genes and foods designed, as such, to enrich and prolong a life resistant to disease, shape the parameters of what is known today as the "new" medicine.[87] In September 2007 a ruling by the British Human Fertilization and Embryo Authority heralded what is expected to be the subsequent creation of part human, part animal embryos—or chimeras—for use in medical experimentation.[88] This scientific advancement has raised considerable concern and fear that some hybrid embryos could well be transferred to wombs of women where they might well develop. Present British regulations require all "human" embryos used in research to be destroyed within fourteen days after their creation.[89] The conditions under which human experimentation can be pursued in order to advance these and other creative and ambitious undertakings will be discussed in Chapter 4.[90]

The *micro* and *macro* issues raised with human organ transplantation are examined in Chapter 5 and presented as a paradigmatic case study of a contemporary issue of distributive justice set within the boundaries of the new medical science. From this analysis, it will be seen that normative standards or principles of just distribution for those needing either organ or tissue transplants should strive to achieve equity rather than equality.[91]

Medical judgments regarding the efficacy of organ allocation should remain paramount.[92] Yet, oftentimes compromises to this principle are made when the urgently ill are given priority of access—this, because presently there are no incentives which encourage patients who are least likely to derive any significant benefits from a transplant from being *triaged* out of any procurement program.[93] Even though policy agreements are advanced for keeping organs close to their source of origin—since it is believed prospective donors are more likely to donate organs when they are used by a person in need from a local social unit—prevailing sentiment remains that allowing organs to be kept within a local or regional area for transplantation is yet another compromise to medical efficacy.[94] Well-intentioned differentation in listing, prioritizing or allocation of organs nonetheless invariably raises socio-ethical issues, for these actions are subject to claims that non-medical judgments about patient differences are being made which, in turn, give rise to blatant or relative judgments about recipient worthiness.[95]

In the final analysis, what should be sought is an organ distribution policy which follows principles that are capable of endorsement by reasonable people—one that seeks to balance competing *micro* and *macro* economic policies of distribution for scarce resources yet, essentially, a policy that promotes to the greatest number of disadvantaged citizens "the increased likelihood of receiving an organ or having a successful transplant."[96]

PARTICIPATORY DEMOCRACY

Noble though the sentiment may be that "active liberty refers to a sharing of a nation's sovereign authority among its people,"[97] and is tied—

of necessity—to connecting frameworks grounded in responsibility, participation and capacity,[98] the hard reality is that ordinary individuals have
little interest in considering complex policy issues and—indeed—have little
aptitude for evaluating complex intellectual matters[99]—and especially those
involving medical science.[100] Consequently, it is unrealistic to expect either
sound and thoughtful ideas or sensible and understandable policies to
be shaped in public discourses under present conditions of "intellectual
disorder."[101] Because of this state, the scientific community is reluctant—
understandably—to accept public oversight and direct participation in regulating the parameters of the new biotechnology and its offspring, the new
medicine.[102] It is well to remember that, even though science promises an
unpredictable future, futures are inevitably unpredictable.[103] Accordingly, it
is well to understand that "doing nothing has just as many consequences as
doing something."[104]

Such a state of affairs means that there can be no direct way to move from
any level of moral assessment to a clear public policy. Instead, all that can
be hoped for is a level of information to be provided. Quite often, then,
owing to a failure to develop adequately the moral dimensions of formulating public policy in a liberal pluralistic society, presumptions in favor of
reproductive autonomy and scientific freedom, for example, are indulged
and, indeed, advanced.[105]

Driven by "painful technologies and sciences," the new medicine runs the
risk of being seen as no longer "patient based."[106] The ideal of philosophical reasoning and meanings for such ethical terms as responsibility, rights,
duties, interests, beneficence and justice is mired often in confusion and
conjecture.[107] Indeed, many of the new ethical questions raised from the
development and practice of the new medicine are set within a "blurred
outline."[108] Perhaps all that can be hoped for is that the Cartesian aspiration of reaching a "clear and distinct idea" be pursued with objectivity.[109]
And from this may well come acceptance of a societal obligation not to
achieve all the good that can be achieved, but—rather—to effect all the good
that can be done within the limits morality imposes upon the development
and use of the technologies of the new medicine.[110]

Although, traditionally, the ethics of medicine has focused on the obligations of physicians to their individual patients, there is—as well—a need
to appreciate broader ethical issues arising from a recognition that
medicine "is always practiced within a social context."[111] "Social medicine"
or, alternatively, "the medicine of society" becomes crucial to shaping the
parameters of application and use in the age of the new medicine.[112]

Distinct from clinical medicine, which is directed toward healing and
relieving human suffering among individual patients, the medicine of
society is concerned with the use of medical knowledge to advance the

health of society.[113] Yet, while these two fields of medicine have differing ends, they enjoy a symbiotic relationship—this, because "the end of each is essential for human well-being."[114] Advancing and pursuing health care, then, is an obligation that "a good society owes its citizens in justice."[115] A balanced moral relationship between the goals of the individual patient and the common good must always be sought.[116] So long as this ethic and point of equilibrium guides the development and use of the new medicine, the moral compass is set correctly and humanely. Applying this ethic is always problematic, however, because "fiscal scarcity" drives the new medical economics and forces a "general tightening of health care ethics as government and business attempt to gain control over their skyrocketing expenditures."[117]

NOTES

1. "Price of good health painful", *Richmond Times Dispatch*, 21 Feb. 2007, p. 1A (discussing a report from economists at the Centers of Medicare and Medicaid Services on health costs).
2. M. Kaufman and R. Stein, "Record share of economy is spent on health care," *Washington Post*, 10 Jan. 2006, p. A1. See generally J. Richmond and R. Fein (2006), *The Health Care Mess: How We Got into It and What It Will Take to Get Out*.
3. See P. Krugman and R. Wells (2006), "The health care crisis and what to do about it," *New York Review of Books*, 23 Mar., p. 38.
4. Ibid., pp. 38, 40.
5. M. Häyry (2002), "Utilitarian approaches to justice in health care," Ch. 4 in R. Rhodes, M.P. Battin and A. Silvers (eds.), *Medicine and Social Justice*.
6. Ibid.
7. Ibid., p. 62.
8. Ibid., p. 54.
9. Ibid.
10. Ibid.
11. Ibid. Utilitarian logic does not discount the life of the individual. Rather, it balances the interest of one individual against the interests of other individuals. G. Winslow (1982), *Triage and Justice*, p. 83 (relying on the ideas of Joseph Fletcher). See generally J. Rawls (1972), *A Theory of Justice*. It has been argued that explicit quantifiable utilitarian principles, together with decision analysis, should be applied by bioethicists in reaching ethical judgments. See J. Baron (2006), *Against Bioethics*.
12. J. Bentham (1973), *An Introduction to the Principles of Morals and Legislation*, Ch. 1. While early utilitarians define happiness as pleasure, twentieth-century followers equated happiness with contentment and enjoyment. Häyry, "Utilitarian Approaches," p. 54.
13. Häyry, "Utilitarian Approaches," p. 54. Interestingly, today, economists are measuring utility as Bentham conceived it: as a quantum of pleasure or pain; and—led by Nobelist Dr. Daniel Kahneman—they ask people about their *fallible memories* of pleasure and pain and, in this regard, depart from Bentham's thesis that the sovereign masters of the actions of all people are pleasure and pain. See "Economics discovers its feelings," *Economist*, 23 Dec. 2006, p. 33.
14. Häyry, "Utilitarian Approaches," p. 55.
15. Ibid., p. 56.

16. Ibid., p. 55.
17. H. Edgar (1998), "Quality of Life Indicators," in R. Chadwick (ed.), *Encyclopedia of Applied Ethics*, **3**, pp. 759–76.
18. Ibid. See also Häyry, "Utilitarian Approaches," p. 55.
19. J. Weinstein (2003), "We ration health care, better to do it rationally," *Washington Post*, 1 June, p. 133.
20. Ibid.
21. Ibid.
22. N. Daniels (1991), "Is the Oregon rationing plan fair?," *Journal of the American Medical Association*, **265**, p. 2232.
23. M.D. Adler (2006), "QALYs and policy evaluation: a new perspective," *Yale Journal of Health Policy, Law and Ethics*, **VI**(1), p. 3.
24. Ibid., pp. 4, 83.
25. Ibid., p. 2.
26. Ibid., pp. 1, 2.
27. Ibid., pp. 2, 5. Allocation deals primarily with statistical lives, while rationing deals generally with identifiable lives. B.R. Furrow, T.L. Greany, S.H. Johnson, T.S. Jost and R.L. Schwartz (2001), *Bioethics: Health Care Law and Ethics*, p. 390. See R. Hahn and S. Wallsten (2003), "Whose life is worth more? (And why is it horrible to ask?)," *Washington Post*, 1 June, p. B3 (discussing the efforts of the U.S. Environmental Protection Agency to use age-adjusted analysis in which the statistical lives of the elderly over 70 would be considered less valuable than those of younger people when undertaking a cost–benefit analysis of proposed clear air anti-pollution legislation). Two other metrics, both seen as discriminatory, are disability-adjusted life expectancy (DALE) and disability-adjusted life-years (DALYs). Francis, L. (2002), "Age rationing under conditions of injustice" in R. Rhodes, M.P. Battin and A. Silvers (eds.), *Medicine and Social Justice*, Ch. 22.
28. Adler, "QALYs and policy evaluation," p. 2.
29. Ibid.
30. Ibid., pp. 2, 3. See generally R.A. Posner (2004), *Catastrophe: Risk and Response*, p. 165, *passim*.
31. President's Council on Bioethics (2003), *Beyond Therapy: Biotechnology and The Pursuit of Happiness*, President's Council on Bioethics, Washington, D.C., p. xviii.
32. Ibid., p. 277. It has been suggested that genetic enhancement should not be viewed as part of basic health care entitlements and, thus, should be excluded from the domain of distributive justice. A. Buchanan, D.W. Brock, N. Daniels and D. Wikler (2000), *From Chance to Choice*, pp. 17, 129. See L. Kass (2003), "The pursuit of biohappiness," *Washington Post*, 16 Oct., p. A25. See also G. Smith and T. Burns (1994), "Genetic determinism or genetic discrimination," *Journal of Contemporary Health Law and Policy*, **11**, p. 23.
33. See G.P. Smith, II (2001), "Setting limits: medical technology and the law," *Sydney Law Review*, **23**, p. 283.
34. Ibid. See also G.P. Smith, II (1987), "The province and function of law, science, and medicine: leeways of choice and patterns of discourse," *University of New South Wales Law Journal*, **10**, p. 103. But see AP [Associated Press] (2003), "Rules are clarified to spur medical advances," *New York Times*, 31 Jan., p. A23 (reporting on how the Food and Drug Administration—responding to a sharp decline in the development of novel treatments and medical devices to spur medical innovation—has clarified, and some claim relaxed, its requirements for approval of research on new products).
35. P. Kitcher (1996), *The Lives to Come: The Genetic Revolution and Human Possibilities*, p. 204. See generally G.P. Smith, II (1993), *Bioethics and the Law: Medical, Socio-legal and Philosophical Directions for a Brave New World.*
36. G.J. Annas (1993), *Standard of Care: The Law of American Bioethics*, p. 253. See R. Stein (2004), "FDA approves artificial heart for those awaiting transplant," *Washington Post*, 19 Oct., p. A3. See generally G.P. Smith, II (1989), *The New Biology: Law, Ethics and Biotechnology.*

37. See G.P. Smith, II (1990), "The Frankenstein myth and contemporary experimentation: spectre, legacy, curse or imperative," *Biolaw*, **2**, §463. But see C. Mooney (2002), "Nothing wrong with a little Frankenstein," *Washington Post*, 1 Dec., p. B1. The science of creating cyborgs—"individuals" with electronically powered legs, arms, hands and eyes—is progressing rapidly. R. Highfield and C. Joyce (2006), "We can rebuild him. We have the technology. Almost," *Daily Telegraph*, 4 Apr., p. 5; Brown (2006), "For 1st woman with bionic arm, a new life is within reach," *Washington Post*, 14 Sept., p. A1.

38. Annas, *Standard of Care*, p. 216. See A.R. Jonsen (2005), *Bioethics Beyond the Headlines: Who Lives? Who Dies? Who Decides?*, See generally G.P. Smith, II (1996), "Utility and the principle of medical futility: safeguarding autonomy and the prohibition against cruel and unusual punishment," *Journal of Contemporary Health Law and Policy*, **12**, p. 1.

39. See A.R. Caplan (1997), *Am I My Brother's Keeper?*, Ch. 17. See also M. Kirby (2000), "The Human Genome," in *Through the World's Eye*, Ch. 4; G.P. Smith, II, (1998), "Harnessing the human genome through legislative constraint," *European Journal of Health Law*, **5**, p. 53; Symposium (1999), "Human primordial stem cells," *Hastings Center Report*, **29**, p. 30; G. Carr (2000), "Survey: the human genome," *Economist*, 1 July, p. 54.

40. A. Atala, S. Bauer, S. Soker, J. Yoo and A. Retik (2006), "Tissue-engineered autologous bladders for patients needing cystoplasty," *Lancet*, **367**, 15–21 April, p. 1241. See generally G.P. Smith, II, (2000), "Genetic enhancement technologies and the new society," *Medical Law International*, **4**, p. 85.

41. W. Haseltine (2001), "Genomics: the path ahead for science, medicine and society," *Brookings Review*, **21**, Winter. See also A. Caplan and Magnus (2003), "New life forms: new threats, new possibilities," *Hastings Center Report*, **33**, p. 7; B. Commoner (2002), "Unraveling the DNA myth," *Harper's*, Feb., pp. 39, 47 (cautioning that the potential consequences of transferring a DNA gene between species before the consequences of its release are fully understood are problematic).

42. See note 41. See also C. Fleming (1988), *If We Can Keep a Severed Head Alive . . . Decorporation and U.S. Patent* no. 4,666,425; G.P. Smith, II (1983), "Intimations of immortality: clones, cryons and the law," *University of New South Wales Law Journal*, **6**, p. 119; R. Bahr (1977), "A new ethical question: head transplants?," *Science Digest*, May, p. 76. See generally L.P. Knowles and G.E. Kaebnick (eds.) (2007) *Reprogenetics: Law, Policy and Ethical Issues*; G. Annas (2000), "The man on the moon, immortality, and other millennial myths: the prospects and perils of human genetic engineering, *Emory Law Journal*, **49**, p. 753.

43. G.J. Annas (2005), "American bioethics after Nuremberg: pragmatism, politics and human rights," Monograph, p. 13. See G.P. Smith, II (1993), "Biomedicine and Biomedical Ethics: De Lege Lata, De Lege Ferenda," *Journal of Contemporary Health Law and Policy*, **9**, p. 233.

44. See note 43.

45. G. Annas and S. Elias (2004), "Politics, morals and embryos," *Nature*, **431**, 2 Sept., p. 19.

46. R. Weiss (2007), "Stem cell policy hampering research, NIH official says," *Washington Post*, 20 Jan., p. A4.

47. R. Weiss (2007), "Scientists use skin to create stem cells," *Washington Post*, 7 June, p. A1. See R. Weiss (2007), "Advance may end stem cell debate: Labs create a stand-in without eggs, embryo," *Washington Post*, 21 November, p. A1 (discussing how human stem cells have been used successfully in developing stem cells).

48. G. Naik (2007), "The devout doctor's prescription," *Wall Street Journal*, 16–17 June, p. A1.

49. Ibid.

50. R. Weiss (2007), "House votes to ease limits on stem cell research," *Washington Post*, 8 June, p. A6.

51. Naik, "The devout doctor's prescription." Senator Norm Coleman's bill incorporates the Landry proposal. Senator Harry Reid has sponsored a rival bill entitled the Stem

Cell Research Enhancement Act which would allow government funds to be used for stem cell research derived from lines taken from viable embryos which fertility clinics would have discarded. Ibid.

52. *Weekly Compilation of Presidential Documents*, **43**, 22 June 2007, p. 821. See J. Fletcher (2007), "Bush moving to bolster stem cell alternatives," *Washington Post*, 20 June, p. A4.
53. See note 52.
54. R. Weiss (2007), "Future of stem cell tests may hang on defining embryo harm," *Washington Post*, 29 July, p. A8.
55. Ibid.
56. Ibid. See also R. Weiss (2006), "Stem cells created with no harm to human embryos," *Washington Post*, 24 Aug., p. A3.
57. See note 54.
58. Ibid.
59. Ibid. (quoting Prof. R. Alta Charo, University of Wisconsin).
60. D.L. Spar (2006), *The Baby Business: How Money, Science, and Politics Drive the Commerce of Conception*. See also Symposium on Assisted Reproduction Technology (ART), *Family Law Quarterly*, **39** (2005), p. 573; G.P. Smith, II (1990), "Assisted non-coital reproduction: a comparative analysis," *Boston University International Law Journal*, **8**, p. 21; R. Stein (2007), "First U.S. uterus transplant planned," *Washington Post*, 15 Jan., p. A1.
61. S.G. Post and R.H. Binstock (eds.) (2004), *The Fountain of Youth: Cultural, Scientific, and Ethical Perspectives on a Biomedical Goal*. See G.P. Smith, II (1996), "Pathways to immortality in the new millennium: human responsibility, theological direction, or legal mandate," *St. Louis University Public Law Review*, **15**, p. 447; G.P. Smith, II (1987), "Death be not proud: medical, ethical and legal dilemmas in resource allocation," *Journal of Contemporary Health Law and Policy*, **3**, p. 47; G.P. Smith, II (1982), "The promise of abundant life: patenting a magnificent obsession," *Utah Journal of Contemporary Law*, **8**, p. 85. See generally L. Weeks (2003), "Putting God on notice," *Washington Post*, 9 Feb., p. F1.
62. G.P. Smith, II (1998), *Family Values and the New Society: Dilemmas of the 21st Century*.
63. G.P. Smith, II (2005), *The Christian Religion and Biotechnology: A Search for Principled Decision-making*.
64. D. Callahan (2003), *What Better Price? Hazards of the Research Imperative*, p. 85. See J. Merz, D. Magnus M. Choo and A. Caplan (2002), "Protecting subjects' interests in genetic research," *American Journal of Human Genetics*, **70**, p. 965.
65. L. Moss and A. Jamieson (2006), "£50 million research to create revolutionary personalized drugs," *Daily Telegraph*, 4 Apr., p. 5.
66. Ibid.
67. See for example E. Black (2003), *War against the Weak: Eugenics and America's Campaign to Create a Master Race*, chs. 20, 21.
68. See for example Smith, *The New Biology*; G.P. Smith, II (1984), "Eugenics and the family: exploring the yin and the yang," *University of Tasmania Law Review*, **8**, p. 4.
69. Practice Bulletin #77 (2007), "Screening for fetal chromosomal abnormalities," *Obstetrics & Gynecology*, **109**, Jan., p. 217.
70. D. Glanton and B. Rubin (2006), "Rise in single mothers driven by older women," *Chicago Tribune*, 17 Dec., p. C1.
71. R. Hertz (2006), *Single by Chance, Mothers by Choice*; J. Mattes (1994), *Single Mothers by Choice*; S. Roberts (2007), "51 percent of women are now living without spouses," *New York Times*, 16 Jan., p. A1.
72. Roberts, "51 percent of women."
73. Mattes, *Single Mothers by Choice*.
74. R. Stein (2006), "Embryo bank stirs ethics fears," *Washington Post*, 6 Jan., p. A1; "Burying babies, bit by bit," *Economist*, 23 Dec. 2006, p. 117.
75. M. Warnock (2003), *Nature and Mortality*, p. 142. See Knowles and Kaebnick, *Reprogenetics*; I. Wilmut (2006), *After Dolly: The Use and Mission of Cloning*, Ch. 8.

76. N. Shute (2007), "Unraveling your DNA's secrets," *U.S. News & World Report*, 8 Jan., p. 51.
77. J. Geraedts (2006), "The need for interaction between assisted reproduction technology and genetics: recommendations of the European societies of human genetics and human reproduction and embryology," *Human Reproduction*, **21**, p. 1971.
78. E. Watters (2006), "DNA is not destiny," *Discover—Science, Technology, and the Future*, Nov., p. 33.
79. Ibid., p. 35.
80. Ibid., p. 36.
81. Ibid.
82. Ibid.
83. Ibid., p. 76.
84. Ibid.
85. Ibid.
86. Ibid. See generally J. Beckstrom (1985), *Sociobiology and the Law*; E. Wilson (1975), *Sociobiology: The New Synthesis*.
87. See K.L. Macintosh (2006), *Illegal Beings: Human Clones and the Law*; F. Bowring (2003), *Science, Seeds and Cyborgs*; Smith, *Bioethics and the Law*; G.P. Smith, II (1983), *Medical-Legal Aspects of Cryonics: Prospects for Immortality*; R. Hartman (2005), "Face value: challenges of transplant technology," *American Journal of Law & Medicine*, **31**, p. 7; Stein, "First U.S. uterus transplant planned"; A. Pollack and A. Martin (2006), "F.D.A. tentatively declares food from cloned animals to be safe," *Washington Post*, 29 Dec., A1; A. Doland (2006), "Face transplant recipient meets cameras, questions," *Washington Post*, 7 Feb., p. A17; J. Anderson (2005), "French doctors defend ethics of first face transplant," *Washington Post*, 3 Dec., p. A16; R. Weiss (2005), "Mice stem cells made without harm to embryos," *Washington Post*, 17 Oct., p. A6. See M. Soares (2001), "Virtually Human," *New Scientist*, 16 June, p. 26 (discussing the creation of the most complex computer model ever attempted—a virtual human being—at the Oak Ridge National Laboratory in Tennessee). See generally Posner, *Catastrophe*, pp. 35–37.
88. R. Weiss (2007), "Britain to allow creation of hybrid embryos," *Washington Post*, **6** Sept., p. A11.
89. Ibid.
90. See generally P. Knudson (ed.) (2006), *PRIM&R through the Years: Three Decades of Protecting Human Subjects* 1974–2005.
91. R. Rhodes (2002), "Justice in transplant organ allocation," in R. Rhodes, M.R. Battin and A. Silvers (eds.), *Medicine and Social Justice*, p. 350.
92. Ibid.
93. Ibid., p. 351. *Triage*, of course, is designed to but screen patients—normally into three groups—in order to determine their priority of treatment: those not expected to survive even with treatment; those who will recover without treatment; and the priority group—or those needing treatment in order to survive. G.P. Smith II (1985), "Triage: endgame realities," *Journal of Contemporary Health Law and Policy*, **1**, p. 143.
94. Rhodes, "Justice in transplant organ allocation," p. 352.
95. Ibid., p. 350.
96. Ibid., p. 348. See also S.J. Younger, M.W. Anderson and R. Schapiro (eds.) (2004), *Transplanting Human Tissue: Ethics, Policy, and Practice*; D.L. Kaserman and A.H. Barnett (2002), *The U.S. Organ Procurement System: A Prescription for Reform*.
97. S. Breyer (2005), *Active Liberty*, p. 15.
98. Ibid., p. 16.
99. See R.A. Posner (2003), *Law, Pragmatism and Democracy*, pp. 106–07.
100. See W. Broad and T. Glanz (2003), "Does science matter?," *New York Times*, 11 Nov., p. F1 (commenting on the inability of most Americans to endorse scientific rationality).
101. See R.A. Posner (2003), *Law, Pragmatism and Democracy*, p. 107. This situation is more understandable when it is realized that half of the U.S. population has an IQ

below 100. See also R.J. Herrnstein and C. Murray (1994), *The Bell Curve: Intelligence and Class Structure in American Life*, Chs. 1–4, 13–16.

102. M. Condic and S. Condic (2003), "The appropriate limits of science in the formation of public policy," *Journal of Law, Ethics and Public Policy*, **17**, pp. 157, 167. See also K. Phillips (2006), *American Theocracy*, pp. 64, 209, reporting on how unsophisticated religious zealots are playing a prominent role in blocking scientific advancement.

103. O. Jones and I. Goldsmith (2005), "Law and behavioral biology," *Columbia Law Review*, **105**, pp. 405, 499.

104. M. Kirby (2000), "Seven ages of a lawyer," *Monash University Law Review*, **26**, pp. 1, 10. See also Michael D. Kirby (2004), *Authority, Principle and Policy in the Judicial Method*, The Hamlyn Lectures, p. 88, n. 386 (quoting Lord Justice Sedley).

105. See G.P. Smith, II (1999), "Judicial decision making in the age of biotechnology," *Notre Dame Journal of Ethics and Public Policy*, **13**, p. 34.

106. A.R. Jonsen (1990), *The New Medicine and the Old Ethics*, p. 158. See generally W. Sage (2001), "The lawyerization of medicine," *Journal of Health Politics, Policy and Law*, **26**, p. 1179.

107. See note 106. See also R.C. Coile, Jr. (1990), *The New Medicine: Reshaping Medical Practice and Health Care Management*.

108. Jonsen, *The New Medicine*. See generally G.P. Smith, II (1978), "Uncertainties on the spiral staircase: metaethics and the new biology," *Pharos Medical Journal*, **41**, p. 10; Smith (1976), "Manipulating the genetic code: jurisprudential conundrums," *Georgetown University Law Journal*, **64**, p. 697.

109. Jonsen, *The New Medicine*, p. 1.

110. M. Harrison and G. Meilaender (1986), "Case studies: the anencephalic newborn as donor," *Hastings Center Report*, **16**, p. 23.

111. E. Pellegrino and D. Thomasma (2004), "The good of patients and the good of society: striking a moral balance," in M. Boylan (ed.), *Public Health Policy and Ethics*, p. 17. See Symposium, Public Health Ethics: Mapping the Terrain, *Journal of Law, Medicine and Ethics*, **30**, p. 170.

112. Pellegrino and Thomasma, "The good of patients," p. 18.

113. Ibid.

114. Ibid., p. 21. See generally G.J. Annas (1988), *Judging Medicine*.

115. E. Pellegrino and D. Thomasma, "The good of patients," p. 27. See A. Cribb (2005), *Health and the Good Society*; G.P. Smith, II (2005), "Human rights and bioethics: formulating a universal right to health, health care, or health protection," *Vanderbilt Journal of Transnational Law*, **39**, p. 1295.

116. E. Pellegrino and D. Thomasma, "The good of patients," p. 34. See R. Hardin (2001), *Trust and Trustworthiness*; D. Barr (2006), "Reinventing in the doctor–patient relationship in the coming age of scarcity," *American Journal of Bioethics*, **6**, p. 33.

117. E.H. Morreim (1991), *Balancing Act: The New Medical Ethics of Medicine's New Economics*, pp. 50, 51. See J. Herring (2006), *Medical Law and Ethics*, Ch. 9; G. Alexander and J. Latos (2006), "The doctor patient relationship in the post-managed care era," *American Journal of Bioethics*, **6**, p. 29.

2. Normative standards and health care resource management*

INTRODUCTION

Controlling costs while limiting access to health care resources and con-
straining choices thereto is the central dilemma confronting health care
policy today.[1] One overriding point is clear: namely, so long as restrictive
levels of use for health resources exist, some principle of "maximum societal benefit" must be set. Accordingly, the individual's unfettered right to
access and equality of use must—to some extent—be compromised in
order to safeguard the general need.[2]

No definitive structure for normative decision making in health
care resource management will be constructed in this chapter. Indeed,
finding what may be considered a "just" solution to the selective
distribution of finite health care resources is a task of great, overpowering magnitude and perhaps a "near impossibility."[3] The health care
compromises made, the values and public policies used to shape them,
and the framework within which they operate presently, will—however—
be analysed. To that end, the economic, medical, ethical and socio-legal
underpinnings of the frameworks or models for decision making will be
examined critically as well as the conflicts and challenges arising from
their application.

The vast complexities and philosophical nuances of the subject
area, together with limitations of space imposed, dictate—necessarily—
an analytical approach that is restricted in the scope and depth of its criticism. What will emerge, however, is a foundational evaluation of the core
considerations, or perhaps principles, which—of necessity—guide in
conflict resolutions regarding allocations of health care resources.
These considerations, in turn, need to be addressed and, where appropriate, re-evaluated to assure that—to the extent possible—a level of
distributive justice can be achieved in accessing and distributing
limited health care resources to all citizens within the national, global or
transnational communities.

INDIVIDUAL OR COMMUNITARIAN RIGHTS?

Americans assume that, as part of their inalienable rights to life, liberty and the pursuit of happiness, any health care plan sponsored by the government must validate and thus support these fundamental rights which in turn support their claim to whatever courses of action are necessary to make them healthy and happy.[4] Thus, "essential care" or a "decent minimum" of health care is thought to be an integral part of the very right to health care.[5] These claims of access to health care are all set within a culture that is technologically driven, individualistic, wasteful and death denying,[6] and one that refuses to accept limits to health care.[7]

The net effect of the near compulsive obsession with "rights talk" or the supremacy of the "ethics of rights" in health care has challenged both the width and the depth of the common or community life. The common good is, thus, compromised—all in order to advance or maintain private entitlements to more and more health "products."[8] These products are in ever growing abundance because of the phenomenal successes of medicine, not its failures.[9]

Since the potential demand for health care is virtually unlimited, finding a compromise between demand and supply associated with the distribution of scarce resources presents one of the most serious ethical problems of the day.[10] Sadly, medicine today is little more than a very, very expensive article of commerce.[11]

In contemporary society, medicine is seen as a marketplace—where emphasis is placed not only on entrepreneurship, efficiency and profit maximization, but upon customer satisfaction and ability to pay. Thus, the ideology of medicine is displaced by the ideology of the market place. Trust is replaced by *caveat emptor*, with price disparities abounding.[12]

In order to correct this imbalance, patients must be placed at the center of the health care marketing system. Today, the focus in health care maintenance is on organizations instead of individual physicians. Individual-oriented medicine is thus being displaced by "institutionally practiced, community-oriented health care."[13] As a consequence, the dialogue and dialectic between the medical profession and the society it serves are strained.[14]

A SOCIETAL SHIFT?

Fundamental to the prevailing ideology of the United States is an aspiration to egalitarianism—where not only are equal legal rights recognized and practiced, but equity of access is also followed. In fact, this is seen as the moral economy upon which the system was erected originally.[15]

It has been posited, perhaps rather wistfully, that society is moving slowly from materialism—where economic values control—to post-materialism, where other values such as ethics are as significant.[16] If ethics have relevance, however, it is to be found within the principle of distributive justice which seeks a fair way to distribute scarce commodities.[17]

Within this new idealized environment, individualism is not recognized as the sole basis for rights. Rather, when taken together with individual responsibilities, individuals recognize responsibilities to the community and engage with a spirt of activism to fulfill those obligations.[18]

It makes good sense to realize that, since individuals form part of any and every community, they must assume their fair share of the burden of paying for the cost of the community's health care in an equitable manner. In this way, accessing health care is seen as a "special public good"—one grounded as such in basic principles of justice as well as on the basis that respect for persons and their essential human dignity requires communal action in order to safeguard the good itself.[19] Moral traditions, thus, can be seen as not only undergirding, but defining, the "common community."[20] Ultimately, there can be "no true common good if all do not have the good in common."[21]

HUES OR STANDARDS OF JUSTICE

There are essentially five standards of justice: commutative, distributive, general or social, modulated and retributive.[22] Some contemporary philosophers view corrective justice as yet another independent standard,[23] while others see it collapsing into distributive justice[24] or not a form of justice at all.[25] Still others consider social justice and distributive justice as either interchangeable or equivalent.[26]

Commutative justice pertains to the level of obligation owed, in clinical medicine, between the physician and the patient. Distributive justice pertains to what is owed by society to its members in the *micro* allocation of health care resources, while general justice charts what a proper standard of obligation and use is for individuals in the *macro* sense of sustaining the common or communal good. Modulated justice, or *epikeia*, pertains to the preservation of equity in the three other standards of justice, while retributive justice, as a hue of social justice, pertains to providing compensation to those suffering injustice under commutative, distributive or general justice.[27] In this regard, it can also be seen as corrective.[28] Efforts to reduce levels of social justice, seen especially in the criminal justice system, are termed restorative justice.[29]

DISTRIBUTIVE JUSTICE IN A JUST SOCIETY

The theory of distributive justice can be traced back historically at least two millennia. Both Aristotle and Plato addressed the question of how a society or group should allocate its scarce resources among those with competing claims or needs, and the Talmud addresses how creditors can make claims on the estate of a deceased creditor.[30] Considered to be but one element in the classic division of justice by Aristotle,[31] the theory of distributive justice was passed down by Aquinas to the Christian tradition.[32] Aristotle and Plato saw justice as neither an instrumental nor a procedural mechanism for achieving fairness or—for that matter—the fulfillment of any type of social contract. Instead, they embraced the classical notion of it as a value—a principle of moral conduct between and among those within human societies.[33]

For most contemporary thinkers, distributive justice attempts to supply to individuals or groups their due proportion of goods, services or opportunities.[34] In this regard, justice is seen as calculating, simply because it measures what is to be given or withheld.[35] "Operational justice" is viewed, then, as entailing the exercise of power as the central mechanism "for giving or taking away according to proportional deserts."[36]

Any discussion of distributional justice within the American health system is linked to the issue of power.[37] Indeed, it has been suggested that "without power there can be no justice, because justice is the form that power actualizes in the conflict between the haves and the have-nots between claim and counterclaim."[38] In order to resolve these inherent conflicts, power must often be exercised coercively through appropriate laws and policy. And, for these actions to be accepted, they must rest on moral reasons that the public—in whose name the policies are effected—could be expected reasonably to accept.[39]

THEORETICAL WEAKNESSES

While the search for an overarching economic theory of distributive justice has been forsaken long ago by "honest economists,"[40] political philosophers nonetheless continue to posit and reposit theories of distributive justice—none of which ever succeeds in structuring a universally acceptable principle of justice.[41] Perhaps the central reason for this failure is that there can never be such a principle in the first place—this, because any philosophical theory of justice must be anchored on some fundamental value which, in turn, is but a subjective determination.[42] Largely for this reason, the term has been seen as but an "empty label" or "shallow echo."[43]

Ultimately, "honest" political philosophers conclude "justice, like beauty, rests in the eye of the beholder."[44]

Even with this acknowledgment of uncertainty, the intellectual debates continue between those libertarians who advocate liberty to the rank of an overriding social value which in turn can never be traded off against other subordinate values, and egalitarian thinkers who posture "equal respect for all" or "equality of opportunity" as the central or core value of a just society to which all other values (including liberty) must be subordinate.[45] For egalitarians, then, this equality of opportunity requires a set minimum: namely, equal access to a range of certain basic commodities including health care, food, shelter and education.[46]

So long as the questions raised by political philosophers remain problematic, they will continue to be raised time and again. Once a question becomes clear and resolvable, philosophical interest is lost.[47] No other nation in the industrialized West, other than the United States, has sought so boldly and naively to attempt to accommodate both the egalitarian and the libertarian theories of justice.[48] It is because of this very accommodation that the American health care system is presently in so much disarray and seemingly incapable of finding one clear focus or direction.[49]

FOUNDATIONS OF THE JUST SOCIETY

All modern theories of the just society rest, fundamentally, on the same foundation—namely, notions or principles of equality.[50] For Aristotle, equality was seen as the very means of justice.[51] Justice, under Rawlsian theory, must always be seen as prevailing over efficiency, and liberty, in turn, must prevail over social and economic advantage.[52] In a just society, then, justice requires fair equality of opportunity and is thus equated with fairness.[53] This, in turn, requires society to guarantee for its members a fair share of what is required for them to pursue their individual ends.[54] Although Rawls fails to include health care as a primary social good, since a fair share of health resources allows for—or includes—liberty and opportunity, it has been asserted that, under the fair equality of opportunity principle, health care is, indeed, a social good to which all, regardless of social rank or status, have an unqualified right.[55] As such, in regulating the design of a health care system, a principle of protecting equality of opportunity is paramount.[56]

In order to assure this opportunity is open to all, and not unduly burdensome, a principle of just sharing designed to equalize the financial costs to illness is advanced. This principle recognizes that all financial burdens associated with medical misfortune should be shared equally by the healthy and the unhealthy alike unless, that is, individuals can "control those misfortunes by their own choice."[57] In today's practical world, however, noble though this sentiment may be, the sick have neither financial nor moral claim on their fellow citizens and this will, no doubt, continue to be the situation for the foreseeable future.[58]

SOCIAL JUSTICE IN PRACTICE

If, under any given theory of justice, there is genuine hope that the practice of public institutions will be effected by its acceptance, there must first be an understanding that the principles of social justice be understood contextually—with proper sensitivity being given to empirical data and various patterns of actual human association.[59] These, in turn, are drawn on the beliefs of ordinary people—tested empirically—about their social attitudes on the fairness of various distributive practices.[60] For example, empirical evidence from throughout the world discloses the fact that "most people when asked to comment on prevailing inequalities appear to believe that greater equality in distribution would be more fair."[61] There is also a popular consensus that, in order to be legitimate, economic inequalities must be deserved in some way and correspond—accordingly—to real differences in social contribution.[62]

In the final analysis, whether social justice seeks to become an operative ideal which guides everyday behavior or is seen as a highway to "full fledged socialism" and but a chief outlet for moral emotion, as Hayek termed it,[63] depends upon one major fact: that is, the extent to which sufficient assurances are given to those concerned that the restraints they show, by following what are considered to be fair principles and procedures, will in turn be matched by similar restraint by others.[64]

Because of pluralistic beliefs about justice, no single principle can be seen as capturing all the judgments individuals make regarding the distributive procedures they, in fact, follow.[65] One popular theory holds simply that, under a self-interest hypothesis, most people will select whichever conception of distributive justice serves best their material interests.[66] In the absence of a consensus on the shape and vitality of distributive principles, what is needed is a fair process to establish legitimacy for critical resource allocation decisions.[67] Thus far, at least in America, this process can be seen as evolving.

JUSTICE AND THE NEW MEDICINE

Efforts to apply justice to the new medicine through genetic control which have the effect of shaping the limits and/or quality of the human gene pool are bound to be met with opposition—especially from those who would view such efforts as violating a more fundamental and profound ethical ideal: namely, that of respect for human life. Within this ideal are to be found such ambiguous terms as "sanctity," "dignity of human life" and "reverence for human life"[68]—all of which, as abstract principles, lack the specificity of a rule but nonetheless have the social power to be taken as either unyielding *a priori* standards of conduct or, in fact, rules for which no exceptions are tolerated.[69]

Love is seen as the "driving force" behind any true vision of a just society which, in turn, validates the dignity of the human person. Indeed, the inner fullness of justice is only attained in love.[70] Since all laws are set with a hierarchy whose foundation is, according to Augustine, to be found in love, the ethics of love is viewed properly as the very essence of justice.[71] In the end, if a spirit of love, humaneness or compassion guides the shape and direction of the new medicine, its response will be a reasonable and proper one—one directed toward minimizing human suffering and maximizing the social good which, in turn, allows attainments of the "good life."[72]

CONFLICTS IN DISTRIBUTION (ECONOMIC ISSUES)

As seen, libertarian philosophers see individual liberty as the predominate social value which can never be traded off, while egalitarian philosophers espouse "quality of opportunity" as the central or foundational value of a just society.[73] It remains for public policy advocates, and especially politicians, to listen carefully to the language of the law and the competing voices of religion and morality, love and friendship, custom and compromise, and of pragmatism and social accommodation,[74] in trying to fashion a sustainable social compromise from these struggles for access to and maintenance of health care.[75]

Because of rising health care costs during the past fifteen years, societal concern has focused on whether the world's health care resources are being distributed fairly and wisely. More and more, contemporary medicine demands of its practitioners—particularly those in America—that the principle of justice be made a distinct factor in the decision-making process.[76] Increasing governmental pressures continue to stress the need to follow cost control policies, eliminate waste and inefficiency and—as noted—implement the principle of distributive justice in patient care. As a consequence of these three competing policy concerns, more and more, patient interests become secondary to health care delivery.[77] The central conflict for physician-gatekeepers, who are responsible for 75 percent of the national expenditures for health care,[78] thus, is to assure and maintain a patient-centered ethic in their professional work while, at the same time, from a *macro* economic standard, safeguard their responsibility to preserve society's resources.[79] Ancillary to this conflict is the harsh reality that implementing distributive justice at the patient bedside, without any real societal consensus on how it is defined and practiced, most often means that an arbitrary process is put in place which depends upon—to a very large extent—the individual value system of the person assigning worth to the medical intervention or procedure put in issue—normally, the physician.[80]

In considering applications of distributive justice, then, physicians are required to evaluate this operative principle at two levels: the statistical patient or the identifiable patient.[81] The more direct example of statistical applications of distributive justice is seen within the process of establishing guidelines for utilization review. Another example is found in the work of capital budget committees. Although decisions made under utilization and budget reviews affect, assuredly, real people, it is considered more appropriate and—indeed—safer by physicians to consider and evaluate their rationing decisions prospectively rather than be forced to evaluate issues of this nature at the bedsides of their patients.[82] Alternatively, when the particular financial resources of each patient are factored into their identifiable medical treatment profile, the second and unstable level of distributive justice is seen in bold relief which may well involve bedside rationing.[83]

Despite widespread differences among countries in the world community in their financing and organization of health care delivery systems, a common observation has been that all countries have a similar problem maintaining efficiency. This problem entails meeting cost inflation in health care expenditures. Efficient use of resources in medical care (or in any other field for that matter) requires that the benefit from the last dollar spent in any activity be no lower than the benefit obtainable from spending an additional dollar on some other procedure or on some other patient. Stated another way, if allocations of health care resources were totally efficient, it would be impossible to increase total medical benefits by diverting any money away from one service, for example chemotherapy, and spending it on another, such as radiology.[84] Thus, most economists hold that treatments should cease when marginal benefits equal marginal cost.[85]

Interestingly, in Britain, countless patients with chronic renal failure die earlier than necessary due to lack of dialysis treatment facilities. Yet large expenditures have been made routinely to prolong the lives of metastic cancer patients for brief periods.[86] Thus, a rationing of care, to some stated or unstated degree, is seen in all health systems, and a conflict of approach as well;[87] for at one level of analysis is the outright denial of economic efficiency as any valid factor in medical practice and, at another level, a recognition that there is a moral impetus behind efficiency. Those who hold the second view conclude correctly that it would be unethical, and indeed fanatical, to foster an approach that allows one person to consume health care resources regardless of benefits conferred while totally ignoring other more valuable and directly beneficial uses of the resource.[88]

Rationing policies encounter the most difficulties in the area of marginally beneficial health care. The reason for this is simple: it is quite difficult and distasteful to fine-tune rationing policies to the degree that they select the treatments, diseases and people for whom marginal benefits are as great as opportunity costs.[89] Quite often age is a quotient in determining success of treatments and, at the same time, a factor in discrimination of health care delivery.[90]

RATIONING AS A FACT

Rationing has been in effect for quite some time and may be seen in three particular settings.[91] First, it is implicit in all systems where limited amounts of money are available for health care, and, secondly, it is practiced daily by clinical physicians who must decide how resources will be used as each case is presented. This is the method of practice in prepaid health insurance programs, and, so long as there are sufficient funds, the front-line physicians will have few challenges made to their clinical judgments. Finally, when third parties fail to fund specific treatments indicated medically, explicit rationing occurs. Even though physicians may be of the mind that certain medical procedures or surgical interventions are indicated, these treatments cannot be undertaken unless the patient can either fund them privately or prevail upon the doctor to complete them free of charge. A system of this design eliminates totally physician discretion for all items explicitly prohibited.[92]

For those individuals who have both money and health insurance, the market place itself structures other methods of rationing that include copayments and deductibles, which force upon patients the ultimate decision whether they are willing to expend additional monies in order to obtain specific care. Consequently, for those citizens who are strained economically or without funds at all and are ineligible for public assistance, rationing of health services is not even an operable issue. There is no access to these services at all! Sadly, it has been estimated that 15.2 percent of the population, or 43.6 million Americans, were without health insurance coverage during the entire year in 2002—up from 14.6 percent in 2001, an increase of 2.4 million people.[93]

Those individuals qualifying under the income criteria for Medicaid programs have few problems with access to the health care delivery programs or the costs thereunder because virtually everything their physician recommends is available—so long as the monies allocated within the program last.[94] It has been thus suggested that—to the extent health problems can be regulated—serious illnesses should be presented at the first part of each fiscal year. Many families that are not wealthy still find that their income levels exceed the qualifying levels for membership in public health programs and are denied consequently even a minimum level of the most critical care because they simply cannot pay. It has been suggested further that, by eliminating some of the available benefits of the Medicaid program not judged to be as important as others, funds could then be released so more people could become eligible for coverage even though overall fewer benefits would be available.[95]

SPECIFIC DECISIONAL FRAMEWORKS

Since no resource is infinite (and health resources are among them), selective distribution is inevitable. When considering issues of health care allocations, two classifications or levels of decision making are seen: *micro* allocation and *macro* allocation.[96] While *micro* issues are often regarded as "patient selection issues" or "choices among patients," regarding the resources available for specific kinds of health care services,[97] *macro* issues are focused on highly political matters such as the amount to which a nation is devoting its health care resources to primary and preventive care—as opposed to new biotechnology medicine—as well as the budget percentages being expended by hospitals.[98]

Lacking a clear and unambiguous definition of rationing, it may nonetheless be seen as a process whereby some are—temporarily and against their wishes—left without types of health care that would otherwise provide a benefit to them.[99] In addition to referring to these general limitations, rationing may encompass, as well, very "specific treatment decisions for particular patients" at the bedside.[100] Alternatively, rationing is seen as a means of providing every citizen with a guaranteed level of basic health care—this, by excluding from coverage those treatments considered to be "outside" the package.[101] One point in this analysis is certain: rationing is the central health care policy issue of the day.[102]

Long viewed as haphazard and unprincipled, rationing occurs today as it always has.[103] Yet the term is softened considerably by referring to it as merely allocations of health care resources.[104] No doubt, the most direct example of massive rationing is to be found in the field of health insurance, which is denied routinely to those who lack it because they work for an employer that simply does not provide it or because their personal level of poverty has yet to fall to that level required for eligibility under Medicaid.[105]

The fundamental question raised in issues of health care resource allocation is, as seen: who decides what care is not worth the costs? The decision maker can be the patient, the physician or third parties (primarily private and governmental insurers).[106] Two central approaches are considered normally: those oriented toward achieving the most productive use of the health resources and those designed to ensure equality of access to treatment through impartial or random selection for all suitable candidates.[107] Among the specific criteria used in determining proper *micro* allocations are: social value (with treatment preference being given to those judged of greatest social value to society), socio-medical (for example, age), psychological balance, nature and quality of supportive environment, medical (determining the basic merits or extent to which a benefit is conferred) and personal (the patient's willingness to accept treatment).[108]

Among the approaches to rationing used widely are: a "first come, first served" system of queues, random selection (which takes no account of the gravity of either the patient's conditions or of the medical benefit), ability to pay, *triage* systems based on medical urgency and—more recently—systems tied to computations of quality adjusted life years (QALYs) which are designed to test the appropriateness of treatment.[109] It has been suggested that treatment considered to be unsafe, unkind, unsuccessful or unwise is inappropriate and should be withheld.[110]

At the *micro* level, *ad hoc* decisions are made routinely and instinctively without need for any profound analysis. Accordingly, the bedside physician will inevitably choose the patient in greater pain for appropriate treatment—this, despite the fact that this will delay simultaneously the treatment of patients in lesser pain.[111] Interestingly, there is no precedential case law measuring societal attitudes with respect to judging the allocation of resources at the *micro* or individual level—since, presumably, decisions are taken in good faith and are based on principles seen as respectable to a responsible body of medical opinion.[112]

In considering how to limit the use of health care costs, ethical conduct which respects a person's autonomy and his right to decide for himself those treatments that he wants or, alternatively, does not wish can well lead to a reduction in costs. Minimally life prolonging treatments which are also invasive and expensive are often refused. Education in "lateral thinking" can also effect cost and resource savings. Thus, assisting individuals to deal with their death fears by offering palliative care options presents a wider range of potentially cost-saving choices available for their care and treatment at the conclusion of their lives.[113]

Other decision making mechanisms for health care resource allocations are found in internal hospital policies—for example, those that set standards for use of do-not-resuscitate orders. It is within these internal guidelines that institutional policies are in turn formulated.[114] As well, hospital ethics committees serve as an important source for setting policies which govern access not only to health care, but to allocations of health resources and egress therefrom.[115] Through medical malpractice decision making, the courts also become a mechanism and structure for determining efficacious uses of resources.[116] Finally, health care advocacy groups are becoming a growing and forceful voice in resource management here.[117]

A CASE IN POINT

The harsh reality of enforcement in health care resource allocation can be seen vividly as an ethical conundrum when either a health care system or a hospital seeks to limit the actual range of treatments available to a patient—this, because either the limitations, in and of themselves, or the actions taken to exceed them can result in meaning that the physician is acting unethically.[118] A hypothetical case reveals this dilemma more forcefully.

Suppose a cardiac surgeon is told by the hospital where he is on the medical staff that he is allowed to implant no more than ten intracardiac assist devices per year. Both the surgeon and the hospital know full well that, generally, some 50 patients will either need directly or could at last benefit from this life-saving treatment—a treatment which implants a defibrillator which, in turn, activates automatically, if a patient should suffer a cardiac arrest. Obviously, here, the surgeon is faced with a serious ethical quandary: to respect the hospital policy of allocation or disregard it to the extent that a medical patient presents in distress whose best interests will be served by use of a "prohibited" device even though he exceeds the quota for the device.[119]

Perhaps the only ethically acceptable way to allocate the defibrillators is to distribute them on a "first come, first served" basis. Others might propose, however, that use of a lottery might be preferred. The idea of pulling a number from a hat or a lotto ping-pong ball from a barrel is, however, abhorrent. Yet, if all individuals, in Canada for example, were given this medical device who needed them, it is estimated the cost to the health care budget could well be as high as 4 percent—this being but one item in the new biotechnology health cabinet.[120]

A corollary to the ethical dilemma just presented is to be found in another area of resource management: namely, medical efficiency. In order to combat gross inefficiency in cardio-thorasic surgeries, it has been suggested that a wider use of cardiac pacemakers be made available through a reusal policy which, in turn, would save millions of dollars. Since within 18 months of receiving a new pacemaker approximately 35 percent of the patients using them die, it has been suggested there are some 35 000 pacemakers available for reuse for other candidates. Even allowing for the fact that not all of these candidates could be accessed, and—assuming—further wastage as high as 70 percent, 10 000 pacemakers could still be reused each year.[121]

ARTIFICIAL HEARTS

When, in September 2006, the federal Food and Drug Administration (FDA) gave limited approval for use of the first totally implantable artificial heart, yet another complicated allocative issue was presented: namely, the cost-effectiveness of such an approval and subsequent use. The device, costing $250 000, will be available to a maximum of 4000 people.[122] Approved under the FDA "humanitarian device exemption," which lowers the bar effectively for such devices, they are then subject to approval only if they are shown to advance "safety" and be of "probable benefit." In calculating the degree of benefit conferred by the device, largely subjective measurements are allowed and include improvement in the quality of life. If not granted the humanitarian exemption, the artificial heart would have had to demonstrate both "safety and effectiveness."[123]

Powered by a battery with no wires or tubes piercing the skin, the new artificial heart—unlike its prototype in 1982 which was powered by a 400 pound air compressor—has its battery recharged with an inductive coil placed against the skin and allows the recipient to be away from an external power source for approximately an hour.[124]

Previous recipients of artificial hearts survived, after implantation, an average of 5.2 months—with the longest living 17 months; and of these 14 patients, ten left the hospital only with occasional day passes, one resided in a hotel near his hospital and one returned home while two died during the initial surgery. With a life expectancy of a month or less when the device was implanted, the net gain for all of them was 4.5 months.[125] Obviously, any honest and accurate computation of quality adjusted years is simply not possible for this procedure. For past recipients of artificial hearts, assuming a total cost of $350 000, the "incremental cost-effectiveness ratio" of the treatment was $940 000 per year of life gained.[126] Improved familial interaction together with improved levels of activity—ranging from moving from bed to chair and walking with assistance—set the parameters of the quality of life achieved with the device.[127] Because of these limited and, indeed, marginal results, the adequacy of truly informed patient consent remains of serious concern to this procedure—this, especially because of the lack of full understanding regarding the wide range of serious complications which may result in additional surgeries and many days of unconsciousness from implantation.[128]

The record of past use of artificial hearts is, to be sure, checkered at best. This, in turn, raises the question whether the long-term value of the investment will be sustained. Indeed, it has been suggested that, instead of approving and developing this expensive therapy, it would be better to spend the monies "vaccinating children and helping people with hypertension get better treatment—things that are of proven benefit but cost much less."[129]

Whether implantation costs (set at $100 000) of the new artificial heart will be covered by insurance companies and Medicare is also another major issue. For the federal Medicare program, at least for the present, controlling regulations list artificial hearts as "uncovered devices."[130] The extent of product liability for defective implantable medical devices remains, as well, a potential drawback to the full development and utilization of this new procedure.[131]

PRIORITIZATION

The pressing question, if such a change as this is advanced, is how to determine those benefits that could be retained. The clearest and most direct approach to resolving this question would be to assemble—as the state of Oregon did—a group of experts or health commissioners to develop a list, in order of importance to health, of medical procedures and surgical interventions. This, then, is labeled *prioritization* or, alternatively, rule-based rationing.[132] A cut-off level could be set by the legislature or even by a private insurance company. Although a legislature would simply make the cut-off (the limit for present or even future funding determined actuarially for the number of citizens eligible in the state), private insurance companies would probably use this priority list by writing policies at different rates and then offering them for various cut-off points on the list.[133]

In the event a legislature chose a cut-off point on the priority list where the population covered by the program was being denied beneficial health care, this could be termed properly *rationing*.[134] Similarly, the private insurance company could be thought of as rationing according to the levels private citizens could afford to pay for themselves. Certainly it is not unfair, in any sense of the word, to expect some limit for a public health program of this design—especially if the program were not restricted unconscionably.[135] Indeed, it can be argued persuasively that, because public funds are expended on health care in recognition of the social good attached to health maintenance, society has every right to administer and control the monies expended in order to assure their wise and just allocation.

NECESSARY HEALTH CARE NEED VARIABLES

Rationing can be avoided as a national policy if an agreement can be reached in identifying "really necessary" health care interventions and a process was then designed to ensure that all patients have equitable access to them. Thus, objective criteria, which could possibly take the form of clinical guidelines, must be established and identify real health care needs, as opposed to mere desires. These guidelines would be termed "necessary care guidelines" and would give the indicators or types of patients for whom specified services would be considered necessary. Applied as standards of care, these guidelines would specify patient management strategies required for patients with certain medical problems. Physician adherence to these guidelines would serve as a defense in a malpractice action.[136] Ideally, these policies or guidelines would be developed by bodies or panels drawing on outcome data, public testimony and expert consensus. In measuring treatment, *net benefit* would be defined in terms of longevity plus quality of life.[137]

ETHICS OF RATIONING HEALTH CARE

Richard Lamm, in suggesting a working ethical principle for distributing health care resources for the elderly, created quite a furor among the elderly when he urged health care resources be distributed along a utilitarian principle so as to maximize the long-run general happiness of the entire community and not only the debilitated, chronically ill, or very elderly as individual members of it. In other words, he argued that the greatest health resources should go to the greatest number of individuals capable of using them effectively. The reality of this harsh statement meant that, in Lamm's view, the elderly have "a moral duty to forgo further health care and to accept their death."[138] Children, he maintained, have more opportunities to flourish and achieve happiness; therefore, it was only logical that they should deserve a greater share of health resources than the elderly. This, of course, once again raises the issue of intergenerational equity or justice.

A society surely cannot consider itself a noble one if it does not respect the individuality of its members—even when to do so creates the appearance of running counter to the general happiness of the community at large. Any society runs the risk of dividing itself if it seeks to withhold health care from the elderly based on the argument that the "return" of such an investment can never be realized economically because of the limited lifespans of the recipients. The Lamm thesis challenges society to reallocate its health care resources in a way that does not abandon the elderly yet achieves a balance in providing long-term health protection and happiness for its members as a whole. Sadly, current evidence discloses that this challenge is going unmet.[139]

INTERGENERATIONAL JUSTICE

The concept of intergenerational equity arises from the association between the increased number of persons over 65 years, the probability that they are frequently using health care resources, and the resultant increase in health care costs.[140] The government is not able to bear, without restraint, the growing social and economic health care costs associated with the elderly. In America, during the presidency of Ronald Reagan, federal funding failed, for the first time, to keep pace with demand—as the demand for resources far out-distanced the available supply.[141] Every dollar given to programs for the elderly meant one less dollar for other groups. Addressable economic issues included then, as now, the proper delivery of care, the allocation of resources, effective and affordable methods of insurance, and defining research priorities.[142]

The fastest growing population in the United States and world-wide is people over the age of 65.[143] A corresponding shrinkage occurs in the population under 65 years of age who will have to bear burdens of providing for the prior and future generations.[144] Furthermore, the elderly are disproportionate consumers of health care as hospitalization of elderly persons on the average costs three times more per health care dollar than of those under 65 years of age.[145] Rationing of heath care resources for them is distinguished from cost containment measures which result in a withholding of medical services considered to be of no "expected patient benefit."[146] Thus, age rationing occurs only in those cases "where elderly patients, are denied access to medical services that are of *expected benefit* to them."[147]

There is some merit to the argument that the elderly must be compensated for their work earlier in life and not be required to make additional health care sacrifices.[148] Owing to their advanced years, the elderly earn some degree of public sympathy and respect because of what they have accomplished before approaching the end of their lives.[149] In coming to this end, they have discharged already many of the obligations that society has required and should not bear a disproportionate burden in their later years.[150]

Arguably, there is a shared intergenerational duty between both the elderly and those who are younger. Assurances against neglect and abuse come from the moral obligations and relationships that the young have with the elderly.[151] At the same time, the elderly are stewards of a world they helped fashion and their purpose should be to aid the young and future generations to come.[152] Therefore, the proper role for all societal groups should recognize a life cycle where the elderly have come before the young and made life easier for those who follow, while the young have the burden of supporting the elderly when they are unable to take care of themselves. The extent of that burden remains the open and truly vexatious question of this century.

PATTERNS OF MODERN RATIONING

Renal dialysis and heart transplantation are perhaps the two most relevant examples of contemporary rationing. When dialysis was in its infancy, it was a scarce and costly intervention with only a few dialysis machines in existence. In efforts to develop a scheme for the use of this new, scarce life-saving technology, different localities adopted varying policies for determining who should have access to the technology. In Seattle, Washington, social worth was used as a criterion in the decision-making process to decide ultimately on the relative value of the lives of those individuals competing for use of the process itself. When Congress was presented with this problem, it simply expanded Medicaid coverage to provide kidney dialysis for all patients in need—with average costs now running in excess of $1.5 billion per year.[153]

Although *de facto* rationing as a current feature of contemporary health care delivery systems is recognized, any further expansions of it should be delayed, it has been suggested, until the irrationalities of the current national system are resolved.[154] This suggestion is impractical simply because rationing is seen as an inextricable (if not unavoidable) given in the present system and its "irrationalities" are beyond correction within any reasonable period of time. Others might suggest that this effort to distribute scarce resources in an equitable manner, that is, rationing, is not irrational at all.[155]

Because health care services, providers of health care, and the means to pay for these services are all scarce, procedures must be established and followed to allow for a fair distribution of them. As observed, physicians engage regularly in rationing by their regulation of the extent of partici-pation in Medicare as well as in health maintenance organizations (HMOs).[156] Historically, during times of military engagement, field physi-cians decided routinely whom they would treat because they were "sal-vageable" and those from whom treatment would be withheld until the others were treated. Some were even denied treatment because of the futility of such actions. And, even today, emergency medicine—as prac-ticed in emergency wards of major hospitals and in times of local or state disaster—utilizes the principle of *triage*.[157] A strong argument could be advanced that, indeed, the very bedrock of modern rationing is to be found, to one degree or other, within the principle of *triage*. Surely an analogy can be seen between a military battlefield and the crisis in health care management because, in both, efforts must be made to balance the costs with the benefits of all actions taken.[158]

THE VALUE OF LIFE

Economists seek to place an actual monetary value for people's lives by employing two models. The first, called the human capital model, calculates the value of life only in terms of productivity or the present discounted values of one's future earnings. The second model is described as willingness to pay. Here, the monetary value of life is directly a function of one's will-ingness to use resources to increase one's chance of survival. Thus, in a hypo-thetical situation in which an individual annually demands an extra $500 in order to perform work that runs an additional 1-in-1000 risk of dying, $500 000 is the monetary value of that person's life. No more than $500 000 need be spent under this hypothetical model to save a particular life.[159]

In 2003, the federal Office of Management and Budget (OMB) focused on this issue of intergenerational justice when it chose to consider the value of human lives within the context of undertaking cost–benefit analysis in order to determine whether new administrative rules and laws were justified within agency rule making. During its study of this issue, it was learned that various regulatory agencies used widely varying values in making their computations.[160] The Environmental Protection Agency (EPA), for example, priced a life at $6 million while the Department of Transportation set $3 million as appropriate. The Food and Drug Administration chose to use a sliding scale based on the number of additional years a new regula-tion could be expected to allow each person to live.[161]

Subsequently, in preparing evaluations of President George Bush's pro-posed Clear Skies Act, aimed at reducing power plant pollution which would have the effect of benefitting mainly those older people with breathing disorders, EPA sought to discount the lives of those over age 70 by 37 percent by using this second model of willingness to pay. Because of a loud and sustained uproar by senior citizens groups, this formula was stopped.[162] Nonetheless, the OMB stated its conviction "to weigh each person's life expectancy in cost–benefit analyses of legislation and regulations."[163]

MEASURING QUALITY OF LIFE

A controversial, albeit growing, view in health economics is that the goal of all service should be to create as many years of healthy life as possible for as many as possible. The underlying basis for this view is, quite simply, the "assumption that for all alike a year of healthy life is equally valuable."[164] The productivity of health care, then, is measured in terms of years of healthy life or quality adjusted life years (QALYs). Thus, when consideration of the cost of receptive treatments is combined with the length of lives extended and the quality of life they enhance, interesting examples can be posited that force striking conclusions.[165] For example, because hip replacements produce QALYs at approximately one-twentieth the cost of renal hemodialysis, the conclusion is obvious: more replacements should be done. Using the same principle, there should also probably be more coronary bypass surgeries for individuals with severe angina and left main vessel disease and more screening and follow-up treatment for mild hypertension because of the qualitative results that follow these procedures.[166]

The aged are disadvantaged significantly by QALYs—this, because quality adjusted life years measure only treatment endpoints without taking into consideration either the proportional loss or the gain in the quality of one's life. Thus, the major moral criticism of QALYs is that they set no value on life *per se*.[167]

An alternative to QALYs has been suggested in what is termed "the saved young life equivalent."[168] Although, arguably, still reducing individuals to numbers, this approach seeks a unit of measurement in which saving a young person's life and restoring him to full health is the controlling paradigm. This position is justified on the grounds that most people would regard this goal, itself, as the maximum benefit an individual can gain.[169] An assessment of comparative treatment values is thus made "in terms of how many expected outcomes of each treatment would be equivalent to SAVE."[170]

Instead of trying to structure a model that seeks to incorporate a defensible method of pricing life and health, QALYs are thought to be a more feasible means of prioritizing health care services. The goal of trying to obtain the most QALYs from a health care system does not force a search for an answer to the central question: namely, what amount of money should be spent per QALY? Thus, quality adjusted life years will be of considerable use in those contexts in which the question of the amount of resources to spend on health care has presumably been answered, that is, when there is a health budget to stay within such as in the British National Health Service, an American prepaid plan, or a rational Medicare plan operating in the twenty-first century.[171] Indeed, some speculate that soon within this century QALYs will be accepted totally and used in planning and organizing health services.[172]

RISK–BENEFIT OR COST–BENEFIT ANALYSIS?

Perhaps the fairest idea for limiting or rationing care is to be found in risk–benefit analysis, which shows the risk and potential benefit of a medical procedure.[173] In developing risk–benefit uses, although age might always be expected to weigh against an older person likely to have fewer years of vigorous life left, it would not be necessarily conclusive.[174]

If, for example, a very elderly man with an aneurysm, failing kidneys and other complications were presented for surgical evaluation, under a cost–benefit analysis, a decision regarding the merits of surgery would be simply tied to cost. Under risk–benefit analysis, if the likelihood of the patient's surviving surgery were practically zero, whereas the likelihood of his living very long even if he did survive the surgery was very low, then surgery to repair the aneurysm would not be found probably cost-effective.[175]

AN ETHICAL DILEMMA AND THE AMERICANS WITH DISABILITIES ACT

Rationing on the basis of quality of life—as opposed to cost, effectiveness or cost-effectiveness—has a strong civil rights advantage; it seeks to measure the value of life to the individual patient as opposed to his usefulness to society. The inherent complexity with this is determining and, thus, adhering to an incompetent patient's life preferences. In those cases where these are not fully determinable, a substituted judgment model is used. Accordingly, the surrogate decision maker construes patient preference and makes a decision the patient would have made if competent.[176] Rationing at this level forces an ethical dilemma: specifically, quantifying the value of life for individuals in varying states of disability and health. Because quality-of-life decisional standards are subject to being colored or influenced by prejudices toward disability, it could be argued that this standard of rationing might well be considered discriminatory and, furthermore, violate the purpose of the Americans with Disabilities Act (ADA), which was designed to eliminate differential treatment based on disability,[177] and thus effect a redistribution of scarce goods so that the disabled receive additional resources to compensate for their limitations.[178]

Although yet to be tested definitively in the courts, the ADA definition of discrimination appears to proscribe implementation of any theory (or health care measure) that advances the notion that the quality of life associated with a treatment should in part determine the priority given to funding the treatment itself. In order to avoid further confusion on this issue, Congress should act decisively to amend the ADA, thereby allowing the states to deal directly with the issue of scarce health care resources and make whatever rational choices are necessary and base them on the most reliable and available measure of qualitative life.[179]

STRUCTURING A DECISIONAL FRAMEWORK

Establishing fair procedures for the distribution of health care resources is a crucial goal for contemporary society to set and, hopefully, to achieve. Accordingly, fairness is to be defined and shaped by four conditions: (1) public accessibility to "limit-setting decisions" and their policies and rationales; (2) clarity in policy rationales which explain how "value for money" is met in distributing health care resources within a society where there are reasonable resource constraints on the resources themselves; (3) a framework for principled decision making which provides a means for resolution of disputes; and (4) a regulatory process which not only assures public access to the initial "limit-setting decisions" but also provides an equitable mechanism for challenging the reasonableness of contested health care distribution decisions.[180]

RESTORING TRUST

Sadly, as a direct consequence of the multiple and conflicting roles a physician is cast in or forced to choose between, because of either the particular managed care program he is practicing under or the professional ethic he espouses, medicine is no longer being seen as caring for people. Indeed, the very acceptance of medicine as a moral value whose end is the healing of vulnerable persons in need of life and whose paramount essence is codified in the virtue of benevolence is thus challenged to its very core.[181]

The politics of economic self-interest compromise—if not extinguish—the sacred trust patients once placed in their physicians. Stated otherwise, the present system promotes the use of expensive, invasive and at-risk treatments and places little effort in patient care. It has been suggested that a new ethic needs to be recognized and embraced by physicians—one that shifts from using medicine if it might assist to one that promotes use only when it will.[182]

BALANCING NEEDS WITHIN THE DEMOCRATIC PROCESS

The ineluctable conclusion to be drawn from this analysis is that, in formulating health care policies, the principle of distributive justice demands decisions such as allocating and rationing health care be made fairly within the political process. It demands, further, that broad grants of discretion (which in turn often promote managerial indecision) to administrative decision makers in the HMOs who, themselves, have varying systems of values, and to bedside medical gatekeepers as well, be limited. It is only by and through deliberate debate within a democracy that assumptions about aging, the value of life for the aged and intergenerational responsibilities of assisting them in their care can be set, tested or—as the case may be—rejected.[183]

"Most people," it has been said, "are ignorant about most matters."[184] This is true particularly with regard to the health care market where consumers are found to be lacking in basic information about not only the quality but the price of medical services. This ignorance, in turn, means consumers lack the expertise to evaluate the professional qualifications of health care providers as well as evaluate necessary information regarding the range of alternative treatments available to them. Even when price information is available, health care consumers have difficulty assessing and, indeed, comprehending what the data means and how it impacts on their accessing health care.[185]

Since the efficient use of medical resources dictates both consumers and health care providers weigh the costs and the benefits of alternative medical treatments, the failure to access health care information regarding these options means—essentially—that physician preferences for particular medical procedures trump the ideal of informed patient consent.[186] And this in turn means that the physician solidifies his position of power as the primary gatekeeper to health care resources.

In the final analysis, what is called for is fair democratic procedures designed to allow average citizens to be sufficiently informed and knowledgeable in order to make choices among just alternatives for health care resource allocations.[187] Aided by careful cost-effectiveness and cost–benefit analyses, tied—as such—to those discernible values ranked clearly as beneficial and those regarded as costly, such a process can in fact work.[188]

Granted, a public dialogue to reach a *consensus* on how medical resources ought to be distributed is unlikely.[189] Yet a "public conversation" on these issues of the type the state of Oregon undertook several years ago is available. No matter within what policy forum the health care resource debate occurs—local, state or national—a fundamental balancing test will, of necessity, be employed: one that weighs, in an equitable and reasonable manner, individual needs with larger societal standards of economic efficiency.[190] By seeking to integrate moral and ethical reasoning with quantitative or economic formulations of needs and resources, the opportunities for a stronger and more contemporary standard of distributive justice will be both enhanced and stabilized.[191]

The ultimate moral issue seen in this debate is not—rather surprisingly—whether too much or too little treatment is offered, but rather how to seek an optimum level of reasonable or appropriate treatment based on the medical condition of each patient. Failing to meet resolutely the inherent difficulty of allocative decisions here foredooms the total decision-making process to a continued state of lethargy where inaction becomes the tragic hallmark of health care management.

If agreement could be reached for setting principles of distributive justice which, in turn, would establish a mechanism for determining how to set fair limits to heath care, societies would then be empowered to check all social decisions and practices against the principles in order to determine whether they conformed with them. In cases where decisions, policies and practices failed to conform, they would be held unjust and subsequent actions then taken to change them. When disagreements arose over interpretation of principles or facts, legal procedures for resolving such disputes would be sought.[192]

Ideally, the establishment of a national minimum standard of health care delineating, as such, what an adequate level of care should be for managed care organizations, the managers within it and the physicians who are practicing under it would be a positive step toward resolving present inadequacies in the system. Once such a standard is in place, there will be some level of expectation that competition will "take place not on establishing the leanest rationing strategy the market will bear (however ethically problematic it may be), but on delivering the agreed minimum standard efficiently."[193] This standard would demand of the physician an ethical obligation to his individual patients "to interpret it in the light of the patient's circumstances and make certain it was offered to them."[194]

Realistically, designing a satisfactory mechanism for defining a morally acceptable threshold standard of care is problematic.[195] Reaching a political consensus on this challenge is even more daunting when the level of public "understanding"—and indeed lethargy—is realized.

CONCLUSIONS

In the final analysis, it is quite possible (and probable) that society has come to review health care as little more than a commodity—a service—much as other commodities in a market economy and for which specific and harsh rationing decisions are imposed on physicians. The direct consequence of this societal redirection means the cornerstones of professional medical ethics—beneficence, patient autonomy and justice—will yield to "social good and economic need."[196] The whole art of healing, once seen as a partnership between the healer and nature itself, is also thus recast as an effort to redesign nature—improving upon it, and aiming it in new startling directions heretofore not found in its history.[197]

The choice implied, inherently, in the rationing of medical goods and services "will reveal more about the kind of people we are, and wish to be, than it would about the ideas we profess."[198] Indeed, there is a growing national belief in, and acceptance of, the inevitability of rationing and an awareness of the attendant ethical issues and dilemmas deriving therefrom within the patient–physician relationship[199]—issues arising inescapably from the very nature of managed care which, itself, challenges the foundational basis of relationship-centered care.[200]

From a transnational perspective, perhaps it is more realistic—when considering the extent to which there should be a governmental obligation to guarantee a citizen's good health—to refer to a right to health protection, with this including a right to access health care together with a right to live under healthy conditions.[201] Ideally, guaranteeing access to health care resources is the foundation upon which all other assertions of health care "rights" and their permutations are built. Lacking a strong determinative framework for both identifying and analysing the essential societal factors representing the conditions under which people can access health care, it is thought unrealistic and impractical to acknowledge an absolute right to health care.[202] International legislative templates go only so far in shaping a response to this issue. Rather, the dynamics of gatekeeping ethics and the centrality of the medical healing partnership between patient and physician must be seen as the paramount elements in assuring distributive justice in both the national and the transnational health care delivery system.[203]

NOTES

*   The foundational arguments put forward in this chapter derive, in part, from a paper entitled, "Economic efficiency, justice, and health care delivery," first presented in Amsterdam, The Netherlands, in 2002 at a Congress of the International Academy of Law and Medicine. These arguments were refined and presented subsequently at a seminar at the Rothermere Institute for American Studies at the University of Oxford in June 2006.

1.   J.F. Childress (1997), *Practical Reasoning in Bioethics*, pp. 259–62.
2.   J.K. Mason, R.A. McCall Smith and G.T. Laurie (2002), *Law and Medical Ethics*, pp. 364–86.
3.   Ibid., p. 386.
4.   G.J. Annas (1998), *Some Choices: Law, Medicine and the Market*, pp. 12–51.
5.   J. Kilner (1995), "Allocation of health care resources," in W.T. Reich (ed.), *Encyclopedia of Bioethics*, rev. edn, **2**, pp. 1067–84.
6.   Annas, *Some Choices*.
7.   W. Gaylin (1993), "Faulty diagnosis: why Clinton's healthcare plan won't cure what ails us," *Harper's Magazine*, **287**, pp. 57–65.
8.   See generally, M.A. Glendon (1991), *Rights Talk: The Impoverishment of Political Discourse*; A. Etzioni (1994), *The Spirit Of Community*.
9.   See W. Gaylin (1996), "Health unlimited," *Wilson Quarterly*, **20**, p. 38.
10. Mason et al., *Law and Medical Ethics*, p. 364. See also C.C. Havighurst, J.F. Blumstein and T.A. Brennan (1998), *Health Care Law and Policy*, p. 179.
11. M. Rodwin (1993), *Medicine, Money and Morals*, pp. 1–20.
12. Annas, *Some Choices*, p. 46. See E. Pellegrino (2001), "The goals and ends of medicine," in R.J. Bulger and J.P. McGovern (eds.), *Physician and Philosopher: The Philosophical Foundation of Medicine—Essays by Dr. Edmund D. Pellegrino*, pp. 56–69; M. Bobinski (2003), "Health disparities and the law: wrongs in search of a right," *American Journal of Law and Medicine*, **29**, p. 363.
13. G. Khushf (2000), "Organizational ethics and the medical profession: reappraising roles and responsibilities," in D.C. Thomasma and J.L. Kissel (eds.), *The Health Care Professional as Friend and Healer: Building on the Work of Edmund D. Pellegrino*, p. 148.
14. Pellegrino, "Goals and ends"; M. Brazier (2003), *Medicine, Patients and the Law*, Ch. 2.
15. D.G. Gill and S.R. Ingman (1994), *Eldercare, Distributive Justice and the Welfare State*, p. 257.
16. M. Somerville (2000), *The Ethical Canary: Science, Society and the Human Spirit*, p. 259.
17. E. Pellegrino (2001), "Access to health care," in Bulger and McGovern, *Physician and Philosopher*, pp. 277–83.
18. Ibid., p. 259.
19. Ibid., p. 268.
20. Childress, *Practical Reasoning*, p. 241.
21. Kilner, "Allocation of health care resources," p. 1071.
22. E. Pellegrino (2002), "Rationing health care: inherent conflicts within the concept of justice," in W.R. Bondeson and J.W. Jones (eds.), *The Ethics Of Managed Care: Professional Integrity and Patient Rights*, pp. 1, 2.
23. See J. Coleman (1982), "Corrective justice and wrongful gain," *Journal of Legal Studies*, **11**, p. 421.
24. P. Benson (1992), "The bases of corrective justice and its relation to distributive justice," *Iowa Law Review*, **77**, p. 515.

25. E. Sherwin (1992), "Why is corrective justice just?," *Harvard Journal of Law and Public Policy*, **15**, p. 839.
26. D. Miller (1999), *Principles of Social Justice*, p. 2; J.S. Mill (1861), *Utilitarianism*, Ch. 5, p. 92, reprinted in H. Plamenatz (ed.)(1949), *The English Utilitarians*, p. 225.
27. Pellegrino, "Rationing health care," pp. 3–5.
28. See generally Coleman, "Corrective justice."
29. J. Braithwaite (2000), "Restorative justice and social justice," *Saskatchewan Law Review*, **63**, p. 185.
30. J.E. Roemer (1996), *Theories of Distributive Justice*, p. 1.
31. Aristotle (1894), *Nicomachean Ethics*, I. Bywater (ed.), v. 4. 1131b25–1132b20.
32. Miller, *Principles of Social Justice*, p. 2.
33. Pellegrino, "Rationing health care," pp. 1–2.
34. W.M. Finnin, Jr. and G.A. Smith (1979), *The Morality of Scarcity*, p. 79.
35. Ibid. See also J. Fiskin (1988), "The complexity of simple justice," *Ethics*, **98**, p. 464.
36. See note 34. Indeed, it has been suggested that the main constituents of distributive justice are the principles of desert, need and equality, together with the establishment of criteria for distribution. Miller, *Principles of Social Justice*.
37. Finnin and Smith, *Morality of Scarcity*, p. 16.
38. Ibid., p. 17. See also Miller, *Principles of Social Justice*, p. 1.
39. Symposium, Public Health Ethics: Mapping the Terrain, *Journal of Law, Medicine and Ethics*, **30** (2004), p. 170.
40. M.A. Hall, M.A. Bobinski and D. Orientlicher (eds.) (2003), *Health Care Law and Ethics*, 6th edn., p. 91.
41. Ibid., p. 92.
42. Ibid.
43. L. Hoyano (2002), "Misconceptions about wrongful conception," *Modern Law Review*, **65**, pp. 883, 905.
44. Hall et al., *Health Care Law and Ethics*, p. 92.
45. Ibid., p. 92.
46. Ibid.
47. Roemer, *Theories of Distributive Justice*, p. 2.
48. Hall et al., *Health Care Law and Ethics*, p. 92.
49. Ibid. (drawing from the work of Ueve Reinhardt). See also Roemer, *Theories of Distributive Justice*, pp. 1–11.
50. D. Smith (2000), "Social justice revisited," *Environment and Planning*, **32**, pp. 1149, 1156.
51. E. Weinrib (1992), "Corrective justice," *Iowa Law Review*, **77**, pp. 403, 406.
52. J. Rawls (1971), *A Theory Of Justice*, pp. 261–2.
53. L.D. Gostin (ed.) (2002), *Public Health Law and Ethics*, pp. 90–91; I.N. Oliver (2002), *Is Death Ever Preferable to Life?*, pp. 132, 133. But see R. Nozick (1974), *Anarchy, State, and Utopia*, p. 6 (discussing anti-egalitarian positions).
54. N. Daniels (2002), "Justice, health, and health care," in R. Rhodes, M.P. Battin and A. Silvers (eds.), *Medicine and Social Justice*, pp. 6, 8; Gostin, *Public Health Law and Ethics*.
55. See note 54.
56. Ibid. See also P. Menzel (2002), "Justice and the basic structure of health care systems," in Rhodes et al., *Medicine and Social Justice*, Ch. 2.
57. Menzel, "Justice and the basic structure," p. 34.
58. See note 22, p. 16. See generally R. Dworkin (1993), "Justice in health care decisions," *McGill Law Journal*, **38**, p. 883.
59. Miller, *Principles of Social Justice*, p. 259.
60. Ibid.
61. Ibid., p. 230.
62. Ibid., p. 259.
63. F.A. Hayek (1976), "The mirage of social justice," in *Law, Legislation and Liberty*, **2**, pp. 64–6, 97, 100.

64. Miller, *Principles of Social Justice*, p. 19.
65. Ibid., pp. 78, 79.
66. Ibid., p. 82.
67. Daniels, "Justice, health, and health care," p. 7.
68. See G.P. Smith, II (1984), "Quality of life, sanctity of creation: palliative or apotheosis?," *Nebraska Law Review*, **63**, p. 709.
69. D. de Nicola (1976), "Genetics, justice and respect for human life," *Zygon*, **11**, June, pp. 115, 124–5. See generally M. Kirby (1986), "Bioethical decisions and opportunity costs," *Journal of Contemporary Health Law and Policy*, **2**, p. 7.
70. Referencing the Synod of [Roman Catholic] Bishops (1971), *Justice in the World*, p. 293, reprinted in D.J. O'Brien and T.A. Shannon (eds.) (1998), *Catholic Social Thought: The Documentary History*. See L. Silecchia (2000), "Reflections on the future of social justice," *Seattle Law Review*, **23**, pp. 1121, 1138. See also J. Fletcher (1966), "Love is the only measure," *Commonwealth*, **83**, p. 427.
71. J. Hall (1978), "Religion, law, and ethics—a call for dialogue," *Hastings Law Journal*, **29**, pp. 1257, 1267.
72. G.P. Smith, II (2005), *The Christian Religion and Biotechnology: A Search For Principled Decision-Making*. See also G.P. Smith, II (1987), "The province and function of law, science, and medicine," *University of New South Wales Law Journal*, **11**, p. 103.
73. Hall et al., *Health Care Law and Ethics*.
74. Ibid., p. 71.
75. Ibid., p. 36.
76. W. Andereck (2000), "Money, medicine and morals," in Thomasma and Kissel, *The Health Care Professional As Friend and Healer*, pp. 233–5.
77. Ibid. See generally D. Callahan (1987), *Setting Limits: Medical Goals In An Aging Society*.
78. E.D. Pellegrino and D.C. Thomasma (1988), *For The Patient's Good: The Restoration of Beneficence In Health Care*, p. 189.
79. Andereck, "Money, medicine and morals," p. 236.
80. Ibid. See generally E.D. Pellegrino and D.C. Thomasma (1993), *The Virtues In Medical Practice*.
81. Andereck, "Money, medicine and morals," p. 236.
82. Ibid., p. 237.
83. Ibid.
84. H.J. Aaron and W.B. Schwartz (1984), *The Painful Prescription: Rationing Health Care*, pp. 83–4.
85. P. Menzel (1990), *Strong Medicine: The Ethical Rationing Of Health Care*, p. 3.
86. Aaron and Schwartz, *Painful Prescription*. See generally S. Frankel and R. West (1993), *The National Health Service: The Persistence of Waiting Lists*.
87. Aaron and Schwartz, *Painful Prescription*, p. 84.
88. Menzel, *Strong Medicine*, p. 5.
89. Ibid., p. 7.
90. N. Dubler and C. Sabatino (1991), "Age-based rationing and the law: an exploration," in H. Binstock and S.G. Post (eds.), *Too Old For Health Care? Controversies in Medicine, Law, Economics and Ethics*, p. 92.
91. M. Weinstein (2003), "We ration health care: better do it rationally," *Washington Post*, 1 June, p. B3.
92. See generally P. Ubel (2000), *Pricing Life: Why It's Time for Health Care Rationing*. R. Lamm (1992), "Rationing of health care: inevitable and desirable," *University of Pennsylvania Law Review*, **140**, p. 1511.
93. U.S. Census Bureau Report, Sept. 2003, pp. 60–223.
94. G.P. Smith, II (1996), *Legal and Health Care Ethics For The Elderly*, Ch. 4.
95. Ibid.
96. Kilner, "Allocation of health care resources," p. 1067.
97. Ibid., pp. 1067, 1075.
98. Ibid., p. 1067. See also Mason et al., *Law and Medical Ethics*, p. 366.

99. Kilner, "Allocation of health care resources," p. 1067.
100. Ibid., p. 1075. See also Hall et al., *Health Care Law and Ethics*, p. 98.
101. R.H. Blank (1997), *The Price of Life*, p. 96.
102. Hall et al., *Health Care Law and Ethics*, p. 98.
103. Ibid., p. 96.
104. Ibid.
105. Ibid.
106. Rodwin, *Medicine, Money and Morals*.
107. Kilner, "Allocation of health care resources," p. 1082.
108. Ibid., pp. 1076–81. See also Mason et al., *Law and Medical Ethics*, pp. 380–81.
109. Blank, *Price of Life*, p. 96. See also Mason et al., *Law and Medical Ethics*, pp. 379–86.
110. Blank, *Price of Life*, p. 96. See R. Crisp (1989), "Deciding who will die: QALYs and political theory," *Politics*, **9**, p. 31.
111. Mason et al., *Law and Medical Ethics*, p. 378.
112. Ibid., p. 385.
113. Somerville, *Ethical Canary*, p. 262.
114. Ibid. See generally G.P. Smith, II (2000), "Euphemistic codes and tell-tale hearts: humane assistance in end-of-life cases," *Health Matrix Journal*, **10**, p. 175.
115. Somerville, *Ethical Canary*, pp. 272–3. See also G.P. Smith, II (1990), "The ethics of ethics committees," *Journal of Contemporary Health Law and Policy*, **6**, p. 157; Gaylin, "Faulty diagnosis."
116. Somerville, *Ethical Canary*, p. 274. See also Moore v. Regents of the University of California, 763 P.2d 479 (Cal. 1990).
117. Somerville, *Ethical Canary*, p. 274.
118. Ibid., p. 262.
119. Ibid.
120. Ibid.
121. Blank, *Price of Life*, p. 84.
122. D. Brown (2006), "Artificial heart gets limited FDA approval," *Washington Post*, 6 Sept., p. A8. See generally A.L. Caplan (1997), *Am I My Brother's Keeper?*, Ch. 3; G. Annas (1987), "Death and the magic machine," *Western New England Law Review*, **9**, p. 89.
123. D. Brown (2006), "Artificial heart gets limited FDA approval," *Washington Post*, 6 Sept.
124. Ibid. Over time, it is hoped a second-generation device, being tested presently in animals, will have a target life of five years and be considerably less expensive.
125. Ibid.
126. Ibid.
127. Ibid.
128. Caplan, *Am I My Brother's Keeper?*, pp. 35, *passim*.
129. Brown, "Artificial heart."
130. Ibid.
131. Case Note, "Product liability: getting to the heart of the matter," *Washburn Law Journal*, **36** (1997), p. 319.
132. Blank, *Price of Life*, p. 98.
133. Ibid., Ch. 4. See also J. Flanagan (1994), "ADA analysis of the Oregon Health Care Plan," *Issues in Law and Medicine*, **9**, p. 397; M.A. Strosberg, J.M. Weiner, R. Baker and I.A. Fein (1992), *Rationing American Medical Care: The Oregon Plan and Beyond*.
134. Gaylin, "Faulty diagnosis."
135. E. Robinson (1992), "The Oregon Basic Health Services Act: a model for state reform," *Vanderbilt Law Review*, **45**, p. 977.
136. E. Hirshfeld (1992), "Should ethical and legal standards for physicians be changed to accommodate new models of rationing health care?," *University of Pennsylvania Law Review*, **140**, p. 1809. For an in-depth consideration of the British approach to rationing, see J. Herring (2006), *Medical Law and Ethics*, Ch. 9.
137. D. Hadorn and R. Brook (1991), "The health care resource allocation debate: defining our terms," *Journal of the American Medical Association*, **266**, p. 3328.

138. M. Waymack (1991), "Old age and the rationing of scarce health care resources," in N. Jecker (ed.), *Aging and Ethics: Philosophical Problems in Gerontology*, pp. 248–9.
139. Ibid., pp. 195–7. See also Lamm, "Rationing of health care," p. 1511.
140. D. Rasinski-Gregory and M. Cotler (1993), "The elderly and health care reform: needs, concerns, responsibilities and obligations," *Western State University Law Review*, **22**, pp. 65, 83.
141. L. Frolik and A. Barnes (1991), "An aging population: a challenge to the law," *Hastings Law Journal*, **42**, pp. 683, 708–709.
142. Callahan, *Setting Limits*, p. 117.
143. D. Thomasma (1995), "The ethical challenge of providing healthcare for the elderly," *Cambridge Quarterly of Healthcare Ethics*, **4**, pp. 144, 148–9.
144. Ibid., p. 148.
145. Ibid.
146. M.R. Wicclair (1993), *Ethics and the Elderly*, p. 80.
147. Ibid. See also Smith, *Legal and Health Care Ethics for the Elderly*; G.P. Smith, II (1996), "Our hearts were once young and gay," *University of Florida Journal of Law and Public Policy*, **8**, p. 1.
148. See Thomasma, "Ethical challenge," p. 156 (noting that the elderly are responsible for building "the roads and bridges, symphonies, and schools we now enjoy").
149. Frolik and Barnes, "Aging population," p. 713.
150. See Thomasma, "Ethical challenge," p. 156 (quoting, "While the elderly may gobble up inordinate relative amounts of healthcare dollars, while doing so, they are not using other resources of society—general resources use equalizes out in the end").
151. See Callahan, *Setting Limits*, p. 83 (noting familial relationships and governmental programs such as social security and Medicare).
152. Ibid., p. 82.
153. Dubler and Sabatino, "Age-based rationing," p. 114.
154. D. Maguire and E. McFadden (1994), "The ethics of health care rationing," in K. Kelly (ed.), *Health Care Rationing: Dilemma and Paradox*, pp. 149–54.
155. A. Haddad (1994), "Ethical issues in health care rationing," in Kelly, *Health Care Rationing*, p. 11.
156. Ibid.
157. G.P. Smith, II (1996), "Utility and the principle of medical futility: safeguarding autonomy and the prohibition against cruel and unusual punishment," *Journal of Contemporary Health Law and Policy*, **12**, p. 1.
158. D. Callahan (1990), *What Kind of Life: The Limits of Medical Progress*; D. Callahan (1992), "Symbols, rationality and justice: rationing health care," *American Journal of Law and Medicine*, **18**, p. 1. Yet one commentator has suggested that today's *triage* is an "empty" principle since the essential premise is reversed— with the seriously wounded being rushed in for treatment, while the merely mutilated must wait. A.R. Jonsen (1990), *The New Medicine and The Old Ethic*, p. 45. See F. Barringer and D. McNeil (2005), "Grim triage for ailing and dying at a makeshift airport hospital" (reporting on Hurricane Katrina), *New York Times*, 3 Sept., p. A4.
159. Menzel, *Strong Medicine*, p. 38. See also R. Perett (1992), "Valuing lives," *Bioethics*, **6**, p. 185. See generally R.A. Posner (2004), *Catastrophe: Risk and Response*, pp. 165–71.
160. J. Fialka (2003), "Balancing act: lives v. regulation," *New York Times*, 30 May, p. A4.
161. Ibid. Professor W.K. Viscusi of Harvard University conducted research which places a $7 million value on human life.
162. Ibid.
163. Ibid.
164. Menzel, *Strong Medicine*, p. 79; Posner, *Catastrophe*, pp. 165–71.
165. R. Hahn and S. Wallstein (2003), "Whose life is worth more? And why is it horrible to ask?," *Washington Post*, 1 June, p. B3.
166. Menzel, *Strong Medicine*, p. 80.

167. Mason et al., *Law and Medical Ethics*, p. 382.
168. Ibid., p. 382.
169. Ibid.
170. Ibid.
171. M. Anderlik (2001), *The Ethics Of Managed Care: A Pragmatic Approach*, p. 125.
172. Menzel, *Strong Medicine*, pp. 80–81. See M. Adler (2006), "Qalys and policy evaluation: a new perspective," *Yale Journal of Health Policy, Law and Ethics*, **6**, p. 1.
173. Kilner, "Allocation of health care resources," p. 1073.
174. A. Smith and J. Rother (1992), "Older Americans and the rationing of heath care," *University of Pennsylvania Law Review*, **140**, p. 1847.
175. E. Rich (1990), "Official suggests risk–benefit rationing," *Washington Post Health Magazine*, 23 Jan., p. 25.
176. M. Cohen (1991), "Terminal care decision-making," in A.M. Dillinger (ed.), *Healthcare Facilities Law*, pp. 703, *passim*. See G.P. Smith, II (2004), "Just say no! The right to refuse psychotropic medication in long term care facilities," *Annals of Health Law*, **13**, p. 1; R. Dresser and J. Robertson (1989), "Quality of life and non-treatment decisions for incompetent patients: a critique of the orthodox approach," *Law, Medicine and Health Care*, **17**, p. 234.
177. U.S. Code, **42**, §§ 12201–12213, Supp. III, 1991.
178. N. Hoffman (2003), "Corrective justice and Title I of the ADA," *American University Law Review*, **52**, p. 1213.
179. N. Stode (1993), "The use of quality of life measures to ration health care: reviving a rejected proposal," *Columbia Law Review*, **93**, p. 985; D. Thomasma (1990), "Ethical judgments of quality of life in the care of the aged," in J. Walter and T. Shannon (eds.), *Quality of Life: The New Medical Dilemma*, Ch. 19.
180. Anderlik, *Ethics of Managed Care*, p. 134.
181. D. Thomasma (1998), "Virtue theory, social practice, and professional responsibility in medicine," in M. Evans (ed.), *Critical Reflection on Medical Ethics*, **4**, pp. 321–38.
182. Anderlik, *Ethics of Managed Care*, p. 5.
183. G.P. Smith, II (1999), "Judicial decision making in the age of biotechnology," *Notre Dame Journal of Law, Ethics and Public Policy*, **13**, p. 93.
184. R.A. Posner (1990), *The Problems of Jurisprudence*, p. 112.
185. B.R. Furrow, T.L. Greaney, S.H. Johnson, T.S. Jost and R.I. Schwartz (2001), *Health Law*, p. 478.
186. Ibid., p. 479.
187. Childress, *Practical Reasoning*, p. 254.
188. Ibid.
189. Blank, *Price of Life*, p. 98. See also P.L. Berger, R.J. Neuhas and M. Novak (eds.) (1996), *Empower People: From State To Civil Society*.
190. Anderlik, *Ethics of Managed Care*, p. 130.
191. E.D. Pellegrino and D.C. Thomasma (1981), *A Philosophical Basis of Medical Practice: Toward A Philosophy and Ethic of the Healing Professions*.
192. Daniels, "Justice, health, and health care," p. 14.
193. J. Bailey (2003), "Managed care organizations and the rationing problem," *Hastings Center Report*, **33**, Jan.–Feb., pp. 34, 40.
194. Ibid.
195. Ibid., p. 185. See generally G.P. Smith, II (2005), "Human rights and bioethics: formulating a universal right to health, health care or health protection?," *Vanderbilt Journal of Transnational Law*, **39**, p. 1295.
196. Pellegrino and Thomasma, *For the Patient's Good*, p. 189.
197. D.C. Thomasma (2000), "The principle of dimension," in Thomasma and Kissel, *The Health Care Professional as Friend and Healer*, pp. 133–47.
198. Pellegrino and Thomasma, *For the Patient's Good*, p. 185.
199. Ibid.
200. D. Thomasma (1996), "The ethics of managed care: challenges to the principles of relationship centered care," *Journal of Allied Health*, **25**, p. 233. See generally N. Hunter

(2006), "Managed process, due care: structures of accountability in healthcare," *Yale Journal of Health Policy, Law and Ethics*, **6**, p. 93.
201. G.P. Smith, II (2000), *Human Rights and Biomedicine*, p. 16.
202. Ibid.
203. Pellegrino and Thomasma, *Virtues in Medical Practice*; Pellegrino and Thomasma, *Philosophical Basis*.

3. The new medicine and scientific research

INTRODUCTION

Substantial scientific evidence indicates man's genetic inheritance acts as a major influence not only upon his behavior but also upon his health.[1] In the United States, for example, it is estimated that 1 out of every 33 babies is born with a discernible genetic deficiency which in turn accounts for more than 20 percent of all infant deaths.[2] Of all chronic diseases, between 20 and 25 percent are predominantly genetic in origin.[3] Down syndrome, for example, is a genetic condition affecting nearly 1 in 800 babies.[4] At least half of the hospital beds in America have been occupied by patients whose incapacities were known to be of a genetic origin.[5] Because modern medicine can alleviate the symptoms of some genetic diseases through sophisticated treatment, many who are afflicted and who would not have survived in the past now survive. Medicine is unable to cure genetic defects *ex utero*,[6] but has been astute in identifying over 4000 inherited disorders.[7] The "new medicine" attempts—largely through genetic diagnostics, screening and manipulation—to alleviate the heartbreak of genetic suffering and thereby attack genetic disease. Unmistakenly, this type of medicine has a eugenic character; but this, as will be seen, is by no means an overpowering negative.[8]

Considerable research into techniques for perfecting genetic engineering has been undertaken in an attempt to develop new treatment for individuals with inherited diseases.[9] Under the rubric of the "New Biology," scientists are investigating and developing many interventions, including gene deletion surgery, splicing and transplantation, cloning *in vitro* or test-tube fertilization, embryo implantation, parthenogenesis, amniocentesis, and experimentation with the scope and application of DNA.[10] Genetic engineering utilizes some of these procedures to reorganize human genes to produce varied, particular characteristics.[11]

In order to combat genetic disease, genetic engineering may, and frequently does, rely upon eugenics, the science that deals with improving heredity. Stated simply, a positive eugenics program seeks to develop superior qualities in man through the propagation of his superior genes,[12] and the positive eugenists seek to produce a "new breed" with keener and more creative intelligence.[13] Conversely, a negative eugenics program attempts only to eliminate genetic weaknesses.[14] When seen in application, positive eugenics programs encourage the fit and "proper" individuals to reproduce, while negative eugenics programs discourage those less fit and those with inheritable diseases from procreating.[15] Abortion is one way of implementing a program of negative eugenics after earlier attempts to regulate have failed.[16]

ASEXUAL REPRODUCTION: CLONING

Research into artificial sexual reproductive techniques, and more specifically cloning, is said to "go to the very nature of the individuality which is implicit in any legal order."[17] Accordingly, ethical and religious objections tie to the nature of cloning as being an unreasonable and "unnatural" interference with "normal" procreative processes.[18] It is not only a form of inbreeding but is said to endanger evolutionary development and the very values of human diversity which come from it.[19]

The word "cloning," which derives from a Greek root meaning "cutting," is defined generally as asexual propagation and is commonly used to develop new varieties of plants.[20] In 1966, a team of Oxford University biologists, headed by Dr. John Gurdon, announced that they had grown seven frogs from the intestinal cells of tadpoles.[21] What had been routine in the garden now existed for one group of animals: a new organism was produced from a single parent.

Several steps would be required to clone a human. First, the nucleus of a donor's egg cell would be destroyed. Second, a nucleus from any convenient cell of the person to be cloned would be inserted into the enucleated egg by microsurgical techniques which scientists today have yet to develop. Third, the new cell, placed in a nutrient medium, would begin to divide; and, fourth, implantation of the embryo into the uterus would follow in approximately four to six days.[22] The cloned individual would be the identical twin of the person who contributed the body cell.[23] The establishment of banks of tissue cultures would permit the cloning of deceased persons.

Present medical ethics require that a researcher be reasonably confident about the outcome of his research, that he undertake research for reasonably humanitarian purposes, and that he obtain the informed consent of the research subjects. These factors do not determine whether cloning is proper. If the rate of pollution of the human gene pool continues to increase through uncontrolled sexual reproduction, however, efforts to produce healthier people may be required to compensate for the increase in the number of people afflicted with genetic diseases.[24] In that event, one could make a strong ethical argument to justify cloning of healthy individuals on the ground that it could achieve the greatest good for the greatest number of people.[25] Fears of the degradation of parenthood and the dehumanization of man by the promotion of genetic bondage or slavery, as a consequence of genetically engineering individuals according to preconceived designs, underscore for some the conclusions that human cloning is a direct assault on the principle of the sanctity of human life.[26] To consider, as well, a ban on cloning because of fears that it might be used for racist purposes has been held as "tantamount to saying that sexual intercourse should be prohibited because it permits the possibility of rape."[27]

Involuntary cloning is of obvious concern—this, because of the relative ease by which it is accomplished. Inasmuch as DNA from only one cell is required to make a clone—and this can be obtained easily from hair, saliva or other cell sources—cloning an individual without his consent or knowledge could, in theory, be done routinely.[28] This concern is allayed, however, when it is realized that physicians would surely not act unethically and assist patients who wish to clone other people than themselves for sport or enjoyment. The vast majority of people would—no doubt—want only to propagate themselves.[29] This desire for clonal self-replication would, however, be met with another competing one: namely, that any cloned children have opportunities for *better* lives than their cloning parent. Thus, this secondary concern may in fact be a "reality check" and serve as a deterrent to the unrestricted popularity and use of cloning.[30]

STATISTICAL UNCERTAINTIES

The success in cloning cows, sheep, goats, pigs and mice is limited—with between 95 and 97 percent of these scientific efforts ending in disaster.[31] Extrapolating from these efforts and applying them to chances for human cloning, it is estimated that almost all of the first 100 clones will end by spontaneous abortion—this, because of extreme physical abnormalities which in turn would place the lives and health of the surrogate mothers carrying the clones at risk. Of the handful of surviving clones, most will have not only grossly enlarged placentas, but fatty livers as well. The associated question then becomes: what is to be done with a malformed clone? With animals, they are destroyed. For flawed human clones, it is thought that they would, with medical intervention, be kept alive. Even for a "normal looking" clone, life under these conditions would not be pleasant.[32]

Genetic imprinting is crucial to the process of successful human cloning for it is a molecular mechanism through which genes inside sperm and egg cells are turned on or off in preparation for early embryonic and fetal development. Regrettably, no test exists presently for determining whether the genes of a cloned embryo are imprinted properly. Thus, it is quite impossible to determine and select out those embryos which are foredoomed to develop abnormally.[33]

Additional ethical issues could arise when a cloned child might be used as a means to an end—when, for example, it has been created to serve as a source for a new and perfectly matched bone marrow transplant for an existing child. Although seen from one perspective as unethical, such actions in and of themselves should not be seen as reasons for banning cloning altogether. Rather, the benefits derived from beneficent actions of this nature would be weighed—in every individual case and jurisdiction—against the social costs and risk of harm to the individual clone from such procedures.[34]

LEGISLATIVE BLUEPRINTS

Behind all of these ethical concerns lie the constitutional values of privacy and personal autonomy—the protection of which is surely a valid secular purpose for legislation. Any state purpose, then, that protects the sanctity of human life contains a combination of religious, moral and secular purposes. If, for example, a legislative ban on cloning achieved a coalescence of these purposes, it might well be expected to encounter difficulty in the courts—especially those which do not view "morality legislation" as proper. Indeed, some statutes have been invalidated because they were found to have an improper purpose of enforcing morals *qua* morals.[35]

Legislation that embodies positive eugenics concepts and permits only individuals with superior genetic endowments to clone would raise a serious constitutional issue. Such a statute would require safeguards against the large-scale cloning of particular types of individuals. To do otherwise would decrease the genetic variation that is so vitally necessary to natural selection and would even threaten man with his own extinction.[36] By discriminating between those with superior genetic traits and all others, however, legislation of this nature would be subject to equal protection challenges. Under standard equal protection analysis, if a court determined that the statutes affected a fundamental right, the state would need to show that the legislation served a compelling state interest.[37] The right to procreate has been declared a fundamental right,[38] but the denial of cloning methods to individuals who are capable of reproducing in the normal manner may not be a sufficient infringement of this fundamental right to trigger the compelling interest requirement.[39] If it were not such an infringement, the state would be required to show only rational relation between the legislation and a legitimate state interest.[40] A court might determine that the state's interest in the propagation of superior traits is impermissible, constitutionally, because it violates the Constitution's nobility clause[41] or the Thirteenth Amendment's prohibition of involuntary servitude.[42] If a court determined that the state has a legitimate interest in the propagation of superior traits, it would probably go on to find that the legislation is related rationally to that purpose.

Persons who carry genes for recessive traits might succeed in claiming that permitting only genetically superior people to clone infringes upon their right to procreate—with that claim triggering strict judicial scrutiny of the cloning law and requiring the state to show a compelling interest for its action.[43] Under this type of judicial scrutiny, at least two constitutional attacks on the statute itself could be made in addition to challenging the state's purpose. It is doubtful whether scientific evidence could provide a rational basis for classification of individuals based on genetic traits.[44] Moreover, the state may be able to achieve its objective through a less intrusive program: its interest in the propagation of superior traits through a positive eugenics program is probably less compelling than its interest in the diminution of inferior traits through a negative eugenics program.[45]

TWO SPECIFIC APPROACHES

Thus, it is seen that there are—essentially—two legislative approaches to the issue of human cloning: enforcing a total prohibition on this form of sexual reproduction in order to safeguard ideals of humaneness and sanctity of life—together with personal privacy and individual autonomy—or promoting a selective regulation of cloning thereby seeking to accommodate the humanitarian goal of providing infertile couples with biologically linked descendants and promote consequentially the improvement of the gene pool.[46]

In March 1997, President Clinton banned the use of federal funds for human cloning,[47] but settled subsequently on a five-year work moratorium.[48] In June of that year, however, the National Bioethics Advisory Commission recommended federal legislation be enacted to allow a limited number of scientists to create cloned human embryos. The use of the embryos by implantation to make cloned human babies would be prohibited however.[49]

The U.S. House of Representatives voted along bipartisan lines (265 to 162) on 31 July 2001 to ban cloning for reproduction as well as for medical research purposes. This action by the House not only prohibits specifically therapeutic cloning but outlaws the sale of treatments developed from it, but imposes for violation thereof a criminal sanction of up to ten years of imprisonment and a civil penalty of not less than $1 000 000.[50] Senator Samuel D. Brownback of Kansas introduced similar proposed legislation which, while calling for an international effort to prohibit human cloning, also calls for further study of the advantages and disadvantages of cloning to produce human embryos for research.[51] Both legislative proposals failed to be enacted and were re-introduced in 2005 and then languished in committee.[52]

Predictably, the cloning issue is enmeshed with the politics of embryonic stem cell research. Yet, a line of distinction is sought by advancing the argument that, since stem cell research is to be limited to cells extracted from embryos otherwise discarded by fertility clinics, it is a less threatening activity in popular society than therapeutic cloning.[53]

While abortion opponents heralded the House action in 2001, the biotechnology industry viewed the action "as a step backward for medical research."[54] At times, the debate appeared to be a discourse in theology more than a political discussion—"with lawmakers expounding on matters like whether embryos created through cloning are embryos at all."[55] Some feminists on the political left oppose all forms of cloning because of their fears science will place undue burdens on those women who choose to donate their eggs either for research or for reproductive purposes. Others support a moratorium—not an outright ban—on research cloning.[56]

Abortion rights were revitalized as an ancillary issue, as well, when the Bush administration began efforts in January 2002 to extend health care to more women during pregnancy and included health insurance coverage for developing fetuses.[57] The effect of such a policy is to define childhood—for the first time in any federal program—as commencing *before* birth. While the Secretary of Health and Human Services stated the policy would assist lower-income or poor mothers in taking care of their unborn children and obtaining medical care, abortion rights advocates criticized the action as nothing more than a ruse for the development of legal grounds for, very simply, outlawing abortion.[58] The Vice President of the National Partnership for Women and Families opined that this new policy "is not about providing prenatal care or expanding coverage for pregnant women . . . [but about] granting legal personhood to a fetus."[59]

CONGRESSIONAL "ACTION" AND INACTION

On 10 April 2002, President George W. Bush called upon the Senate to ban all types of human cloning either for reproduction or for medical research.[60] Hinting that he would use a veto to achieve this goal, the

President aligned himself with many congressional Republicans who think as he does,[61] and particularly with the bill proposed by Senator Brownback—this, in opposition to most Democrats who defend therapeutic or research cloning.[62]

Despite heavy lobbying on both sides of the aisle, and growing fears that the two types of cloning have merged in the public's mind[63]—together with a realization in the American scientific community that US biologists will need to emigrate to laboratories in Australia, Japan, Israel and certain European countries if the Brownback prohibitions were enacted into law[64]—the Congress found itself paralysed and unable to act.[65] This inactive course of events has given a new focus and impetus to state legislative programs designed to tackle and resolve the cloning issue[66] even though the final result may well be a crazy patchwork quilt of various responses. When all is said and done, however, most informed observers fully expect Congress, over time, to act by banning reproductive cloning and thereby preventing hopefully a science fiction scenario being developed wherein corporations engage in selling standardized people specially engineered genetically for specific job purposes (for example, captive organ donors, hyper-violent soldiers, assembly line drones).[67]

ADMINISTRATIVE UNCERTAINTIES

It has been determined that the federal Food and Drug Administration has the authority to regulate human cloning. Thus, any efforts undertaken to attempt research in this area must be initiated with the filing of a formal application to the FDA which would then undertake a lengthy review. Anyone failing to follow this procedure will be prosecuted.[68]

A number of legal scholars hold to the opinion that there is little evidence to support this assertion of authority by the FDA over cloning. Indeed, it is contended that there is no basis in present food and drug laws which would provide a legal basis for preventing physicians from attempting to clone human beings and, furthermore, if a court challenge were to be made, the FDA would lose.[69] The director of the FDA's Center for Biologics Evaluation and Research argues, however, that the administration's regulatory authority derives from the Public Health Service Act which delegates to it the power to regulate "biological products" used to treat medical conditions. A cloned human embryo is defined by the FDA as a "somatic clone" and is, consequently, to be considered a "biological product" intended to treat infertility.[70]

There is a growing consensus among scientific leaders on this issue that the FDA will be more reasonable than will Congress if and when it decides to impose a blanket prohibition on cloning.[71] As observed, any congressional action limiting the right of scientists to pursue their intellectual interests would have to be drawn very narrowly in order to avoid a successful First Amendment challenge.[72] Thus, if the government views the central issue of cloning as a health and safety issue, there should be a law setting forth minimal safety standards for scientific work in this field.[73]

Ultimately, it may well be up to the US Supreme Court to decide whether there are acceptable limits to be placed on human reproduction. In the past—as seen—the Court has recognized procreative liberties as "fundamental rights" and cautioned the government that any abridgement of these rights cannot be undertaken or validated unless a truly compelling state interest can be shown.[74]

MARKET STRATEGIES FOR CONTROL?

At the national level of debate, various suggestions have been made to regulate participation in genetic technologies.[75] Total bans have been suggested as the most direct means of curtailment. Targeting directly health care professionals and institutional providers (for example, hospitals and IVF clinics), legislation could be enacted not only making it a crime to provide genetic enhancements, but allowing a loss of medical licenses and hospital accreditation for convictions thereof. If genetic enhancements were tested as proprietary products similar to drugs or medical devices, marketing denial of them could be imposed by the Food and Drug Administration.[76] The enforcement of such prohibiting regulations would be complicated, however, by the ongoing need to distinguish valid therapeutic uses of genetic modification through assisted reproductive technologies from invalid enhancement uses.[77]

Licensing has been proposed as an alternative to legislative prohibitions on genetic enhancements. Accordingly, under this scheme, a licensing system would be imposed for the ownership and/or use of dangerous enhancement products. As suppliers, providers of this service would be required to obtain a license which, in turn, would impose restrictions on use as well as impose reporting requirements. Those seeking a license would be required to justify the social benefits deriving from their use of enhancement technologies and would be required, furthermore, to report to the licensing board in order to provide assurance of satisfactory performance.[78] Obviously, this scheme would be open only to those having adequate financial resources to participate in the first instance.[79]

In order to equalize opportunity for use of genetic enhancement therapies, a final suggestion has been made to establish either a national enhancement lottery or a subsidization program. These would provide people, otherwise lacking in sufficient resources, with an opportunity for access to enhancements.[80] Under one format, the government would seek to subsidize enhancements for certain "underprivileged" genetic classes. The other strategy would provide a national lottery where everyone would be given one chance in a drawing—with the winner being entitled to use those public resources necessary to purchase legally a tailored-to-need enhancements package in the private market.[81] Here, there are obvious problems of fairness in not only determining the standards used for selecting the "underprivileged" for participation in such a program but—as well—the first order determination of the national need (and justification) for a vast commitment of resources to correct genetic "deficiencies" or abnormalities within the general population.[82]

THE NEW EUGENICS

With the introduction of contemporary molecular biology into prenatal testing, society is being led—inescapably—into eugenics, albeit from a far differently focused perspective than seen in Nazi Germany during World War II.[83] There are, to be sure, fears that this new *laissez-faire* eugenics will seek to transform the population in a particular direction—thus not advancing an inherent goal of eugenics to avoid suffering, but rather reflecting and advancing a particular set of social values.[84] Today, parents may—through genetic screening or *in utero* testing—learn whether a prospective offspring will be born with, for example, neurofibromatosis or Hurler syndrome, and knowing this may take what action is deemed appropriate.

Utopian Eugenics seeks to uncover those considerations which should or may guide reproductive choices. Thus, for example, a high priority of this science is assessing the array of fetal characteristics which would lead responsible people to terminate a pregnancy.[85] Utopian Eugenics seeks not to coerce parents, but rather to educate them and—furthermore—seeks no societally imposed restrictions on reproductive choice.[86] Accordingly, this science seeks to foster an understanding—by and through education—that "abortion is appropriate when the fetus suffers from a genetic disease."[87] When it is determined that a fetus had no chance of self-determination, as with early-onset neurodegenerative disorders, or in cases where a low quality of life combines with a large impact on the lives of others (as when it tests positive for degenerative muscular disease and the parents-to-be are already struggling to make a decent living for themselves and other existing children), Utopian eugenists would suggest a clear case for abortion exists.[88] And, they in turn, would stress—by way of justifying their position—that the prevention of "disease has nothing to do with imposing social values, for whether or not something is a disease is a matter of objective fact."[89]

However one chooses to view the field of molecular biology—as an out-and-out attack on the right-to-life movement or an exciting aspect of modern science—one fact is indisputable: namely, the field itself presents an "unimaginable ocean of truth" with which contemporary society must deal. It cannot be sealed off and closeted as a forbidden zone of simply theoretical knowledge.[90]

A DUAL RELATIONSHIP

It would appear that eugenics enjoys clearly a dual relationship with genetics; for it does not only have a negative force, but the threatening potentiality of its unrestrained application is of minor consequence when the positive sequence of its potential contributions is both appreciated and utilized. The dynamic vectors of force seen in the application of modern eugenics through efforts of genetic advancement and "engineering" must be restrained and placed in equilibrium in order to alleviate fears of unbridled slippery slopes of scientific advancement pursued blindly.[91] Viewed as not only an aid to the tragedy of infertility in family planning, but as a tool for enhancing the health of the future members of society, vital research and experimentation must continue apace in eugenics and genetics. To attempt to sever one from the other assures an impotent, as opposed to a virile, response to both the challenge and the mystery of amazing development of the new reproductive biology.[92]

The failure of the early eugenics movement can be attributed to its endorsement of principles and initiatives which had the ultimate effect of both devaluing and marginalizing large segments of the public. Today, the new genetics—feared and shadowed by the eugenic records of the past—must state with clarity and purpose its central policy: namely, to ensure that its maximum benefits are obtained while avoiding the exclusion and stigmatization of any individual.[93] Fears of promoting and, indeed, developing a "genetic ghetto" should not hold back the untold opportunities for good coming from research and advancement in eugenics and genetics.[94] In order to safeguard this needed compatibility, a spirit of accommodation must be fostered—one that accommodates genetic advances and, at the same time, integrates individuals with disabilities. Accepted as such, eugenics becomes a moral obligation society must both accept and act upon.[95]

THE SCOPE OF SCIENTIFIC REVIEW

The central question which arises in relation to current scientific advances in biotechnology under the rubric of the "new medicine" is whether genetic engineering should be promoted and encouraged as a basic recognition of the freedom of scientific inquiry and right of privacy. Significant potential dangers are present in conjunction with the almost limitless opportunity for scientific advancement within the technology of recombinant DNA, referred commonly to as genetic engineering. The fear that the proverbial "mad scientist," working independently or with an enemy foreign power, could isolate and then proceed to duplicate a cancer organism and possibly place it in public water supplies is not easily dismissed. Acts of thoughtless negligence in a laboratory could result in the "escape" of a deadly microbe, which in turn could give rise to a "parade of horribles." Chance occurrences are always inherent in any scientific intervention.[96] When the chance of harmful accident is calculated, the primary consideration is whether the merit of the intervention justifies beginning or continuing the experiment.[97]

The sanctity of creation and the fundamental right of privacy in procreation, which is an acknowledged basic or fundamental freedom, may be altered by compelling state interests.[98] Is there a more compelling state interest than the desire to stop a "chromosomal lottery" which saddles the economy each year with 4 million Americans born with diabetes or 50 000 born with discernible genetic diseases?[99] State interests in minimizing human suffering and maximizing the social good should be properly validated.[100]

Opponents of unrestricted genetic research attack specifically its proponents as being both scientifically and socially irresponsible, and the ultimate promoters of a serious environmental disaster.[101] They suggest that nature has developed strong barriers against genetic interchanges between species, and that extreme caution ought to be used during experimentation in this area.[102] Others argue that mankind's genetic inheritance is its greatest and most indispensable treasure which must be protected and guaranteed at any cost. These opponents submit that the evolutionary wisdom of the ages must not be threatened irreversibly or abridged in order to satisfy the ambition and professional curiosity of some members of the scientific community.

Autonomy, self-determination and a basic sense of freedom must be tempered by logic, objectivity and a disinterested search for knowledge, a search that may result in the minimizing of human suffering and maximizing of social good.[103] But what is the social good in this equation? It is suggested that the social good, within this context, could be equated with an economic policy that lessens the financial burden on citizens to support and maintain genetically defective citizens. The wisest policy is, by consensus, that which promotes a good—social, economic or otherwise—for the greatest number. Thus, human need and well-being shape the degree of positive good resulting from one policy as opposed to another.[104] Alternatively, a determination could be made in order to structure what is right or wrong, good or evil, according to whether the consequences of an act or public policy add to, or detract from, the aggregate human well-being.[105]

ENCOURAGING EXPERIMENTATION

Recognizing that a sustained level of progress for society would depend upon a continuing standard of technological evolution as well as individual technological contributions of exceptional merit and benefit, the Founding Fathers endeavored to codify this attitude within the United States Constitution. By structuring a system of checks and balances within the Constitution which would promote both perspectives, contributions which were truly exceptional could be promoted by grant of a limited monopolization as authorized by the Patent Clause.[106] However, the grant of limited monopolization was intended to be consistent with the guarantees of the Fifth and the Fourteenth Amendments, that recognize the right of all citizens to develop their individual skills in pursuit of a trade or calling, and thus establish this right as an inalienable property right.[107]

On 16 June 1980, by a 5–4 vote, the United States Supreme Court decided that new forms of laboratory life were eligible for patents.[108] The decision may be regarded as ratification of some of the accomplishments of the "biological revolution" which has allowed a broader understanding of life and promoted a greater ability to manipulate various forms. However, both the majority opinion and the dissent stressed that they addressed only the question of whether the current patent laws evinced a congressional intent to deny patents to those inventions determined to be alive.[109] More particularly, the Court chose to tie itself to the United States Code section which provides: "Whoever invents or discovers any new and useful process, machine, manufacture, or composition of matter, or any new and useful improvement thereof, may obtain a patent therefor, subject to the conditions and requirements of this title."[110] Out of this statute emerged the issue of whether a manufactured microorganism constituted "a 'manufacture' or 'composition of matter'" within the meaning of the statute.[111]

In the past, the Patent Office has included living things within the statutory subject matter. For example, in 1873, United States Patent No. 141 072 was issued to Louis Pasteur. Claim two of the patent application reads:

"Yeast, free from organic germs of disease, as an article of manufacture."[112] There are other examples, in other patents, of claims having been granted for viruses and cultures.[113]

Today, there are more than 100 patent applications related to products of genetic engineering.[114] *Chakrabarty* sets the pace for a wide variety of new "man-made" organisms which can facilitate socially desirable processes such as growing wheat in arid lands, leeching ores to assist mining companies in reaching remote parts of the earth, and producing a "bug" that will ferment corn starch or corn syrup into ethanol, an alcohol used in both whiskey and gasohol. There was also a patent application for a bacterium that metabolizes ethylene into ethylene glycol (antifreeze).[115]

A FURTHER INNOVATIVE APPLICATION

In May 1987, the United States Patent and Trademark Office announced that it "considers non-naturally occurring nonhuman multi-cellular living organisms, including animals, to be patentable subject matter."[116] This policy was viewed by the Patent Office as an effort to keep pace with the startling new advances in biotechnology, and thereby encourage innovation and not determine its ethical implications. Others, such as animal rights advocates, were concerned that animals were being considered as products and not sentient beings.[117] Some feared that the new policy would enable a select number of biotechnology companies to dominate the livestock industry, thereby eliminating small independent breeders and threatening to eliminate genetic diversity among farm animals,[118] since with the patents the central issue becomes who either owns or is in control of breeding livestock.[119]

Theologians quarreled with the Patent Office policy because it not only equated heavenly made creatures with manufactured goods of the market place, but took a giant step on the slippery slope that would lead to the patenting of genetically altered human beings and man's full assumption of God-like powers. The clear specification of the policy that its application was only for "nonhuman life" was of no assurance here.[120] Informed members of the scientific community, however, saw the Patent Office as merely continuing the reasonable exploitation of nature.[121]

If enacted into legislation by the Congress, the Transgenic Animal Patent Reform Act of 1988[122] would have excluded human beings from patentable subject matter, provided immunity from patent infringement to farmers who purchased patented farm animals and sought subsequently to reproduce them, and endeavored to clarify the authority of the Patent and Trademark Office to require biological material deposits from patented animals.[123] The most serious defect of this proposed legislation, which did succeed in passing the House, was its failure to define the term "human being." Thus, the extent to which genetic material constitutes a human being remains an open question.

> Should an animal that contains one-half of a human code be considered human? How about one-quarter human genetic material? Should genetically altered fetuses be considered patentable subject matter under current patent law? Although such animals are not being patented . . . such technology will exist in the near future.[124]

A cellular biologist at the New York Medical College announced in 1998 that he had applied for a patent on a method for making creatures that are part human and part animal, or chimeras. While he had never created such a creature—and with no present intent to undertake the task—his goal was to force a national debate on the commercialization of life with the US Patent and Trademark Office to re-examine the country's current position on this issue.[125] Indeed, patent law experts suggest that there is nothing in the US Patent Code precluding someone being awarded a patent on a partially human creature. The Patent Office has awarded previously several patents on animals with minor human components, including laboratory mice engineered with human cancer genes or human immune system cells. While not empowered to take ethical criteria into account when considering a patent application, the Patent Office held this application to a high standard of proof of feasibility.[126] Accordingly in 2005, the office rejected the earlier claim filed in 1998 for a chimera, stating that the hybrid had not yet been created and, furthermore, would be too closely related to a human to be patentable.[127] It remains, ultimately, for Congress and the courts to determine how questions of this nature regarding the ownership of life forms are determined.

CONGRESSIONAL DIRECTION

On 23 January 2004, President George W. Bush signed into law H.R. 2673, the Consolidated Appropriations Act.[128] Within this legislation was a provision prohibiting the US Patent and Trademark Office from issuing patents "on claims directed to or encompassing a human organism." Known as the "Weldon Amendment," after its author, Congressman David Weldon of Florida, this legislation makes it considerably more difficult for biotech firms to profit from their ongoing attempts to, through use of cloning, create human embryos—this, simply because investors will be less willing to support, financially, such research, since there is no hope for a return on their original investments. Interestingly, the National Right to Life Committee played a significant role in lobbying support for this amendment.

Even though, as seen, the US Patent and Trademark Office has had a long-standing policy against granting a patent on a "human being," there has been a growing fear by some that, when an application is made for a patent on a cloned or genetically modified human embryo, the courts—using *Chakrabarty* as precedent—will likely order the Patent Office to grant the patent, unless, that is, Congress acts to prohibit it specifically.

In explaining his position on the Weldon Amendment, the congressman himself asserted that the amendment would not prohibit the issuance of patents on stem cells or genes, but would only prohibit the issuance of patents on human organisms, embryos, fetuses or human beings.[129] And, indeed, previously in 1998 and 2001, patents claiming preparations of human stem cells have been granted.[130]

Yet a major concern is that the broad language of the Weldon Amendment prohibiting, as it does, the patenting of "human organisms" could nevertheless be interpreted as broadening the current Patent Office prohibition to proscribe also the patenting of human cells or human cell lines, such as embryonic stem cells. Since human cells are allowed to divide and multiply, creating larger cell masses, the question then becomes, at what point do these cell lines cross over the line from being a collection of human cells to a human organism? Heretofore, the Patent Office has supported patenting lines of this composition.[131]

CONTINUING CONCERNS

It is expected, as well, that the near future of biotechnology will give rise to work in laboratories in the United States where virus and bacteria genes will be transferred to plants in an effort to enable them to produce their own particular insecticides or fertilizers. After field testing, these "transgenic" plants will be used by farmers in the place of conventional crop varieties.[132] Further successful research will be undertaken that manipulates the primordial cells producing sperm and eggs to enable breeders to determine the sex and other preferred characteristics of their animals; and routine gene transplants from one species to another will be accomplished.[133]

A part of the continuing debate over the long-range effects of genetic engineering was seen rather dramatically in 1995, when leaders from more than 80 religious denominations—including Protestant, Catholic, Jewish, Buddhist, Muslim and Hindu groups—formed a Joint Appeal against Human and Animal Patenting.[134] The appeal grew from concerns over the long-term consequences of *Chakrabarty* and the US Patent and Trademark Office's positions on non-human multicellular organisms and sought, essentially, to advance the prominence of the idea that human genes are integral to the maintenance of sanctity in God's creations. Thus, patenting of life forms fails to recognize the soundness of life itself.[135] Interestingly, this action is seen as but a codification of the decades-old controversy concerning whether risks associated with new technologies outweigh their benefits.[136] At the same time, it serves as a reminder that the force of religious values and ethics in the public arena is ongoing.[137]

THE FEDERAL POSITION

As a response both to Louise Brown's extracorporeal conception in 1978 and to a grant application for *in vitro* fertilization (IVF) research, the then Department of Health, Education, and Welfare (HEW) (now the Department of Health and Human Services) and its Ethics Advisory Board decided to study the complex ethical, legal, social and scientific issues raised by the IVF process.[138] The final report of the Department was ultimately "buried in the bureaucracy."[139] Yet today, given the sometimes strident pro-life mood of a vocal segment of society, there is pessimism that a strong positive movement will occur at the federal regulatory level.[140] Owing largely to the leadership of former Congressman (then Senator) Albert Gore of Tennessee, hearings were conducted in August 1984 on the issue of embryo transfers and the legal, ethical and medical responses to such procedures.[141] Although no firm or conclusive steps were taken as a consequence of these hearings, they served to focus attention on the need for continuing dialogue in this area.

Because of a *de facto* moratorium set in 1975, no federally funded research was undertaken on IVF.[142] Even though the 1979 Report of the Ethics Advisory Board of HEW concluded that federal support of research on humans designed to establish the safety and the effectiveness of IVF procedures would be ethically permissible so long as certain conditions were met,[143] the Report has never been accepted nor the moratorium ended; there is no real likelihood such action will be taken soon.[144]

It should be noted carefully that the involvement by the federal government and its Department of Health and Human Services is structured presently by general regulations protecting human subjects which apply to any IVF research, development, or other related activities that might in the future be conducted by the Department, or by the federal government outside the Department.[145] To ensure additional protection in research projects that involve fetuses and/or pregnant women, the Ethics Advisory

Board of the Department will be required to review every such proposal for IVF "as to its acceptability from an ethical standpoint."[146]

Subsequent specific protections have been provided fetuses who are the subject of proposed experimentation and IVF research.[147] Although limited to research efforts funded in whole or in part by the federal government,[148] these guidelines make a significant distinction with regard to potential legal rights of implanted embryos.[149] The distinction is apparent in the definition of a fetus as "the product of conception from the time of implantation (as evidenced by any of the presumptive signs of pregnancy, such as missed menses, or a medically acceptable pregnancy test)."[150]

As a consequence of this structured definition, research undertaken on fetuses *in utero* and *ex utero* is prohibited unless the purpose of the activity is to meet the particular health needs of the at-risk fetus or there is minimal real or potential harm to the fetus by the research, and the purpose is to obtain biomedical knowledge not otherwise obtainable.[151] Research undertaken on non-viable fetuses *ex utero* is prohibited unless vital functions will not be maintained artificially, experimental activities that would terminate vital functions are not used, or the research purpose is to obtain otherwise unobtainable significant biomedical knowledge.[152] The obvious implication of these restrictions on embryonic and fetal research is that the scientific pursuit of mankind is handicapped significantly. Private research into the mysteries and the opportunities of the new reproductive biology continues. But, without a balanced regulated scheme and sources for federal research funding, the initiative and the momentum for scientific advancement are curtailed.

PRESIDENTIAL DIRECTION (THE BUSH ADMINISTRATION EXTENSION)

On 13 November 1989, the administration of President George H.W. Bush, through Dr. Louis W. Sullivan, Secretary of Health and Human Services, advised the National Institutes of Health (NIH) that, because of a belief that allowing federal scientists to conduct research using fetal tissue transplants would actually increase the incidence of abortion across the country, the ban on fetal tissue research would be extended.[153] The Secretary stated that his department "should not be funding activities which encourage or promote abortion."[154] Even though the ban is limited in application to federal scientists, many members of the medical research community are of the opinion that extension of the fetal tissue research ban will produce a "chilling effect" on this exciting field of research even for privately funded undertakings.[155] What is seen very clearly here is the inextricable relationship between abortion, fetal research[156] and experimentation and, even more importantly, a similar inextricability between politics and morality.[157]

THE CLINTON ACTION

On 22 January 1993, President William Clinton lifted the moratorium on federal funding of research involving transplantation of fetal tissue from induced abortions.[158] With the execution of this presidential memorandum, untold opportunities are now created for developing effective treatments for such diseases as Parkinson's and Alzheimer's as well as disorders of the nature of diabetes and leukemia.

After the moratorium was lifted in 1993, Congress proceeded later that year to enact the National Institutes of Health Revitalization Act which authorized expressly the Secretary of Health and Human Services to support research on the transplantation of human fetal tissue "regardless of whether the tissue is obtained pursuant to a spontaneous or induced abortion or pursuant to a still birth."[159] The Act requires written consent of the woman donating the tissue. And, in the event the tissue is obtained pursuant to an induced abortion, assurances must be received that the woman's consent to the abortion was obtained before a request for donation of the tissues was made. The donor may not place restrictions on the tissue recipients and—furthermore—must affirm that she has not been informed of the identity of the recipients—this to ensure these individuals are aware that they are working with or receiving human fetal tissue.[160] Interestingly, the Act does not require consent of the father of the fetus before research is undertaken.[161]

TOWARD A STANDARD OF REASONABLENESS

Man's dehumanization and depersonalization will not be fostered as a consequence of the continued quest for mastery of the genetic code and the study and use of non-coital reproduction processes. Indeed, so long as procreation continues to remain the central driving force in a marital relationship and the family the very core of a progressive society, efforts will be undertaken to expand the period of fecundity and combat infertility itself. Genetic planning and eugenic programming are more rational and humane alternatives, as seen, to population regulation than death by famine and war.

Man must endeavor to execute his investigatory and manipulative or creative powers within the scientific laboratory with a rational purpose and in a spirit of humanism. He should seek to minimize human suffering, thereby continuing to the social goal of allowing each member of society an equal opportunity to achieve their maximum output within the economic market place, and to maintain personal integrity and seek spiritual tranquility. Genetic engineering that contributes to the social good should be utilized fully. There can be no real doubt that genetic manipulation provides a perilous opportunity that may either threaten freedom or enhance it—all depending upon the balance struck between its use for individual need satisfaction and societal good.[162]

Restraining scientific inquiry should be limited only to action taken considered to be unreasonable. Accordingly, an undertaking would be regarded as unreasonable when the long- and short-term costs of its effects would outweigh the enduring benefits that would derive from its study and implementation. Viewed, then, as being not only an aid to the tragedy of infertility in family planning, but a tool for enhancing the health of a nation's citizens, vital scientific research must continue in the new, non-coital reproductive technologies and in efforts to engineer man's genetic weaknesses out of the line of inheritance. Healthier and genetically sound individuals have a much better opportunity for pursuing and achieving the "good life" and making a significant contribution to society's greater well-being.

STRUCTURING RESPONSES (FEDERAL GUIDELINES)

Drawing upon positive recommendations made by the National Bioethics Advisory Commission in September 1999, the National Institutes of Health issued Guidelines for Research Using Human Pluripotent Stem Cells on 25 August 2000, and thus lifted effectively the moratorium on embryonic stem cell research in the United States.[163] These guidelines allow for the federal funding of human embryo cell research but forbid use of federal funds to destroy human embryos directly—yet they permit federal research on stem cells taken from embryos by privately financed researchers. The guidelines provide, additionally, that all cells be derived from embryos that have, first, been frozen—this being designed as such to discourage women from creating fresh embryos expressly for research purposes.[164]

Presently in the United States, early stage embryonic stem cells are obtained—as a practical matter—from the donated or purchased embryos produced in private laboratories such as fertility clinics. These clinics are an excellent source for the acquisition of stem cells—inasmuch as they produce an oversupply of embryos for *in vitro* fertilization, and destroy ultimately the unused ones.[165] Interestingly, as a matter of current concern, it has been estimated that it would take 280 human eggs to produce a single line of embryonic stem cells. Human eggs are in short supply and difficult enough to obtain for routine IVF purposes let alone to meet the additional demands of therapeutic cloning.[166]

Adult stem cells, skin, nerve tissues and even cadavers and human fat can produce stem cells.[167] These sources have not, however, shown the same range of potential as embryos and fetal cells.[168] Indeed, a recent report from the National Institutes of Health—requested by the Secretary of Health and Human Services—concludes by affirming the previously stated scientific consensus that research on stem cells derived from both human embryos (derived typically from five-day-old embryos or discarded ones from fertility clinics) and adult tissue holds great scientific promise. Inasmuch as adult stem cells are rare and do not proliferate as readily as embryonic cells, they are less advantageous to successful stem cell research, however, the report concluded.[169]

A POLITICAL DILEMMA

In the early spring and summer of 2001, President George W. Bush—together with the National Conference of Catholic Bishops—began to stress the need for more scientific work to be undertaken on the utilization of adult stem cells for ultimate transplant purposes.[170] There was a real worry the President would, in fact, block all federal funds for research on embryonic stem cells.[171] One major reason for this concern was the expectation by some that allowing the remains of individual abortions as a viable research source might encourage women to terminate their pregnancies because of their knowledge that the discarded fetal tissues could not only be used to help desperate patients and advance medical research, but even be a source of financial reward.[172]

Another more direct political reason for President Bush to have concerns over the federal support for biomedical research using cells derived from human embryos was White House uneasiness that any federal subsidy would have the effect of infuriating conservative voters, anti-abortion groups and especially the Roman Catholics—all considered important to the subsequent re-election bid sought by the President.[173] The challenge was to craft a compromise which would recognize the Catholic views regarding their moral objections to research of this nature yet not forfeit totally the significant potential for scientific benefits from this scientific study. For Roman Catholics, frozen embryos are seen as life, and not a mere potential for life, and for them this is the fundamental issue concerning embryo research.[174]

Early in the debate, it was suggested that the White House could cease federal support of embryonic stem cell research with donated embryos after a certain date or, alternatively, pay for research only on stem cell lines already derived from human embryos. The first proposal appeared very feasible—this because there were already enough frozen embryos in fertility clinics to produce embryonic stem cell lines for research and therapeutic purposes if scientists were given direct access to them. Once cell lines are made, they—in effect—become immortal and may be propagated forever.[175] The second proposal was more complicated. Inasmuch as only perhaps a dozen human embryonic stem cell lines were thought to be in existence, scientific needs for efficacious research mandated from 100 to 1000 such cell lines be made. Thus, a severe shortage in the stem cell "market place" would be encountered at the very outset.[176]

THE BUSH COMPROMISE

On 9 August 2001, President Bush announced his long-awaited decision on embryonic stem cell research which limits, essentially, scientific research to cells already extracted and disallows government support of the destruction of new embryos. Federal funding would be allowed, however, for research to be conducted on more than 60 genetically diverse stem cell lines in existence throughout the world.[177]

As noted, stem cell lines are colonies of continually dividing cells created from embryos. Embryonic stem cells are extracted from microscopic embryos no bigger than 200 to 300 cells. These stem cells are then grown atop embryonic mouse cells known as "feeder" cells. Because they have been in close contact with mouse cells, the human cells pose a small but real risk of transferring deadly animal viruses to people. Thus, under Food and Drug Administration guidelines for xenotransplants it would be difficult—though not impossible—to use the feeder cells in human clinical tests.[178]

Under the Bush guidelines, federal dollars may be used to study these very versatile and medically promising cells only if they came from donated fertility clinic embryos that were already destroyed by 9 August 2001. Much scientific skepticism abounds however about the existing stocks of stem cells available and, as noted, their purity. While Congress banned federal financing of human embryo experimentation in August 2000, the Clinton administration sought to carve out an exception to the congressional ban by allowing federal funding for stem cell research undertaken from the privately financed sources that obtained embryos. Interestingly, this policy was never enforced.[179]

RESOLUTIONS AND CONTINUING POLITICAL CONFLICTS (NEW GUIDELINES FOR RESEARCH)

In 2005, the National Research Council and the Institute of Medicine issued a much anticipated report[180] designed to provide guidelines for responsible research of human embryonic stem (HES) cell research—or those cells taken from a five-day-old fertilized egg that may be tweaked to become any organ within the body. Although compliance is voluntary, all institutes conducting this type of research are being urged to establish adequate oversight committees to ensure that these guidelines are followed.

Among the central guidelines in the report are those which: direct the establishment of embryonic stem cell research oversight (ESCRO) committees; forbid nuclear transfer undertaken to pursue reproductive cloning; forbid the use of human embryos for research grown in culture for longer than 14 days—or until the point when the body axis and central nervous system begin to form; require donor consent be obtained before a blastocyst is used to generate stem cells and—further—inform donors that they have the right to withdraw their consent at any point before a stem cell line is derived; refuse to allow payments to donors; and mandate the ESCRO committees to maintain a complete registry of stem cell lines which not only includes verification of informed consent but a complete medical history of all donors.[181]

The guidelines also allow for the introduction of human embryonic stem cells into non-human mammals only under circumstances where no other experiment can provide the needed information. Regarding scientific work which mixes human and animal cells in order to create so-called chimeras—undertaken, as such, to test the therapeutic potential of human stem cells in animal models—the guidelines preclude transplantation of animal embryonic stem cells into a human blastocyst. Approval by an appropriate ESCRO committee must first be obtained before any human embryonic cells are placed into an animal. Further prohibitions disallow human embryonic stem cells being introduced into non-human primates and forbid breeding of animals into which human embryonic stem cells have been introduced.[182]

The Hinxton Group—composed of some 60 scientists, physicians, philosophers, lawyers and others from throughout the world—has also proposed ethically acceptable norms to conduct stem cell research.[183] While not superseding existing national or state laws, these principles could codify a set of basic rules in those jurisdictions lacking stem cell laws—including, interestingly, most of the United States.[184]

Fundamental to the principles put forth is recognition that restrictions on this type of research should be rare, well justified and, when imposed, sufficiently flexible in order to accommodate changes in this rapidly evolving field and—furthermore—scientists should have the freedom to undertake scientific work abroad when such activity is banned in their own country.[185]

BUSH v. CONGRESS: THE SUMMERS OF 2006, 2007

After passage by both houses of the Congress of the Stem Cell Research Enhancement Act of 2005, on 19 July 2006,[186] President Bush proceeded to veto the proposed legislation—with his veto being sustained by the House of Representatives.[187] Although it was crafted as a legislative scheme to provide for human embryonic stem cell research, regardless of the date on which the stem cells were derived from a human embryo, President Bush declared research of this nature "crosses a moral boundary that our decent society needs to respect," with the destruction of day-old embryos being akin to murder.[188]

This legislation, if enacted, would have expanded the supply of embryonic stem cells by allowing federally funded research on cells derived from embryos created for fertility treatments or donated from *in vitro* fertilization clinics. Such embryos would have had to be in excess of the clinical needs for infertility treatments and otherwise destined to be discarded. Additionally, they would have had to be obtained by written consent and acquired without payment to donors.[189]

With an estimated 400 000 frozen embryos stored within infertility clinics because couples producing them have completed their pursuit of having a family and therefore do not wish additional biological children, few embryo adoptions are to be anticipated. The reason for this is simply attributed to the fact that most couples seeking IVF want a genetic connection to their child. Consequently, these excess embryos will be used for either scientific research or discarded.[190]

While signing into legislation the Fetus Farming Prohibition Act of 2006, which imposes a ban on fertilizing eggs in women or in test tubes specifically to yield embryos for research,[191] and willing to sign the Alternative Pluripotent Stem Cell Therapies Enhancement Act, a bill which would have directed the National Institutes of Health to continue cutting-edge research designed to yield stem cells without requiring embryonic destruction,[192] the President was denied this opportunity, for leading Democrats in the House of Representatives blocked the effort because of their opinion that this bill was little more than a "political fig leaf" which was meant to serve as a "distraction" for the President's veto.[193]

As seen in Chapter 1, in June 2007, when presented with essentially the same version of the stem cell legislation that he had vetoed in 2006, once again President Bush exercised his veto.[194] He sought to temper the concerns of many in the scientific community who have objected to embryonic research restrictions by issuing Executive Order 13435. Essentially, this Order directs the Secretary of Health and Human Services and the Director of the National Institutes of Health to develop a plan for new scientific research from alternative sources on stem cells for treatments of disease "derived without creating a human embryo for research purposes or destroying, discarding, or subjecting to harm a human embryo or fetus."[195]

REGULATING REPRODUCTION IN THE UNITED STATES

The extent to which the states may regulate validly IVF procedures and embryo transfers depends upon whether these acts are viewed as fundamental rights. Thus, the threshold question is whether they are "rights" guaranteed by the Constitution as part of the "right to marital privacy."[196] Various Supreme Court decisions seem to grant "the right . . . to marry, establish a home and bring up children" as among those liberties granted by the Fourteenth Amendment.[197] Based upon these cases, it could be argued that any state regulation on IVF and embryo transfers would be an intrusion upon the fundamental right to marital privacy.[198] "[I]f the decision to beget a child is a protected area of privacy, presumably the actual method of begetting also would be protected. Thus, any statute affecting this delicate area would have to serve a compelling state interest and must do so by the least restrictive means."[199]

A more conservative analysis of the Supreme Court decisions in this area recognizes, at the threshold, that the right to privacy is not mentioned explicitly in the United States Constitution. No right of sexual freedom is found within the ambit of procreative rights recognized by the Supreme Court; nor has the Court fashioned a general right of personal privacy which is sufficiently broad-based to encompass sex outside marriage.[200]

LEGISLATIVE POSITIONS AMONG THE STATES

It is doubtful that Congress could ever enact effective legislation on the legal status of an embryo because society is not of one mind; nor is there a consensus as to when "life" should be protected legally. Judicial interpretation of this issue has aroused national debate with the decision in *Roe v. Wade*.[201] Despite the lack of agreement regarding when life begins, those children born of an IVF procedure using either donor ova or donor sperm should be recognized as children of the family in which they are born. No issue of illegitimacy should be raised; nor should the donors be held to any level of financial support of the child. Similarly, the child should have no right of inheritance against the donors. The best interests of the IVF child are served and, more importantly, the strength of the family unit is enhanced and its stability assured.[202]

After *Roe*, some 25 states enacted fetal research laws designed primarily to control research on aborted fetuses.[203] Several statutes extend their protective coverage to research on embryos.[204] If cumbersome safeguards effecting excess embryo preservation are required, the initiation of medical-scientific programs utilizing IVF procedures could be discouraged.[205] Moreover, in a number of these states, the very legality of IVF as a medical procedure to overcome infertility is in question.[206] And, interestingly, by 1 April 2005, some 12 states had also passed laws addressing reproductive cloning, research cloning and therapeutic cloning.[207]

PRESERVING GENETIC INTEGRITY

The publication of Aldous Huxley's *Brave New World* in 1946 pre-dated the discovery by James Watson and Francis Crick of deoxyribonucleic acid (DNA)[208] by seven years. Commentators to this day continue to view the significance of advances in recombinant rDNA technology through the lens of Huxley's totalitarian society[209]—a genetic caste system made possible by genetic technology.[210] The alternative characterization of such technology as a grail to treat or heal inherited diseases is perhaps less alarming but fails similarly to describe adequately the current state of technology from the perspective of both identifying specific genetic traits and developing therapy.[211] In 1993 for example, on the fortieth anniversary of the discovery of DNA, the Human Genome Project attained new levels of success in its mapping of the human genome.[212] The accelerated pace of mapping that began in the early 1970s[213] continued owing to innovations in genome mapping and sequencing with the first draft of the project being completed in June 2000.[214]

The salutary effect of this technology, the ability to catalog and analyse the genotype of a particular individual, creates the potential for abuse of such information. Indeed, for some, the eugenics movement to this day casts a shadow over the Human Genome Project. The risks of abuse engendered by the mapping of the human genome and emergent rDNA technology do not extend to social engineering and development of a "superior" human, a process necessitating germ-line modification. Rather, the potential abuse may result from discrimination based on the dissemination of key information about the genotype of an individual—information which reveals the risk factors inherent in that individual.[215] Genetic data is a particularly sensitive category of health care information.[216] Unlike information about a specific transient condition or illness, data pointing to a genetic disorder will affect, and may stigmatize, a person throughout his or her entire life.[217] The handling of genetic information by the state or its agents, therefore, implicates individual liberty interests deriving from fundamental constitutional rights to equality and privacy.[218]

In this context, genetic discrimination has been defined as "discrimination against an individual or against members of that individual's family solely because of real or perceived differences from the 'normal' genome in the genetic constitution of that individual."[219] Because some individuals are asymptomatic or presymptomatic and, therefore, not readily identified, genetic discrimination is most likely limited to two contexts: employment and insurance. Both employers and insurers may believe such discrimination is warranted for the profitable conduct of business.[220] Furthermore, both employers and insurers normally have access to detailed medical records of employees and customers.[221]

An employer, for example, may reject a job applicant based on information obtained through genetic testing for several reasons: increased medical and insurance premiums, absenteeism, lowered productivity, increased risk in the line of duty and increased liability for workers' compensation.[222] In the area of insurance, genetic testing undermines potentially the principle that both the insurer and the insured ought to possess equal knowledge of a particular insured's risk of becoming ill.[223] The availability of the genotype of a particular individual either to the insurer or to that individual alone presents the possibility of adverse selection.[224] For example, an individual who knows he is at risk for developing Huntington's chorea will buy a greater amount of life or health insurance, knowing that he or she is at greater risk of death or serious illness.[225] Conversely, insurers will either refuse to offer coverage or drop those individuals in a genetic high-risk category.[226]

Although discrimination is arguably fair when an individual chooses to engage in a high-risk activity such as smoking or sky-diving, refusing to provide insurance to individuals because of a genetic trait is inequitable and contrary to public policy.[227] First, carriers of defective genes may never develop full symptoms that affect their ability to function.[228] More importantly, however, such disparate treatment and resulting risk minimization vitiate the purpose of traditional private insurance as a risk-spreading mechanism.[229]

While there are, to be sure, risks associated with the pursuit and development of the new genetics, man's dehumanization and depersonalization will not be fostered as a consequence of the Human Genome Initiative. Rather, so long as science pursues its basic quest for knowledge with the purpose of establishing truth and integrity and with promoting the goal of minimizing human suffering and maximizing social good, then the noble integrity of evolution and genetic progress will be preserved and irrational fears of eugenic supremacy advanced through programs of genetic screening dispelled. Restraining scientific inquiry and the application of its results should be limited only to actions considered unreasonable.

THE HUMAN GENOME INITIATIVE: MORE PROMISES AND PERILS

The human genome refers simply to the chromosomal collection of 23 pairs of chromosomes that all humans carry within which all human genes reside—and more specifically those genes that contribute so directly to traits such as height, eye color and the shape of body parts as well as human behavior. Diseases develop when alterations of the genes, known as mutations, occur.[230] In all, more than 12 000 disease conditions have been found to have their origins in single gene defects.[231]

The Human Genome Initiative is an undertaking coordinated by the United States Department of Energy and the National Institutes of Health and funded by the US Congress in 1990 which set as a goal the complete "mapping" of *all* 50 000 to 100 000 human genes within 15 years. Although it was not fully funded at the $3 billion set originally, Congress provided sufficient funds for there to be every reason to conclude that the deadline for its completion would be met.[232] Interestingly, there is no single human genome project in the United States. Rather, three major organizations—the National Institutes of Health (NIH), the Department of Energy (DOE) and the Howard Hughes Medical Institute—are about the business of funding specific aspects of an overall "initiative" on genome mapping, with simultaneous work efforts being undertaken in other countries as well as a private organization denominated the Human Genome Organization (HUGO).[233]

As seen previously, by March 1993, some 2736 of the targeted genes had been in fact "mapped" or, in other words, located precisely on one of the 23 chromosomes. Of these, 682—when they occur in mutant form—have been found to be associated with human disease. And researchers have decoded, in 321, part of the "sequence" (or precise chemical structure) which thus allows the first step to have been taken in determining how a gene works actually.[234]

On 14 April 2003, marking the fiftieth anniversary of the discovery of the DNA double helix by James Watson and Francis Crick, the Human

Genome Project was declared "officially complete."[235] Much improved from the working draft issued in 2000, and completed in 13, instead of 15 years,[236] the final phase of the project is still not finished totally—this, because about 1 percent of the genome has proven impossible to sequence and will remain as such until new technologies are developed to meet this task.[237] While the code has been deciphered, the research is just beginning and will tackle projects, among others, to develop a map of common human genetic variations that will pinpoint specific genes linked to asthma, cancer, diabetes and heart disease and—furthermore—catalog all of the genome's working parts which in turn could be the birthplace of genes.[238]

The driving motive behind the Human Genome Initiative is quite simple and direct: the identification and eradication of all genetically based disease. With more than 12 000 conditions being recognized as having their origins in single gene defects,[239] the ultimate success of the Initiative holds awesome opportunities for improving the health of all world citizens and minimizing their human suffering from disease.[240] Yet the secrets of the genome—when revealed—will, as observed, generate a whole array of what-if fears: from the unbridled use of genetic information to advance a program of positive eugenics[241] to concerns that disclosure of an individual's genetic profile and his susceptibility to illness (even alcoholism) will, in turn, form the basis for discriminatory action or stigmatization, resulting in a possible refusal by an insurer to pay medical costs if one elects not to undergo a recommended treatment or if a child with a prenatally identified genetic defect were to be born.[242]

Equally worrisome is the fear that the widespread delineation of genetic profiles will result in the centralization of that genetic information—much as today credit information is centralized.[243] Since DNA sequence databases are prone to error, there is also concern that, even in the event gene mapping were to become routine, "comparison of an individual's genetic profile to an error-ridden prototype could have the same stigmatizing effect as do false positives on drug tests and tests for the HIV antibody."[244]

The emerging genomic technology—while positive in its potential for good—also raises the concerns about its misuse. Genetic engineering is being transformed rapidly into a synthetic genome technology where, for example, science is able to "synthesize" a small genome to create a virus. Over the course of time, it is conceivable that artificially synthesized chromosomes will be placed within humans. Synthetic genomics may be able—further—to provide microbes with an ability to reduce carbon dioxide in the atmosphere, eat radioactive waste or clean up factory pollutants and unleash "good" viruses to attack cancers and infections caused by "bad" viruses and bacteria.[245]

There is a potential for environmental harm if these new synthetic organisms were to escape into the environment. Inadvertent and undesirable gene leakage has already proven costly to manage in dealing with the genetic engineering of seeds and plants. As synthetic microbial genomic technology develops, policies must be established and enforced which will contain the spread of organisms and their genes that have been engineered.[246]

Of equal concern is the use of this new technology for bioterrorism. With the genome for smallpox being capable of synthesis shortly, the sequence for constructing it—having already been published—makes its availability wide open to use by not only terrorists but even by disgruntled citizens. Careful thought must be given and protections developed in order to determine who learns the technology, the extent to which publications of its use and potential application are disseminated and who may acquire it. To wait until the research for this new technology is fully developed before acting may well mean that it is too late to attempt to control it.[247]

Finally, there is the issue of control and ownership. Battles over the ownership of individual genes and gene sequences provide a dramatic prelude to the scope of challenges which will arise surely over these new synthetic life forms. It is a safe argument to make, however, that, if these new microbes are made at government expense, accessibility to them ought to be a natural part of granting patents or commercial control over them.[248]

GENETIC KNOWLEDGE

Once a "disease gene" is discovered, the new release of it normally incorporates a suggestion that treatments to arrest it are forthcoming. Yet discovering the mechanism of a disease is not the same as knowing how to change that mechanism. With genetic information of this type, however, at least a chance is created for developing an effective therapy to combat the genetic disease.[249]

The "heuristics of fear" all too often blot out rational analysis of emerging genetic knowledge and add little to the need to promote medically and ethically informed public discussion[250] within "communities of moral discourse" where scientific, as well as medical, ethical and political, issues can be engaged in "by informed and intelligent persons who represent different interests and different perspectives on the nature of humanness and well-being."[251] Caution should always be the watch-word, however, in examining genetic assumptions, and over-simplification of genetic findings should be avoided.[252]

As much as law should seek to avoid ambiguity, it should not rely on science for definitive answers; for science—within its own sphere—simply does not offer unambiguous resolutions.[253] Two forms of uncertainty are inherent in any scientific undertaking: one is conceptual and derives from fundamental changes in those concepts engendered by the new biotechnologies, and the other is termed occurrence and applies to select issues that cannot be addressed readily.[254]

The image of neutrality that science has sought to cultivate or "sell" is largely a myth created in an attempt to maintain autonomy and thus blunt increasing pressures from both church and state for intervention and control.[255] Indeed, the history of science is replete with cases where not only the choice of research topics but the nature of scientific theories as well as the representation of results from research have been socially constructed and shaped by cultural forces to reflect various societal assumptions of the times.[256]

In 1990, the federal government's Center for Biologics, Evaluation and Research at the Food and Drug Administration approved efforts to undertake human gene therapy.[257] Recognized as a radical and unproven method of fighting disease, the therapy involves the transfer of genetic information contained in DNA into specific cells to replace absent or deficiently functioning genes within these cells.[258] Initial experimentation trials will focus on the treatment of two different diseases: adenosine deaminase (ADA), a rare and congenital immune system defect, and metastic melanoma, an advanced malignant cancer virtually untreatable once it invades secondary organs.[259]

GENETIC ENGINEERING FORMS

Applications of genetic engineering are of four types: somatic cell gene therapy (SCGT), germ-line gene therapy (GLGT), enhancement genetic engineering (EGE) and eugenic engineering.[260] Each of these applications raises complex ethical and scientific issues.[261] The most amenable approach to solving the effects of a broad spectrum of inherited diseases is to be found with somatic cell gene therapy—yet it is the only one of the four that is yet to be justified through scientific verification and ethical acceptance.

Somatic cell gene therapy involves the gene transfer into the somatic (body) cells of a human to correct a genetic defect.[262] If the therapy is developed fully, it would result—when used—in replacing defective or absent enzymes or proteins (the product of genes) that are necessary to a cell's proper functioning. Already in 1992, within the National Institutes of Health and its Recombinant DNA Advisory Committee, some 11 gene therapy trials had been approved and seven more were under consideration.

It is expected that, within the immediate future, applications will quadruple.[263] Still in its infancy, germ-line therapy seeks to insert a gene into the reproductive cells of germ cells of an afflicted patient.[264] In addition to combating genetic disease, this type of gene therapy could treat others such as cancer as well as heart and vascular disease. While germ-line changes have been accomplished successfully in mice, it has yet to be performed in humans.[265]

In January 1992, medical history continued to be made—for, in Memphis, Tennessee, a two-year-old child who was suffering from a neuroblastoma tumor was treated with bone marrow cells that had been altered genetically.[266] History was made previously in September 1990, when a four-year-old child received the world's first gene therapy.[267] Termed gene therapy, or the alteration of the genetic material of a patient in order to combat disease at its cellular source, this medical procedure or a variation of it called gene marking has been performed thus far on 22 patients and—as such—has become a viable strategy for uncovering new approaches to fighting incurable diseases. This therapy is being tested, developed and applied not only in America, but notably in Canada, China, Italy, France and Japan.[268]

Enhancement engineering is effected by the insertion of a gene into a patient's reproductive tissue, thus assuring that the disorder in the offspring would in turn be corrected. For example, in order to "enhance" a known characteristic, an additional growth hormone gene could be inserted into a normal child. While the enhancement of somatic cells is technically feasible and has, as observed, been validated with animal experiments, the enhancement of germ-line cells has yet to be shown to be technically feasible.

The fourth level of engineering—recognized as eugenic in focus—seeks, by definition, to "improve" complex human traits coded by a large number of genes (for example, personality, intelligence) and is not thought to be feasible for the foreseeable future. Indeed, the processes associated with it may be so complex that it may never prove feasible.[269]

TOWARD A PRINCIPLE OF BIOLOGICAL DETERMINISM

In today's society, a new and discernible preoccupation with biological determinism is seen, spurred by successes in developing genetic tests that have found the markers indicating predispositions to certain single gene disorders such as Huntington's disease and the hopes that complex conditions such as cancer, drug dependency and mental illness will be—with the successes of the Genome Project—predictable. Building upon the limited successes with Huntington's chorea, a number of states now mandate new-born infant genetic testing for conditions such as phenylketonuria (PKU).[270]

Biological determinism evolves from the principle of genetic essentialism that posits personal traits—such as mental illness, homosexuality, aggressive personality, exhibitionism, dangerousness, shyness, stress—have a genetic or biological disposition and, indeed, are predictable and determinable at conception; thus the social context in which the traits adhere is minimized under this principle.[271] In a word, biological determinism recognizes essentially that one's fate is determined by one's genetic inheritance.[272]

The issues raised by the near staggering advances of the new genetic medicine should not be seen as presenting unique ethical problems in the sense of dilemmas not heretofore seen. The fundamental issues of ethical concern in this field were, indeed, recognized in the late 1960s with the introduction and widespread use of amniocentesis and carrier screening. The new genetics will—most assuredly—magnify the range, complexity and frequency of these problems, however, for one very crucial reason: the failure of medical geneticists to form, and thereby validate, agreements, protocols or compacts in writing designed to codify normative standards for decision making. Instead, a blind adherence to oral traditions is pursued with the end result being indecisiveness. Clearly, without a fundamental set of ethical standards agreed to as such by the scientific community, the power-brokers in human genetics will continue to be less accountable to the public for their actions.[273]

JUDICIALLY DERIVED PRIVACY INTERESTS

The public dissemination of genetic information and its potential for stigmatization implicate another constitutional interest: the individual's stake in maintaining the privacy of such information. Conceivably, discrimination could be avoided if no information were available upon which distinctions could be made between those individuals with "normal" genotypes and those with abnormal genetic characteristics. In contrast to equal protection, there appears to be little protection in the area of employment or insurance apart from theoretical constitutional restraints upon public employers, and scattered state constitutional and statutory privacy provisions.[274] These federal constitutional restraints, however, reveal several bases upon which courts might discern a fundamental privacy interest applicable to the genetic material of a particular individual. They also provide support for legislative measures to protect the privacy of genetic material.

Privacy has been identified in a number of Supreme Court cases as a fundamental value of the provisions of the Bill of Rights.[275] However, it was not until *Griswold v. Connecticut* that the Court derived an independent right to privacy from the confluence of several provisions of the Bill of Rights.[276] This "penumbral" zone of privacy has been held to include a woman's right to terminate a pregnancy,[277] consensual male sodomy,[278] a depositor's interest in not disclosing bank records,[279] or a taxpayer's interest in not disclosing tax records.[280]

LEGISLATIVE EFFORTS TO RESOLVE CONFLICTS

In 1990, the US House of Representatives considered the Humane Genome Privacy Act, which was designed to resolve the significant problems of maintaining confidentiality of genetic information in the workplace. More specifically, the purpose of the bill was "to safeguard individual privacy of genetic information from the misuse of records maintained by agencies or their contractors or grantees for the purpose of research, diagnosis, treatment, or identification of genetic orders."[281] This bill was not enacted into legislation.

The Genetic Privacy and Nondiscrimination Act of 1995 was introduced by the then Senator Mark O. Hatfield of Oregon but died in committee.[282] Developed essentially from a draft Genetic Privacy Act prepared by Professor George J. Annas and his associates at the Boston University School of Public Health, this proposal aimed to place legal safeguards on the collection, analysis and storage of DNA and genetic information. It is from analysis and storage of DNA sampled (for example, blood, saliva, hair and other tissue) that genetic information is derived—for these samples contain an individual's private genetic information. Thus, any custodian of such samples has complete power to analyse and re-analyse them in an effort to derive new genetic information as more advanced tests are, in fact, developed. The central tenet of the original Genetic Privacy Act, as proposed by Professor Annas, was to forbid the acquisition of DNA samples or genetic information about another individual unless "that individual specifically authorizes the collection of DNA samples for the purpose of genetic analysis, authorizes the creation of that private information, and has access to and control over the dissemination of that information."[283]

In subsequent years, various initiatives have been undertaken to legislate in this volatile area of genetic privacy—all to no avail.[284] In 1996, however, some measure of success in protecting against genetic discrimination was achieved by passage of the Health Insurance Portability and Accountability Act.[285] More specifically, this legislation provides protections for those who wish to undergo genetic testing but fear discrimination by health insurers in the event their test results indicate an increased risk for developing a serious disease. The law curtails sharply the right of group health insurers to limit coverage of new employees because of "pre-existing" conditions. Such conditions are considered pre-existing if their diagnosis or treatment occurs six months before enrollment.[286]

Senator Olympia J. Snow introduced the Genetic Information Nondiscrimination in Health Insurance Act of 2001, which was not enacted into legislation even though it passed the Senate.[287] Again, in 2005, the Senator re-introduced the proposed legislation as the Genetic Information Nondiscrimination Act of 2005, S. 306, and it passed the Senate but was "held at the desk" and never reached the House of Representatives.[288]

CONCLUSIONS

In exploring the non-coital reproductive sciences, a balance should be struck between the unfettered use of science for individual satisfaction and the promotion and maintenance of the social good. Thus, embryo research and experimentation—which contribute to the goal of minimizing human suffering and maximizing the social good deriving therefrom—must be pursued in a reasonable manner. So long as the central driving force in marital relationships continues to be procreation and the family unit remains at the core of a progressive society, efforts will be pursued which seek to expand the period of fecundity, combat infertility and assure that inherited genetic deficiencies are not passed on to future generations. Genetic experimentation and planning, in conjunction with eugenic programming, are more rational and humane than alternatives to population regulation through death, famine and war or an abdication of genetic autonomy to the countervailing doctrines of gene sovereignty and biological determinism.[289]

Socially responsible scientific inquiry should be restrained only when the scientist "is clearly able to foresee that the particular line of work is leading to a kind of scale of dangers" that would constitute a "limitation" or, in other words, present "dangers of cataclysmic physical or psychological proportions" for mankind as a whole.[290]

While some would view research and experimentation in human embryology and reproductive biology as promoting a genetic disaster or cataclysm, the better view is that such work advances the goal of minimizing human suffering and maximizing the quality of purposeful and meaningful existence free of inherited genetic disabilities.[291] Certain aspects of the new human reproductive biology (for example, cloning) might well require greater degrees of reasonable self-restraint. By and large, however, the nature and degree to which restraint is mandated must be determined by the individual scientist who should be guided or, as the case directs, constrained by the cultural norms of the society in which he lives.

Preemption of scientific work in human reproductive biology by the state is short-sighted and repressive of the principle of free scientific inquiry. Instead of developing a scientific regulatory scheme relying on legislative prohibition, rule-making committees within the pertinent medical and scientific profession should be established to monitor and control scientific inquiry. Perhaps the best model would be a simple organization approached easily on a consultative and advisory basis and designed to assist biologists, scientists and medical researchers make their own decisions.[292]

President Clinton renewed hope in the scientific community during the summer of 1995 by issuing an executive order creating a new National Bioethics Advisory Commission charged with studying ethical issues arising from experiments on human biology and behavior and the relations of these issues to the goals of the federal investment in science and technology. More specifically, the Commission considered how best to use and manage genetic information derived from the Human Genome Project as well as the scientific, legal and ethical implications of patenting human genes and the feasibility of human cloning.[293] The Commission concluded its work on 3 October 2001.[294] Whether its legacy will meet with greater success than its most recent predecessor depends in large part upon the degree to which politics can be disengaged from the ultimate recommendations it will make. Previously, in August, President George W. Bush announced yet another new bioethics advisory commission would be established and it was constituted officially in January 2002. Charged with exploring the "intersections of medicine and morality," the Council considered—initially—the ethics of human cloning and of experimentation on clonal embryos.[295] With charges that the membership of the Council is "politically stacked" to the conservative right, questions have been raised already as to the level of objectivity that will be brought to their deliberations.[296]

In January 2004, the Council produced its much anticipated report on new reproductive medicine and surprised many of its critics—especially the American Fertility Association—by *not* recommending new restrictions on egg and sperm donation or surrogacy arrangements.[297] Rather, it chose to stress the need—among the members of the reproductive medicine community—to place greater attention on professional reforms and maintenance of ethical standards. Urging, specifically, the need for thoughtful boundaries to be imposed on new forms of reproduction, with a heavy burden of persuasion being set for those wishing to cross it in the name of scientific advancement, the Council recommend Congress prohibit, temporarily, the gestation of human embryos in animal wombs and the fertilization of human eggs with animal sperm and *vice versa*. Additionally, the President's Council called for a ban on any transfer of an IVF embryo to a woman's womb for any purpose other than to produce a live born baby—this, designed as such, to prevent farming of fetuses for body parts. For women participating in the IVF procedures, more effective frameworks for assuring informed consent were urged—especially disclosures regarding not only the risks, but the costs of such fertility treatments.[298]

In order to combat misleading rates of success reported by IVF clinics in the 1980s and the misuse of embryos and eggs—oftentimes even discarded without patient permission—the federal Fertility Success Rate Act of 1992 was enacted. It provides a useful mechanism for assuring that clinic success rates for prospective patients and policy makers alike is a matter of public record.[299]

Two central issues regarding future uses of IVF remain: the need to develop safe practices and sound ethical guidelines for chromosomal and genomics screening of embryos as couples seek increasingly to screen embryos in order to ensure a healthy child and the need to reduce the high incidence of multiple pregnancies.[300] All too often, infertile couples—wishing to maximize their chances of achieving pregnancy—either ignore or downplay the risks of a multiple pregnancy. Such pregnancies with two or more fetuses not only carry heavy, significant extra burdens and major risks for both the woman and the offspring, but also impose a greater societal burden leading, as such, to greater overall health care costs and maintenance concerns.[301]

Since it is highly unlikely that laws will be enacted limiting the number of embryos allowed to be created in IVF clinics—this, because of the prevailing American attitude toward privacy in medical decision making—guidelines designed to reduce multiples will have to be issued and respected by professional organizations of IVF physicians. In 1999, the American Society of Reproductive Medicine took a bold step forward in regulating this area of concern by recommending that patients younger than 35 years of age with a good prognosis of success have not more than two embryos transferred in IVF procedures. Those between the ages of 35 and 40 with an average prognosis of success should be limited to three transfers. For patients who have had previous difficulties or are 40 years or older, four embryo transfers would be allowed.[302] These recommendations, although but of an advisory nature, should—over time—have the effect of reducing greatly the high incidence of multiple IVF births.[303]

The ultimate challenge for contemporary lawyers in the Age of the New Biology is to become more aware and, indeed, educated to the challenges

and complexities of these scientific and technological advances in reproductive biology. No doubt the central focus of this energy should be a
serious attempt to tackle the extent to which there is a fundamental constitutional and/or international human right to procreative liberty, health
assistance in biological reproduction and the point in the biological developmental chart at which the state is obligated to assert its protective interest to "life."[304]

While ever mindful of the perhaps unavoidable mixture of religion into
science and the new laws of reproductive biology, every step must be taken
to assure as pragmatic a view as possible is adhered to in the ultimate structuring of legislative responses and judicial interpretation. Scientific objectivity, if not verifiability, should be not an ideal but a given in this area of
decision making.[305] If this is attained, law, science, medicine and religious
ethics will have formed a dynamic collaboration which will go far toward
assuring that all citizens have an equal opportunity to achieve their
maximum potential within the economic market place, their physical
suffering minimized and spirituality tranquility preserved.

As seen, advances in rDNA technology and screening techniques have
created a new genus in the taxonomy of genetic information, information
that is particularly susceptible to misuse by both state and private entities.
As with any new invention—whether a genetically altered plant or a laboratory technique for identifying mental illness—such technical capability
and concomitant information are often met with fear. Similarly, those individuals identified by such technology as genetically distinct from the social
norm are at risk for disparate and intrusive treatment.[306]

The perception by both public and private institutions that identifying
and singling out persons with genetic abnormalities serve either public or
private commercial interest in turn sets the stage for an erosion of fundamental privacy rights based on such genetic information. Whatever the
risks from the perspective of individual rights, however, it is increasingly
clear that rDNA techniques and the valuable knowledge they generate
provide great hope for alleviating human suffering both as diagnostic measures to avoid genetically related illness and as therapeutic techniques to
cure such illness. Discerning a rational course between the often conflicting
interests of individual rights and the greater social good in the application
of rDNA technology presents particularly difficult problems regarding
how to apply existing constitutional precedent and public policy to this new
technology. Indeed, the factual permutations raised by the use of rDNA
and screening techniques appear at first consideration novel and strange.

Closer examination, however, reveals recurring constitutional and policy
questions. For example, to the extent such genetic markers are immutable
characteristics which subject a class of individuals to any stigma, the Equal

Protection clause of the Fourteenth Amendment arguably recognizes the need for heightened judicial scrutiny of government action affecting such a suspect class.[307] Exacting judicial scrutiny imposes on the state and its agents a higher standard of rationality. As with any suspect class like race or alienage, such scrutiny attempts to discern the extent to which fear or prejudice may have supplanted rational discourse in the making of public policy.

Similarly, fundamental privacy rights recognize an individual's interest in not disclosing personal information that might hold him up to unnecessary public scrutiny and reputational damage. This principle applies with particular force to an individual's interest in concealing from public scrutiny the makeup of his genetic map. Although these rights, especially as defined by the Fourth Amendment, are qualified, when balancing society's interest in obtaining and using genetic information, courts and legislatures should give great weight to the private nature of such information given its personalized and sensitive nature.[308]

Finally, in the legislative sphere, the logical complement to recognizing rights of equal protection and privacy for individuals with genetic abnormalities is the extension of those rights as protections not only against state action but also against private entities. Specific amendments to the ADA[309] and the federal Privacy Act[310] could have the effect of preventing genetic discrimination in the workplace and thus clarifying, definitively, any further ambiguities arising in administrative rulings or interpretations by the Equal Employment Opportunity Commission (EEOC) here. As important, such legislation would further advance the principle that, absent some compelling reason, private individuals and institutions will be charged with treating individuals whose genetic maps diverge from the norm as they would a person with a completely normal genotype.

Obviously, the wide number of social dislocations produced by the biotechnological advances of the New Biology neither must nor should be a serious matter of constitutional concern.[311] Rather, efforts should be undertaken with resolve to sharpen ethical constructs for principled decision making within the professional bodies concerned with the development and management of the New Biology. The state legislatures and courts should—in partnership with medical scientists, ethicists, philosophers and the other architects of the new biological sciences—endeavor to regulate, and thereby resolve, the complexities of these biotechnological sciences.[312]

To be sure, the constitutional challenges raised as a direct consequence of the startling advances in bio-science are unique for they hold every promise of changing some of the most fundamental principles of the political order of the United States—challenges "that the individual human being is autonomous and exercises free will, that all people are entitled to equal treatment, that individuals enjoy a legitimate expectation of privacy in their dealings with the state and that freedom of scientific inquiry and expression can flourish along with freedom of religion."[313]

While the Human Genome Initiative will provide startling genetic maps, it remains for the law to sequence or identify the policy issues inherent in the complex issues of medical genetics and then to proceed to map them (or, in other words, determine them and then resolve them to the extent possible within legal doctrines).[314] This, in turn, forces a need to examine critically the true social significance of the concepts of normality and abnormality.[315] With this all comes a fear—rational or irrational—that laws will be passed requiring everyone to submit to gene therapy or even, as the case may warrant, "provide personally identifiable genetic material for purely scientific uses."[316] Yet, interestingly, individuals are less likely to be interested in knowing about their genetic profiles if they are obsessed with an overriding fear that such knowledge will then be used (or has a real potential for misuse) to punish them. Society will thus be forced to develop both ethical and legal norms designed to protect those of its members at higher risk from genetic discrimination.[317]

From a more positive side, universal access to the wide opportunities of genetic services will allow persons "to act on the perception that it is good to want to know about genetic risks."[318] Accordingly, when the benefits of genetic diagnosis and treatment become more evident over time, genetic information will, in turn, become far less threatening and stigmatizing.

In order to meet these new challenges, law and sciences must march together as full partners and not—as in the past—with law behind the scientific cadence. All too often, as former Chief Justice Warren E. Burger has observed, "The law does not search out as do science and medicine; it reacts to social needs and demands."[319] It is thus vitally incumbent upon the law to develop a contemporary agenda for social change and changing socio-political needs instead of responding simply to or reacting to change itself—especially so here with the Age of the New Genetic Medicine.[320] In the final analysis, then, it is well to recognize that "Each new power won by man is a power *over* man as well" and that within every risk taken is an opportunity for untold success.[321]

NOTES

1. See S. Stanley (1981), *The New Evolutionary Timetable*; T. Dobzhansky (1973), *Genetic Diversity and Human Equality*; H. Muller (1961), "The human future," in J. Huxley (ed.), *The Humanist Frame*, p. 401. See also Nuffield Council on Bioethics (ed.) (2002), *Genetics and Human Behaviour*, Ch. 12.
2. "Birth defects," Centers for Disease Control and Protection, http://www.cdc.gov/ncbddd/bd/faq/.htm (accessed 1 Aug. 2006).

3. A. Robinson (1971), "Genetics and society," *Utah Law Review*, p. 487. Approximately 30 000 severely defective infants are born each year and afflicted with grave handicapping conditions that range from spina bifida to anencephaly. T. Ellis (1981), "Letting defective babies die: who decides?," *American Journal of Law and Medicine*, 7, p. 393, n. 1.

4. "Birth defects."

5. See notes 2 and 3 and accompanying text; J. Rivers (1972), "Grave new world," *Saturday Review*, 8 Apr., pp. 23, 26.

6. J. Waltz and C. Thigpen (1973), "Genetic screening and counseling: the legal and ethical issues," *Northwestern University Law Review*, **68**, pp. 696–8.

7. B. Furrow, S. Johnson, T. Jost and R. Schwartz (1991), *Bioethics Health Care Law and Ethics*, p. 168.

8. See K. Wailoo and S. Pemberton (2006), *The Troubled Dream of Genetic Medicine*; M. Sandel (2004), "The case against perfection," *Atlantic Monthly*, Apr. p. 51.

9. L. Kass (1971), "The new biology: what price relieving man's estate?" *Science*, **174**, pp. 779, 780. See also R. Blank (1983), *The Political Implications of Human Genetic Technology*.

10. Symposium, "Reflections on the New Biology", *UCLA Law Review*, **15** (1968), p. 267. See J. Rifkin (1998), *The Biotech Century*, Ch. 4.

11. Waltz and Thigpen, "Genetic screening," p. 696; see also M. Frankel (1973), *Genetic Technology: Promises and Problems*; J. Fletcher (1978), "Ethics and recombinant DNA research," *Southern California Law Review*, **51**, p. 1311. Among current gene therapy applications are those for macular degeneration, non-insulin-dependent diabetes, dwarfism, hemophilia, anemia, Parkinson's disease, Huntington's disease and amyotrophic lateral sclerosis. M. Lysaght and P. Aebischer (1999), "Encapsulated cells as therapy," *Scientific American*, **280**, Apr., p. 58. See also P. Parenteau (1999), 'Skin: the first tissue-engineered products, the organogenesis story," *Scientific American*, **280**, Apr., p. 59.

12. See W. Vukowich (1971), "The dawning of the brave new world—legal, ethical and social issues of eugenics," 1971 *University of Illinois Law Forum*, pp. 189, 222. See also A. Buchanan, D.W. Brock, N. Daniels and D. Winkler (2001), *From Chance to Choice: Genetics and Justice*, Ch. 4.

13. C. Frankel (1974), "The specter of eugenics," *Commentary*, **57**, pp. 25, 30. See E. Brody (1993), *Biomedical Technology and Human Rights*, Ch. 5; M. Malinowski (2003), "Choosing the genetic makeup of children: our eugenics past, present, and future," *Connecticut Law Review*, **36**, p. 125.

14. See note 13. To be justifiable, the acceptance or rejection of eugenic policies should be based upon more than one criterion. The following requisites should be a part of every eugenic program: scientific validity (e.g. a demonstration of sufficient genetic variation to allow for selection of the attribute in question); moral acceptability (i.e. a demonstration that the attributes chosen for selection are properly considered socially desirable); and ethical acceptability (i.e. a demonstration that programs needed to institute a eugenic program do not compromise individual rights and liberties presently sanctioned by both public policy and law). See M. Lappe (1976), "Why shouldn't we have a eugenic policy?," in A. Milunsky and G. Annas (eds), *Genetics and the Law*, pp. 421, 425. See also F. Osborn (1960), "Qualitative aspect of population control: eugenics and euthenics," *Law and Contemporary Problems*, **25**, p. 406.

15. G.P. Smith, II (1968), "Through a test tube darkly: artificial insemination and the law," *Michigan Law Review*, **67**, pp. 127, 147. See generally Buchanan et al., *From Chance to Choice*, Ch. 5; J. Rifkin (1998), "Who will decide between defect and perfect?," *Washington Post*, 9 Apr., p. C4. See T.A. Shannon and J.J. Walter (2003), *The New Genetic Medicine: Theological and Ethical Reflections*.

16. T. Dobzhansky (1962), *Mankind Evolving*, p. 245. See also T. Dobzhansky (1961), "Comments on genetic evolution," *Daedalus*, **90**, pp. 451, 470–73. See G. Will (2005), "Eugenics by abortion," *Washington Post*, 14 Apr., p. A27 (reporting on a case in Britain in 2001 where a 28-week-old fetus was aborted legally because it was found that it would be born with a cleft lip and palate and would—under the law—suffer, as such,

from a physical or mental abnormality which, its parents determined, would seriously handicap it and noting as well that in Britain more babies with Down syndrome are aborted than are allowed to be born and in America 80 percent of such babies diagnosed prenatally with this condition are aborted).

17. Comment, "Asexual reproduction and genetic engineering: a constitutional assessment of the technology of cloning," *Southern California Law Review*, **47** (1974), pp. 476, 499. See also J. Robertson (1998), "Liberty, identity and human cloning," *Texas Law Review*, **76**, p. 1371.
18. Comment, "Asexual reproduction."
19. Ibid., p. 560.
20. G. Taylor (1968), *The Biological Time Bomb*, pp. 23–5. See G.P. Smith, II (1983), "Intimations of immortality: clones, cryons and the law," *University of New South Wales Law Review*, **6**, p. 119.
21. G. Leach (1970), *The Biocrats*, p. 94.
22. J. Watson (1971), "Potential consequences of experimentation with human eggs," 28 Jan., Papers 1, 3, 4, Harvard University Biological Labs. See also R. Cowper (1972), *Clone*; W. Walters (1982), "Cloning, ectogenesis, and hybrids: things to come," in W. Walters and P. Singer (eds.), *Test-Tube Babies: A Guide to Moral Questions, Present Techniques and Future Possibilities*, p. 110.
23. J. Lederberg (1966), "Experimental genetics and human evolution," *American Naturalist*, **100**, pp. 549, 562; J. Watson (1971), "Moving toward the clonal man," *Atlantic Monthly*, May, pp. 50, 51.
24. J. Lederberg (1971), "Genetic engineering or the amelioration of genetic defect," *Pharos*, **34**, pp. 9, 12.
25. J. Fletcher (1971), "Ethical aspects of genetic controls," *New England Journal of Medicine*, **285**, pp. 776, 779.
26. V. Kiernan (1997), "The morality of cloning humans: theologians and philosophers offer provocative arguments," *Chronicle of Higher Education*, 18 July, p. A3; B. Broadway (1998), "A rush to judgment on human cloning," *Washington Post*, 7 Feb., p. C8; U.S. Senate Hearings on Ethics and Theology, "A continuation of the national discussion on human cloning," Subcommittee on Public Health and Safety, Committee on Labor and Human Resources, 17 June 1997, #41-668CC.
27. J. Harris (1998), *Clones, Genes and Immortality*, p. 32.
28. Robertson, "Liberty, identity," pp. 1446–7.
29. D. Orentlicher (1999), "Cloning and the preservation of family integrity," *Louisiana Law Review*, **59**, pp. 1019, 1025. See L.R. Kass (2002), *Life, Liberty and the Defense of Dignity*, Ch. 5. The American Medical Association has taken the position that it is unethical for physicians to participate in genetic enhancement procedures unless they are able to provide a clear and meaningful benefit to either the fetus or the child. AMA Council on Judicial and Ethical Affairs (1994), "Ethical issues related to prenatal genetic testing," *Archives of Family Medicine*, **3**, pp. 633, 641
30. G. Annas (2000), "The man on the moon, immortality, and other millennial myths: the prospects and perils of human genetic engineering," *Emory Law Journal*, **49**, pp. 753, 765. See Sandel, "Case against perfection." Parthenogenesis is another form of asexual reproduction which, if perfected with humans, would allow a woman to conceive without any physical contact with a man or impregnation by his sperm. In what is termed "the virgin birth," a woman would produce an egg cell for conception, jolt it electronically or by pharmacological assistance, and then have it implanted in her womb for gestation. Laboratory experiments with sea urchins, frogs and mice have yielded success. D. Rorvik (1971), *Brave New World*, p. 95. See J. Cibelli, K. Grant, K. Chapman et al. (2002), "Parthenogenetic stem cells in nonhuman primates," *Science*, **295**, 1 Feb., p. 819.
31. R. Weiss (2001), "Human cloning bid stirs experts' anger," *Washington Post*, 7 Mar., p. A1.
32. Ibid. See R. Highfield (2001), "Scientists back worldwide ban on baby cloning," *Daily Telegraph*, 20 June, p. 10 (reporting that, while a clone is most likely to bear a striking resemblance to the original progenitor, it will differ at least as much as identical twins in

terms of personality and other high mental attributes). See also I. Wilmut (2006), *After Dolly: The Uses and Misuses of Human Cloning*; M. Amer (1996), "Breaking the mold: human embryos, cloning and its implications for a right to individuality," *UCLA Law Review*, **43**, p. 165; "Will cloning beget disaster?," *Wall Street Journal*, 2 May 1997, p. A14.

33. See note 31.

34. Orentlicher, "Cloning and the preservation," 1024–5. See also AMA Council on Judicial and Ethical Affairs, "Ethical issues related to preatal genetic testing." See generally R. Weiss (2000), "Test-tube baby born to save ill sister," *Washington Post*, 3 Oct., p. A1.

35. Stanley v. Georgia, 394 U.S. 557 (1968); Baird v. Eisenstadt, 429 F.2d 1398 (1st Cir. 1970), *aff'd on other grounds*, 405 U.S. 438 (1972).

36. See note 35.

37. Comment, "Asexual reproduction," p. 561.

38. Ibid., pp. 550, 556.

39. Skinner v. Oklahoma, 316 U.S. 535, 541 (1942).

40. Lederberg, "Experimental genetics," pp. 550–2. See generally M. Rothstein (1996), "Preventing the discovery of plaintiff genetic profiles by defendants seeking to limit damages in personal injury litigation," *Indiana Law Journal*, **71**, p. 877.

41. Lederberg, "Experimental genetics," p. 556. See Shapiro v. Thompson, 399 U.S. 618, 638 n. 20.

42. Skinner v. Oklahoma, 316 U.S. at 581–2; U.S. Constitution, Art. I, §9, Ch. 8; U.S. Constitution Amend. XIII. See generally G.P. Smith, II (1999), "Judicial decisionmaking in the age of biotechnology," *Notre Dame Journal of Law, Ethics and Public Policy*, **13**, p. 93.

43. Skinner v. Oklahoma, 316 U.S., p. 556.

44. Ibid., p. 579. See also Blank, *Political Implications*, pp. 93–109, 117–22.

45. Vukowich, "Dawning of the brave new world," pp. 189, 222. If the challenged legislation incorporated negative, rather than positive, eugenic concepts so that it only restricted carriers of recessive debilitating defects from cloning, the constitutional problems would be minimized. The legitimacy of the state interest could not be challenged on the ground that it creates an elite group and therefore violates the nobility clause of the United States Constitution. A court could find readily that such a statute is related rationally to a legitimate state interest—specifically, diminishing the propagation of inferior traits. Scientific evidence more readily can provide a rational basis for the classification of those carrying debilitating effects than for those possessing superior genetic traits. Whether the state's interest in a negative eugenics program is sufficiently compelling to sustain the validity of the statute under a strict scrutiny test, however, is uncertain. Ibid., pp. 198–201, 208.

46. Comment, "Asexual reproduction," p. 480. See generally R. Weiss (1998), "Fertility, innovation or exploitation?," *Washington Post*, 9 Feb., p. A1. See also G. Annas (1998), "Why we should ban cloning", *New England Journal of Medicine*, **339**, p. 118; J. Robertson (1998), "Human cloning and the challenge of regulations," *New England Journal of Medicine*, **339**, p. 119 (arguing for the use of human cloning if undertaken according to guidelines designed to ensure safety and efficacy).

47. R. Weiss (1998), "Human clone work will be regulated", *Washington Post*, 20 Jan., p. A1. S. 368 (1997) and H.R. 922 (1997) sought a permanent ban of federal funding for human cloning, while H.R. 923 sought to impose an outright ban on human cloning. See generally S. Newman (1997), "Human cloning and the family: reflections on cloning existing children," *New York Law School Journal of Human Rights*, **13**, pp. 523, 525.

48. Weiss, "Human clone work." See T. Gugliotta (1998), "United against human cloning, Hill leaders differ on specifics," *Washington Post*, 4 Feb., p. A4.

49. R. Weiss (1997), "Panel backs some human clone work," *Washington Post*, 4 June, p. A1. In 1997, the California State Assembly became the first state to legislate a prohibition on cloning a human being as well as the purchase or selling of an ovum, zygote, embryo, or fetus for the express purpose of cloning a human (California Health and Safety Code §24185) (Deering 1997). The second state to legislate here was Michigan—imposing a $10 000 000 fine and a ten-year prison term for violations. Michigan Compiled Laws §750.430a (2004).

Other states (led notably by Iowa, Louisiana, Michigan, Missouri, Rhode Island and Virginia) have also imposed restrictions on clonal experimentation. S. Stolberg (2002), "As Congress stalls, states pursue cloning," *New York Times*, 25 May, p. 1.

50. H.R. 2505.
51. S. 790, Human Cloning Prohibition Act of 2001. Senator Brownback reintroduced a similar bill in the 2002 session as S. 199; and Senator Arlen Specter sponsored S. 2439 as the Human Cloning Prohibition Act of 2002. Interestingly, the American Medical Association has chosen to endorse clonal therapeutic research but not human cloning. Reuters (2003), "Doctors group backs cloning for research," *Washington Post*, 18 June, p. A4. See A. Capron (2002), "Placing a moratorium on research cloning to ensure effective control over reproductive cloning," *Hastings Law Journal*, **53**, p. 1057.
52. H.R. 1357, S. 658.
53. S. Stolberg (2001), "House backs ban on human cloning for any objective," *New York Times*, 1 Aug., p. A1. See J. Brainard (2001), "Scientists' partial victory on stem cells may be undercut by ban on cloning," *Chronicle of Higher Education*, 17 Aug., p. 21. See generally R.M. Green (2001), *The Human Embryo Research Debates: Bioethics in the Vortex of Controversy*, Ch. 7. See A. Pollack (2004), "Scientific and ethical questions cloud plans to clone for therapy," *New York Times*, 13 Feb., p. A1 (discussing the alleged successful research efforts of South Korean scientists to successfully clone human embryos and then isolate from one of them a colony of stem cells). But see, A. McCook (2005), "Hwang faked results says panel," *Scientist*, 23 Dec., p. 1223.
54. Stolberg, "House backs ban."
55. Ibid. See L.B. Andrews (1999), *The Clone Age: Adventures in the New World of Reproductive Technology*, Ch. 12.
56. S. Stolberg (2002), "Some for abortion rights lean right in cloning fight," *New York Times*, 24 Jan., p. A25. See also R. Weiss (2002), "Cloning creates odd bedfellows," *Washington Post*, 10 Feb., p. B1; R. Weiss (2002), "Debate over cloning puts the political in science," *Washington Post*, 10 June, p. A9; S. Stolberg (2002), "Bush's bioethics advisory panel recommends a moratorium, not a ban on cloning research," *New York Times*, 11 July, p. A21.
57. A. Cooperman (2002), "HHS proposes insurance for fetus," *Washington Post*, 1 Feb., p. A1. See C. Wetzstein (2003), "New poll shows tilt to protect unborn", *Washington Times*, 16 Jan., p. A4 (reporting that a poll of 1000 adults showed 66 percent said they favored "restoring legal protection for unborn children"; and from this comes the conclusion that nearly 70 percent of all Americans support this position).
58. See Cooperman, "HHS proposes insurance for fetus." See A. Goldstein (2002), "Bush to extend health care benefits to fetuses," *Washington Post*, 28 Sept., p. A4. The final rule was promulgated 2 October 2002. See 67 C.F.R. §61956-01.
59. See note 57. In order to make this proposal moot, some congressmen endeavored, later unsuccessfully, to extend the State Children's Health Insurance Program to prenatal care. See note 57, Cooperman; see note 58, Goldstein. Interestingly, President Bush signed the Born Alive Infants Protection Act in August 2002, requiring that, if a fetus survives an abortion procedure, it must be considered a person under federal law. 1 U.S.C. §8 (2002). See generally H. Silverstein and, L. Speitel (2002), "Honey, I have no idea": court readiness to handle petitions to waive parental consent for abortion," *Iowa Law Review*, **88**, pp. 75, 77–9 (observing that, while 32 states mandate parental involvement when pregnant minors seek abortions, with 18 requiring parental consent before the termination of a minor's pregnancy, the statute includes a bypass mechanism whereby a minor may petition a judge to waive parental participation).
60. S. Stolberg (2002), "Bush makes fervent bid to get Senate to ban cloning research," *New York Times*, 11 Apr., p. A28.
61. Ibid.
62. Ibid. In one national survey of 800 adults, 63 percent agreed with the President's position and 29 percent disagreed. R. Novak (2002), "The people vs. cloning," *New York Post*, 22 Apr., p. 31.
63. R. Weinberg (2002), "Of clones and clowns," *Atlantic Monthly*, June, pp. 54–7.

64. Ibid., p. 59. See also R. Mishra (2002), "Clone research quietly builds in world's labs," *Boston Globe*, 21 June, p. A1.
65. S. Stolberg (2002), "Total ban on cloning research appears dead," *New York Times*, 14 June, p. A31; H. Dewar (2002), "Human cloning bill sidetracked," *Washington Post*, 19 June, p. A4.
66. See Stolberg, "As Congress stalls."
67. R. Carlson and G. Stimeling (2002), "Will genetic medicine make us happier?," *Orlando Sentinel*, 16 June, p. G1.
68. R. Weiss (1998), "Human clone work will be regulated," *Washington Post*, 20 Jan., p. A1; J. Schwartz (1997), "FDA sets safety framework for cell and tissue therapies: rules would cover attempted human cloning," *Washington Post*, 1 Mar., p. A3. See Wilmut, *After Dolly*.
69. R. Weiss (2001), "Legal barriers to human cloning may not hold up," *Washington Post*, 23 May, p. A1.
70. Ibid.
71. Past legislative efforts have not succeeded—with one of the foremost problems being uniform enforcement and the unpleasantness associated with convicting an individual for creating life. For a listing of failed federal attempts here see M. Mehlman (2000), "The law of above average: leveling the new genetic enhancement playing field," *Iowa Law Review*, **85**, n. 126.
72. Weiss, "Legal barriers."
73. Ibid.
74. See for example, Griswold v. Connecticut, 381 U.S. 479 (1965); Roe v. Wade, 410 U.S. 113 (1973); Carey v. Population Services International, 431 U.S. 678 (1977). See also G.P. Smith, II (1998), *Family Values and the New Society*, Ch. 4.
75. Mehlman, "The law of above average," *Iowa Law Review*, **85**, pp. 517, 519, *passim.*
76. Ibid., pp. 559, 560, *passim.*
77. Ibid., p. 568.
78. Ibid., p. 571.
79. Ibid., p. 573.
80. Ibid.
81. Ibid., p. 574.
82. Ibid. See E. Rakowski (2002), "Who should pay for bad genes?," *California Law Review*, **90**, p. 1345.
83. P. Kitcher (1996), *The Lives to Come: The Genetic Revolution and Human Possibilities*, pp. 193–5. See G.J. Annas and M.A. Grodin (eds.) (1992), *The Nazi Doctors and the Nuremberg Code*. It is estimated that, from 1933 to 1945, the Nazis sterilized 3 500 000 individuals. P. Reilly (1991), *The Surgical Solution: A History of Involuntary Sterilization in the United States*, p. 109. In America, during the period of eugenic sterilization, 60 000 Americans were subject to sterilization. Reilly, *Surgical Solution*, pp. 49, 165. See also H. Bruinius (2006), *Better for All the World*. See Buchanan et al., *From Chance to Choice*, Ch. 2.
84. Kitcher, *Lives to Come*, p. 199. See generally National Research Council (1997), *Evaluating Human Genetic Diversity*.
85. Kitcher, *Lives to Come*, pp. 199–203. See M. Ruse (1997), *Monad to Man: The Concept of Progress in Evolutionary Biology*.
86. Kitcher, *Lives to Come*, p. 202.
87. Ibid., p. 204.
88. Ibid., p. 209.
89. Ibid., p. 204.
90. Ibid., p. 326. See generally Symposium, "The Genetics Revolution: Conflicts, Challenges and Conundra", *American Journal of Law and Medicine*, **28** (2002), p. 145; P. Kitcher (1993), *The Advancement of Science*.
91. T. McGarity and K. Bayer (1983), "Federal regulation of emerging genetic technologies," *Vanderbilt Law Review*, **36**, p. 461; Comment, "Governmental control of research in positive eugenics," *Michigan Journal of Law Reform*, **7**, p. 615.

92. Buchanan et al., *From Chance to Choice*, p. 325.
93. Ibid., pp. 328–9. See Malinowski, "Choosing the genetic makeup."
94. Buchanan et al., *From Chance to Choice*, p. 333. See J.R. Nelson (1994), *On the Frontier of Genetics and Religion*; M. Ridley (2000), "The new eugenics," *National Review*, 31 July, p. 34.
95. See generally G.P. Smith, II (1996), "Pathways to immortality in the new millennium: human responsibility, theological direction or legal mandate?" *St. Louis University Public Law Review*, **15**, p. 447; G.P. Smith, II (1985), "Genetics, eugenics and public policy," *Southern Illinois Law Review*, p. 435.
96. R. Neville (1978), "Philosophic perspectives on freedom of inquiry," *Southern California Law Review*, **51** pp. 1115, 1128–9.
97. See generally Cohen (1978), "Restriction of research with recombinant DNA: the dangers of inquiry and the burden of proof," *Southern California Law Review*, **51**, pp. 1081, 1098; "Genetic engineering: innovation and risk minimization," *George Washington Law Review*, **57** (1988) p. 100.
98. See Roe v. Wade, 410 U.S. 113 (1973); G.P. Smith, II (1986) "Procreational autonomy v. state intervention: opportunity or crisis for a brave new world?," *Notre Dame Journal of Law, Ethics and Public Policy*, **2**, p. 635; G.P. Smith, II and Iraola (1984), "Sexuality, privacy and the new biology," *Marquette Law Review*, **67**, p. 63.
99. See B. Glass (1966), "The effect of changes in the physical environment on genetic change," in J. Roshansky (ed.), *Genetics and the Future of Man*, p. 43.
100. See G.P. Smith, II (1981), *Genetics, Ethics and the Law*, p. 2.
101. See generally T. Howard and J. Rifkin (1977), *Who Should Play God?*; P. Hilts (1981), "Genetic scientist is punished for test violations," *Washington Post*, 23 Mar., p. A1.
102. R. Sinsheimer (1976), "Recombinant DNA—on our own," *Bioscience* **26**, p. 599.
103. R. Sinsheimer (1977), "Potential risks," in National Academy of Science (ed.), *Research with Recombinant DNA*, p. 78.
104. J. Goodfield (1977), *Playing God*, p. 71.
105. See J. Fletcher (1978), "Ethics and recombinant DNA research," *Southern California Law Review*, **51**, pp. 1131–9.
106. See generally T.L. Beauchamp and L. Walters (1978), *Contemporary Issues in Bioethics*; G.P. Smith, II (1978), "Uncertainties on the spiral staircase: metaethics and the new biology," *Pharos*, **41**, p. 10.
107. See Irons and Sears (1980), "Patent re-examination": a case for administrative arrogation," *Utah Law Review*, pp. 287–8.
108. Diamond v. Chakrabarty, 447 U.S. 303 (1980).
109. Justice Brennan, writing in dissent, surveyed the Patent Act of 1793, as re-enacted in 1952, the Plant Patent Act of 1920, and the Plant Variety Protection Act of 1970 and concluded that there existed a strong congressional limitation against patenting bacteria. Ibid., p. 322.
110. 35 U.S.C. §101 (1976).
111. Diamond v. Chakrabarty, p. 307.
112. Diamond v. Chakrabarty, p. 314, n. 9 (1980). See also R. Dresser (1988), "Ethical and legal issues in patenting new animal life," *Jurimetrics*, **28**, p. 399; D. Daus, R. Bond and Rose (1966), "Microbiological plant patents," *Idea*, **10**, p. 87.
113. Daus et al., "Microbiological plant patents," p. 94, n. 36. See A. Pottage (1998), "The inscription of life in laws: genes, patents and bio-politics," *Modern Law Review*, **61**, p. 740.
114. See D. Daus (1985–86), "Patents for biotechnology," *Idea*, **26**, p. 263; M. Barinaga (1987), "Making transgenic mice: is it really that easy?," *Science*, **245**, p. 590.
115. See generally D. Nelkin (1978), "Threats and promises: negotiating the control of research," *Daedalus*, **107**, p. 191; L. Roberts (1989), "Ethical Questions Haunt New Genetic Technologies," *Science*, **243**, p. 1134; Pottage, "Inscription of Life."
116. U.S. Patent and Trademark Office (1987), "*Notice: Animals—Patentability*," *Official Gazette U.S. Patent and Trademark Office*, **1077**, 21 April, p. 8. While it permitted the patenting of animal organisms, the patenting of humans was not approved. See

C. Wallis (1987), "Should animals be patented?," *Time*, 4 May, p. 110. See also T. Ingold (1988), *What Is an Animal?*. See also "Evolving biotechnology patent laws in the United States and Europe: are they inhibiting disease research?," *Indiana International and Comparative Law Review*, **12** (2001), p. 183.

117. See note 116.
118. Ibid.
119. Ibid. See also P. Elmer-Dewitt (1989), "The perils of trading on heredity, *Time*, 20 Mar., pp. 70–71; Comment, "Biotechnology and the legal constitution of the self: managing identity in science, the market and society," *Hastings Law Journal*, **51** (2000), p. 909.
120. See note 119. Codifying the present rules of the U.S. Patent and Trademark Office that human organisms are not subject to patents, the Congress included a provision in an amendment within a package of spending bills which—while continuing to bar the issuance of patents—will not interfere with stem cell research itself. AP [Associated Press] (2003), "Hill negotiations agree to bar patents for human organisms," *Washington Post*, 25 Nov., p. A18; R. Weiss (2003), "Funding bill gets clause on embryo patents," *Washington Post*, 17 Nov., p. A4.
121. U.S. Patent and Trademark Office (1987), *"Notice: Animals—Patentability,"*; Wallis (1987), *"Should Animals be Patented?"*; Ingold (1988), *"What is an Animal?"*; AP (2003), "Hill negotiations agree to bar patents for human organisms,"; Weiss (2003), "Funding Bill gets clause on embryo patents."
122. H.R. 4970 (sponsored by Representative Kastenmeier).
123. "House passage of animal patent bill," *Patent, Trademark and Copyright Journal* (BNA), **36** (897), 15 Sept. 1988, p. 499.
124. Congressional Record, **134**, H7439, Daily edn., 13 Sept. 1988, Remarks of Rep. C. Rose.
125. R. Weiss (1998), "Patent sought in making of part-human creatures," *Washington Post*, 2 Apr., p. 2. See also D. Magnus, A. Caplan and G. McGee (eds.) (2002), *Who Owns Life?*
126. See generally R. Goldstein (2002), "Integration and differentiation of human embryonic stem cells transplanted to the chick embryo," *Developmental Dynamics*, **225**, p. 1; J. Seibold (1998–99), "Can Chakrabarty survive the Harvard Mouse?," *University of Florida Journal of Law and Public Policy*, **2**, p. 81 (discussing the first patent of a multicellular organism known as the "Harvard Mouse" in 1988).
127. R. Weiss (2005), "U.S. denies patent for a too-human hybrid," *Washington Post*, 13 Feb., p. A3.
128. Public Law 108-199, Division B, §634.
129. Congressional Record, **149**, H7274, Daily edn., 22 July 2003, Statement of Congressman Weldon.
130. See for example J.A. Thomson, U.S. Patent No. 6 200 806, issued 13 Mar. 2001, and J.A. Thomson, U.S. Patent No. 5 843 780, issued 1 Dec. 1998, both of which are assigned to the Wisconsin Alumni Research Foundation.
131. See for example, *In re Bergy*, 568 F.2d 1031, 195 U.S.P.Q. 344 (CCPA 1977). See also Amgen Inc. v. Chugai Pharmaceutical Co. Ltd., 13 U.S.P.Q. 2d 1737, affirmed in part, revised in part, vacated in part, 927 F.2d 1200, 18 U.S.P.Q. 2d 1016 (Fed. Cir. 1991), *cert. denied*, 112 S.Ct. 169 (1991).
132. W. Schneider (1987), "A patent on life forms gets genes into business," *International Herald Tribune*, 9 June, p. 1.
133. Ibid. See also R. Wasowski (1988), "The evolution of patentable compositions of matter: the United States Patent Office accepts genetically altered animals as patentable subject matter under 35 U.S.C. §101," *Administrative Law Journal*, **2**, p. 309.
134. S. Goldberg (1999), *Seduced by Science*, pp. 15–17. See E. Andrews (1995), "Religious leaders prepare to fight patents on genes," *New York Times*, 13 May, p. A1.
135. K. Day (1995), "Church groups to fight patenting of life forms," *Washington Post*, 13 May, p. A3. See generally D. Whitaker (2002), "The patentability of embryonic stem cell research results," *University of Florida Journal of Law and Public Policy*, **13**, p. 361.

136. Goldberg, *Seduced by Science*, p. 15.
137. A.R. Chapman (1999), *Unprecedented Choices: Religious Ethics at the Frontiers of Genetic Science*, pp. 211–23. See B. Waters and R. Cole-Turner (eds.) (2003), *God and the Embryo: Religious Voices on Stem Cells and Cloning* (various denominational positions are presented in the appendices).
138. Ethics Advisory Board of the Department of Health, Education and Welfare (1979), "Report and conclusions: HEW support of research involving human in vitro fertilization and embryo transfer," Federal Register, **44**, 35033. See R. McCormick (1991), "Who or what is the pre-embryo?," *Kennedy Institute of Ethics Journal*, **1**, Mar., p. 1.
139. H. Krause (1985), "Artificial conception: legal approaches," *Family Law Quarterly*, **19**, pp. 185, 190.
140. S. Abramowitz (1984), "A stalemate on test-tube baby research," *Hastings Center Report*, **24**, p. 5.
141. See "Hearings on Human Embryo Transfer, Subcommittee on Investigations and Oversight, U.S. House of Representatives" Committee on Science and Technology, 98th Cong., 2nd Sess. 142 (1984).
142. Abramowitz, "Stalemate."
143. Ethics Advisory Board, "Report and conclusions" 33057. Among these conditions were that the embryo be sustained *in vitro* beyond the implantation stage and that IVF, followed by embryo transfer, be used only by married couples who had donated their sperm and ova. Abramowitz, "Stalemate."
144. Ambramowitz, "Stalemate," p. 6. See J. Fletcher and K. Ryan (1987), "Federal regulations for fetal research: a case for reform," *Law, Medicine and Health Care*, **15**, p. 126.
145. 45 C.F.R. §§46.101–124, 46.301–306(g), 46.401–409 (1991).
146. 45 C.F.R. §46.204(d) (1991). See also 45 C.F.R. §46.205 (1991).
147. 45 C.F.R. §§46.102–206 (1985). *In vitro* fertilization is defined as "any fertilization of human ova which occurs outside of the body of a female, either through a mixture of donor human sperm and ova or by any other means." Section 46.203(g) (1991).
148. 45 C.F.R. §46.101(a) (1991).
149. G. Blumberg (1984), "Legal issues on nonsurgical human ovum transfer," *Journal of the American Medical Association*, **251**, p. 1178.
150. 45 C.F.R. §46.203(c) (1991).
151. 45 C.F.R. §§46.208(a)(1)–(2) (1991).
152. 45 C.F.R. §§46.209(b)(1)–(3) (1991).
153. M. Specter (1989), "Fetal-tissue research ban formally extended," *Washington Post*, 3 Nov., p. A5.
154. Ibid.
155. Ibid. See M. Specter (1990), "Abortion issue chills research: fetal tissue fund ban sidelines U.S. experts," *Washington Post*, 27 Mar., p. 1; R. Marcus (1990), "Fetal protection policies: prudence or bias?," *Washington Post*, 8 Oct., p. A1.
156. See note 155.
157. G.P. Smith, II (1986), "Procreational autonomy v. state intervention: opportunity or crisis for a brave new world?," *Notre Dame Journal of Law Ethics and Public Policy*, **2**, pp. 635, 638. See generally, Richard Locayo (1989), "Pro choice? Get lost: antiabortion views are a must at Health and Human Services", *Time*, 4 Dec., p. 43.
158. *Weekly Compilation of Presidential Documents*, 25 Jan. 1993, p. 87. The National Bioethics Advisory Committee recommended in May 1999 that the congressional ban on funding for human embryo research be lifted to allow research to be conducted on leftover embryos from fertility clinics if they were no longer wanted by their genetic parents. *International Herald Tribune*, 24 May 1999, p. 2.
159. 42 U.S.C.§289g-1(a)(2)(2). See C.H. Coleman, J.A. Menikoff, J.A. Goldner and N.N. Publer (eds.) (2005), *The Ethics and Regulation of Research with Human Subjects*, pp. 657–8.
160. 42 U.S.C. §289g-1(c).
161. Coleman et al., *Ethics and Regulation*, p. 658. See generally, Symposium (2007), "Intergenerational Equity and discounting," *University of Chicago Law Review*, **74**.

162. The following sources serve as references for the presentation of arguments favoring and opposing the use of *in vitro* fertilization as an aid for genetic improvement: A. Nichols and T. Hogan (eds.) (1984), *Making Babies: The Test Tube and Christian Ethics*; R. McCormick (1981), *How Brave a New World?*, Chs. 1, 16; E. Harris (1983), "In vitro fertilization: the ethical issues," *Philosophical Quaterly*, **33**, p. 217.

163. 65 C.F.R. §51.976 (2000). See R. Weiss (2000), "U.S. to issue new rules for research on embryo cells," *Washington Post*, 23 Aug., p. A1. The new rule not only disallows payment to embryo donors, but precludes—as well—donors from determining, in advance, who will receive the stem cells. This will prevent—hopefully—the creation of a market in embryo cells. Embryo donors are, furthermore, required—in giving their consent to the procedure—to fully understand that not only will their embryos not survive the scientific investigation but embryonic cells may be kept alive indefinitely and could be made into tissues which in turn could be transplanted into patients. A special advisory committee of scientists and ethicists designated as the human pluripotent stem cell review group will review all embryo cell grant applications to the NIH. If approved, the applications will then be sent to the NIH Scientific Advisory Committee for final action.

164. Weiss (2000), "U.S. to issue new rules for research on embryo cells."

165. R. Park (2001), "Just press print," *Economist*, 3 Mar., p. 76.

166. Ibid.

167. A. Lau (2001), "Living cells grown from dead brains," *Washington Times*, 4 May, p. A5; R. Weiss (2001), "Human fat may provide stem cells," *Washington Post*, 10 Apr., p. A1; "Cadavers are latest source of versatile stem cells," *Washington Post*, 6 Nov. 2000, p. A19.

168. Weiss, "U.S. to issue new rules."

169. R. Pear (2001), "Stem cell study divides U.S. officials," *International Herald Tribune*, 28 June, p. 6. What had been reported by two South Korean scientists as the first ever successful effort at cloning human embryos and the extraction of universal stem cells from them was later found to be a fraud. See R. Weiss (2004), "Natural human embryos cloned," *Washington Post*, 12 Feb., p. A1; McCook, "Hwang faked results says panel."

170. R. Weiss (2001), "New potential for stem cells suggested," *Washington Post*, 27 Apr., p. A2. See R. Weiss (2007), "Scientists see potential in amnistic stem cells," *Washington Post*, 8 Jan., p. 1 (reporting on the development of non-embryonic stem cells from amniotic fluid and discarded placentas as a very promising source for research); S. Holland, K. Labacqz and L. Zoloth (eds.) (2001), *The Human Embryonic Stem Cell Debate: Science, Ethics and Public Policy*. See also L. Mumola (2000), "Adult stem cells found to have same transforming properties as embryonic ones," *Catholic Standard*, 13 July, p. 7; "The Vatican's Pontifical Academy for Life's declaration on the production and the scientific and therapeutic use of human embryonic stem cells," http://www.vatican.va (accessed 25 Aug. 2000).

171. R. Weiss (2001), "Fetal cell research funds are at risk," *Washington Post*, 26 Jan., p. A3. See R. McGough (2001), "A case for federal funding of human embryonic stem cell research: the interplay of moral absolutism and scientific research," *Journal of Contemporary Health Law and Policy*, **18**, p. 147.

172. Weiss (2001), "Fetal cell research funds are at risk." See also N. Wade (2001), "Stem-cell advances are likely to heighten ethics debate," *New York Times*, 27 Apr., p. A1; R. Faden et al. (2003), "Considerations of justice in stem cell research and therapy," *Hastings Center Report*, **33**, p. 13 (discussing the availability of stem cell research therapies for every patient who needs them—as they might benefit only white Americans).

173. Pear, "Stem cell study divides U.S. officials."

174. R. Doerflinger (1999), "The ethics of funding stem cell research: a Catholic viewpoint," *Kennedy Institute of Ethics Journal*, **9**, p. 137. See generally E. Herold (2006), *Stem Cell Wars*, Ch. 6.

175. Pear, "Stem cell study divides U.S. officials."

176. Ibid. See generally J. Robertson (1999), "Ethics and policy in embryonic stem cell research," *Kennedy Institute of Ethics Journal*, **9**, p. 109. As of August 2002 only three

colonies of embryo cells were readily available to US researchers and only nine research facilities had applied for federal grants to conduct embryonic research on the cells. As a result of this state of affairs, Australia, the UK and Israel have moved forward as the leaders in the field. J. Gillis and R. Weiss (2002), "Stem cell research not yet booming," *Washington Post*, 6 Aug., p. 1. But See C. Connolly (2002), "California to enact bill promoting stem cell research," *Washington Post*, 22 Sept., p. A12 (reporting that the legislation is designed to make California a safe haven for human embryonic stem cell research including cells extracted from cloned embryos but does not permit reproductive cloning. Senate Bill 253 was signed into legislation by Governor Gray Davis on September 22 codifying this position). Health and Safety Code, §125118 (2006). See also §§125 300 *et seq.* See also D. Vergano (2004), "States divide into stem-cell debates: patchwork of laws may slow research," *USA Today*, 21 Apr., p. D1 (reporting on the efforts of some 33 state legislatures to alternatively condemn, condone or fund embryonic stem cell research).

177.   George W. Bush (2001), "Address to the nation on stem cell research," *Weekly Compilation of Presidential Documents*, **37**, Aug., p. 1141. See S. Stolberg (2001), "Tangled issues in Congress: cloning and stem cell study," *New York Times*, 31 July, p. A17. The National Institutes of Health posted on its website a stem cell registry listing 72 colonies or stem lines at 11 institutions in five countries (http://escr.nih.gov/). *Washington Post*, 8 Nov. 2001, p. A14. In March 2002 in a little-noticed ruling, the National Institutes of Health determined that scientists receiving federal monies for stem cell research could study new lines, even deriving them from embryos in their university laboratories, so long as they did not commingle their federal funds with private monies. With this simple clarification, an important barrier to this type of research has been lifted. Heretofore, the few academic researchers conducting embryonic studies did so in their private research laboratories with independent funds—fearful, as such, that using equipment in their university facilities would jeopardize their government grants. S. Stolberg (2002), "Ruling by U.S. widens study of stem cells," *New York Times*, 7 Aug., p. A1. See generally O. Snead (2005), "The pedagogical significance of the Bush stem cell policy: a window into biological regulation in the United States," *Yale Journal of Health Policy, Law, and Ethics*, **5**, p. 491.

178.   J. Gillis (2001), "Stem cell research faces FDA hurdle," *Washington Post*, 24 Aug., p. A1. See R. Weiss (2002), "Scientists say access to embryo cells lacking," *Washington Post*, 26 Sept., p. A19 (noting none of the cell lines approved by Bush have real therapeutic potential because they were cultivated with mouse cells, thus making them all but ineligible for transplantation into humans).

179.   R. Weiss (2003), "Stem cell studies test Bush policy: scientists push use of newer colonies," *Washington Post*, 22 Apr., p. B1; R. Weiss and J. Gillis (2004), "New embryonic stem cells made available," *Washington Post*, 4 Mar., p. A2 (detailing how, using private monies, Harvard University researchers created 17 new colonies of human embryonic stem cells—this obtained from 344 three-day-old to five-day-old human embryos donated for research use by a local fertility clinic). See also R. Lakshmi (2001), "India plans to fill void in stem cell research: scientists say restrictions in U.S. may give them advantage in development" (where there are few constraints on stem cell research), *Washington Post*, 27 Aug., p. A7. In 2002, it was announced that the UK was set to become the world's first stem cell bank in 2003 as record science spending will allow the country to become the world's leading public funding source for research in this field. M. Henderson (2002), "Stem cell scientists given £40 million boost," *The Times*, 10 Dec., p. 12. See also J. Brainard (2001), "Scientists" partial victory on stem cells may be undercut by ban on cloning," *Chronicle of Higher Education*, 17 Aug., p. 21.

180.   *Guidelines for Human Embryonic Stem Cell Research* (2005).

181.   Ibid., Ch. 6.

182.   Ibid. The executive summary and full report of the guidelines can be browsed at books.nap.edu/catalog/11278.html (accessed 1 Aug. 2006).

183. R. Weiss (2006), "Universal stem cell principles prepared," *Washington Post*, 2 Mar., p. A12.
184. Ibid.
185. Ibid. The Hinxton Principles, numbering 19, and consensus statement are found at www.hopkinsmedicine.org/bioethics (accessed 1 Aug. 2006).
186. H.R. 81, S.B. 471, codified as 42 U.S.C. §498C (2006). C. Babington (2006), "Senate passes stem cell bill: Bush vows veto," *Washington Post*, 19 July, p. A1.
187. C. Babington (2006), "Stem cell bill gets Bush's first veto," *Washington Post*, 20 July, p. A14.
188. Ibid. A Gallup poll in May 2006, however, found 61 percent of Americans accepted the morality of pursuing embryonic stem cell research. A. Stone (2006), "Senate defies veto threat, sends stem cell bill to Bush," *USA Today*, 19 July, p. 1. This level of public approval is consistent with other polling results on this issue. See Johns Hopkins Genetics and Public Policy Center (eds.) (2005), *Values in Conflict: Public Attitudes on Embryonic Stem Cell Research*, pp. 5–6. See also L. Browder (2006), "Stem cells in Senate spotlight", *Washington Post*, 16 July, p. B7.
189. Babington, "Senate passes stem cell bill: Bush vows veto."
190. Babington, "Stem cell bill gets Bush's first veto."
191. S. 3504, Public Law 109-242.
192. S. 2754. See Weiss, "Scientists see potential," p. 1.
193. Babington, "Stem cell bill gets Bush's first veto." Regardless of the failure of this funding bill for alternative sources of embryonic stem cell research, the President directed the Secretary of Health and Human Services and NIH Director to proceed with its present ongoing work in this area. R. Novak (2006), "Stem cells: no one-two punch," *Washington Post*, 24 July, p. A13.
194. Ch. 1, notes 52, 53. See J. Fletcher (2007), "Bush vetoes stem cell research legislation," *Washington Post*, 21 June, p. A4.
195. *Weekly Compilation of Presidential Documents*, **43**, 22 June 2007, p. 821.
196. See J. Nowak, R. Rotunda and J. Young (1983), *Constitutional Law* 2nd edn., p. 740. See also K. Lorio (1982), "In vitro fertilization and embryo transfer: fertile areas for litigation," *Southwestern Law Journal*, **35**, pp. 973, 983.
197. Zablocki v. Redhail, 434 U.S. 374, 384 (1978). See for example Carey v. Population Services International, 431 U.S. 678, 685 (1977); Roe v. Wade, 410 U.S. 113, 153 (1973); Eisenstadt v. Baird, 405 U.S. 438 (1972); Loving v. Virginia, 388 U.S. 1, 12 (1967).
198. Lorio, "In vitro fertilization," pp. 1007–8.
199. Ibid.
200. B. Hafen (1983), "The constitutional status of marriage, kinship and sexual privacy," *Michigan Law Review*, **81**, p. 463, at 538. See generally J. Dolgin (1996), "Suffer the children: nostalgia, contradiction and the new reproductive technologies," *Arizona Law Journal*, **28**, p. 471.
201. *Roe*, 410 U.S. 113.
202. See generally G.P. Smith, II (1968), "Through a test tube darkly: artificial insemination and the law," *Michigan Law Review*, **57**, p. 127.
203. See D. Vetri (1988), "Reproductive technologies and United States law," *International and Comparative Law Quarterly*, **37**, pp. 505, 520.
204. See for example Minn. Stat. Ann. §145.422(2) (2005).
205. See for example Comp. Laws Ann. §333.2685 *et seq.* (2001). See L. Andrews (1984), "The stork market: the law of the new reproduction technologies," *ABA Journal*, **70**, pp. 50, 54–5. G. Blumberg (1984), "Legal issues on nonsurgical human ovum transfer," *Journal of the American Medical Association*, **251**, p. (1979) 1178; D. Flannery, C. Weisman, C. Lipsett and A. Braverman, "Test tube babies: legal issues raised by in vitro fertilization," *Georgetown Law Journal*, **67**, p. 1295.
206. See for example 18 Pa. Stat. Ann. §3213(e) (Purdon 2000).
207. Johns Hopkins Genetics and Public Policy Center (2005), *Cloning: a Policy Analysis*, pp: 39–42.

208. J. Watson and F. Crick (1953), "Genetic implications of the structure of deoxyribonucleic acid," *Nature*, **171**, p. 964.
209. K. Nobles (1992), "Birthright or life sentence: controlling the threat of genetic testing,"
Southern California Law Review, **65**, p. 2081.
210. See generally D. Nelkin and L. Tancredi (1989), *Dangerous Diagnostics: The Social
Power of Biological Information*.
211. D.J. Kevles and L. Hood (eds.) (1992), *The Code of Codes: Scientific and Social Issues
in the Human Genome Project*.
212. "The aim is to get genes to do the work: Newsday interview with James D. Watson,"
Newsday, 6 July 1993, p. 59. See also "Changing your genes," *Economist*, 25 Apr. 1992,
p. 11.
213. C. Cookson (1992), "The men who would play God," *Financial Post*, weekly edn., 10
Feb., p. S37.
214. "Genetic code of human life is created by scientists," *New York Times*, spl. edn., 27 June
2000, p. 1; N. Wade (2000), "Now, the hard part: putting the genome to work," *New
York Times*, 27 June, p. D1. The National Human Genome Research Institute of the
National Institutes of Health announced in May 2002 that six more species would have
their entire genetic code deciphered: the chimpanzee, the chicken, the honeybee, the sea
urchin, the protozoan Tetrahymena thermophila and a family of fungi. Building upon
the successes achieved in identifying and placing in order virtually 3.1 billion "letters"
of the human genetic code, the NIH expects—with this new project—to enhance their
understanding of evolutionary processes and thereby uncover the causes of many
human diseases. R. Weiss (2002), "More species chosen for Genome Project,"
Washington Post, 23 May, p. A3.
215. See P. Billings, M. Kohn, M. de Cuevas, J. Beckwith, J.S. Alpen and M.R. Natowicz
(1992), "Discrimination as a consequence of genetic testing," *American Journal of
Human Genetics*, **50**, pp. 476, 479, 481. The findings of this study affirm the existence
of discrimination against individuals who are completely asymptomatic, their only
"abnormality" being in their genotype.
216. L. Andrews (1987), "The future of confidentiality of genetic information," in *Medical
Genetics: A Legal Frontier*, p. 209.
217. Ibid., pp. 187–8, 209. Unlike an infectious disease, a genetic disorder is generally
immutable. See generally A. Iles (1996), "The Human Genome Project: a challenge to
the human rights framework," *Harvard Human Rights Journal*, **9**, p. 27.
218. Andrews, "The future of confidentiality of genetic information," Iles, "The Human
Genome Project." See N. Holtzman (1988), "Recombinant DNA technology, genetic
tests and public policy," *American Journal of Human Genetics*, **42**, p. 624. See generally,
G.P. Smith, II (1988), "Biotechnology and the law: social responsibility in freedom of
scientific investigation," *Mercer Law Review*, **36**, p. 437.
219. M.R. Natowicz (1992), "Genetic discrimination and the law," *American Journal of
Human Genetics*, **50**, pp. 465, 466. See G. Laurie (2002), *Genetic Privacy: A Challenge
to Medico-Legal Norms*, Chs. 3, 4.
220. See note 219. See U.S. Congress, Office of Technology Assessment (1990), *Genetic
Monitoring and Screening in the Workplace*, OTA-BA-455, Washington, D.C.: U.S.
Government Printing Office. See generally O. O'Neill (1998), "Insurance and genetics:
the current state of play," *Modern Law Review*, **62**, p. 716. Interestingly, more than 250
voluntary genetic support organizations were operating in 1996. J.D. Weiss and J.S.
Mackta (1996), *Starting and Sustaining Genetic Support Groups*.
221. See note 220. See M. Rothstein (1990), "Genetic screening in employment: some legal,
ethical and societal issues," *International Law Journal of Bioethics*, **1**, p. 239. It is to be
remembered that, while not all employment discrimination is inefficient, this does not
mean "that it is or should be lawful." R.A. Posner (1992), *Economic Analysis of Law*,
4th edn, p. 337.
222. Nobles, "Birthright," p. 2089. A more accurate measure of safety risk instead of utilizing genetic testing would be a test of an individual's actual capacity to function in a
safety-sensitive job. Council on Ethical and Judicial Affairs (1991), "Use of genetic

testing of employers," *Journal of the American Medical Association*, **226**, 2 Oct., pp. 1827, 1828.

223. Nobles, "Birthright". Over time, as the costs of genetic testing decrease and their degree of accuracy increases, insurers may well be expected to find it not only cost-effective to screen genetically prospective clients but indeed a competitive necessity. S. O'Hara (1993), "The use of genetic testing in the health insurance industry: the creation of a biological underclass," *Southwestern University Law Review*, **22**, p. 1211.

224. Nobles, "Birthright," p. 2090.

225. Ibid.

226. Ibid., p. 2909. Florida, Louisiana, New Jersey and North Carolina have enacted legislation prohibiting discrimination in employment and insurance based on carrying the sickle-cell trait, hemoglobin C trait, thalessemia, Tay Sachs or cystic fibrosis. Fla. Stat. §448.076 (West 2002); La. Rev. Stat. §§22:652.1 (West 2004); N.J. Stat. §§10:5-12, 10:5-5 (West 2002); N.C. Gen. Stat. §§58-51-45, 58-58-25, 95-28.1 (Matthew Bender 2005). See R. Lillquist and C. Sullivan (2004), "The law and genetics of racial profiling in medicine," *Harvard Civil Rights–Civil Liberties Law Review*, **39**, p. 391. See also K. Hudson (2007), "Prohibiting genetic discrimination," *New England Journal of Medicine*, **356**, May, p. 2021, commenting that 35 states have enacted laws prohibiting genetic discrimination in employment and 47 have laws against discrimination in health insurance.

227. Nobles, "Birthright," 2090.

228. Ibid.

229. Ibid. See generally D. Elliott (2002), "The genome and the law: should increased knowledge change the law?," *Harvard Journal of Law and Public Policy*, **25**, p. 61.

230. J. Beckwith (1991), "Foreword: The Human Genome Initiative: genetics' lightning rod," *American Journal of Law and Medicine*, **17**, pp. 1, 2. See M. Singer and P. Berg (1991), *Genes & Genome: A Changing Perspective*.

231. C. Barrad (1993), "Genetic information and property theory," *Northwestern University Law Review*, **87**, pp. 1037, 1043.

232. S. Lubove (1992), "*Genomic Wildcatters*," *Forbes*, 3 Feb., p. 97; J. Watson (1990), "The Human Genome Project: past, present and future," *Science*, **248**, p. 44.

233. See Medical Research Council (1991), *Human Genome Research: A Review of European and International Contributions*. The most comprehensive analysis of the Human Genome Initiative is to be found in Office of Technology Assessment, U.S. Congress (1988), *Mapping our Genes: Genome projects—How Big, How Fast?*", Washington, D.C.: U.S. Government Printing Office.

234. D. Koshland (1989), "Sequences and consequences of the human genome," *Science*, **246**, p. 189; note 214.

235. R. Weiss (2003), "Genome Project Completed," *Washington Post*, 15 Apr., p. A6.

236. Ibid.

237. Ibid.

238. F. Collins, G. Green, A. Guttmacher and M. Gayer (2003), "A vision for the future of genomics research," *Nature*, **422**, 24 Apr., p. 835.

239. Barrad, "Genetic information," p. 1043.

240. See G.P. Smith, II (1976), "Manipulating the genetic code: jurisprudential conundrums," *Georgetown Law Journal*, **64**, pp. 697, 733.

241. See G.P. Smith, II (1989), *The New Biology: Law, Ethics, and Biotechnology*, Ch. 5.

242. Barrad, "Genetic information," p. 1046.

243. Ibid., p. 1047.

244. Ibid.

245. A. Caplan and D. Magnus (2003), "New life forms: new threats, new possibilities," *Hastings Center Reporter*, **33**, Nov.–Dec., p. 3.

246. Ibid.

247. Ibid.

248. Ibid.

249. J. Brown (1993), "Filling in gene map, but far from home," *Washington Post*, 8 Mar., p. A3.

250. See H. Jonas (1984), *The Imperative of Responsibility: In Search of an Ethic for the Technological Age*; J. Gustafson (1992), "Genetic therapy: ethical and religious reflections," *Journal of Contemporary Health Law and Policy*, **8**, pp. 183, 190.
251. Gustafson, "Genetic therapy," pp. 199, 200.
252. R. Dreyfus and D. Nelkin (1992), "The jurisprudence of genetics," *Vanderbilt Law Review*, **45**, pp. 313, 347, 348.
253. Ibid., pp. 343, 345. See Richard A. Posner (2004), *Catastrophe: Risk and Response*, pp. 93, *passim*.
254. President's Commission for the Study of Ethical Problems in Medicine and Biomedical and Behavioral Research (1982), *Splicing Life: A Report on the Social and Ethical Issues of Genetic Engineering with Human Beings*, Washington, D.C.: U.S. Government Printing Office, p. 22.
255. Dreyfus and Nelkin, "Jurisprudence of genetics," pp. 339, 340.
256. *Washington Post*, 14 Nov. 1990, p. 1. See generally L. Anderson (1985), "Human gene therapy: scientific and ethical considerations," *Journal of Medicine and Philosophy*, **10**, p. 275.
257. D. Cournoyer (1990), "Gene therapy: a new approach for the treatment of genetic disorders," *Clinical Pharmacology and Therapeutics*, **47**, p. 1.
258. See note 256. See also *Washington Post*, 31 July 1990, p. 3; *Washington Post Health Magazine*, 25 Sept. 1990, pp. 8–9.
259. See note 256.
260. Ibid. Anderson, "Human gene therapy."
261. Ibid.
262. R. Herman (1992), "Gene therapy is no longer a rarity," *Washington Post Health Magazine*, 21 Jan., p. 7.
263. Anderson, "Human gene therapy," p. 283. Current gene therapy applications include those for hemophilia, molecular degeneration and amyotrophic lateral sclerosis. M. Lysaght and L. Aebischer (1999), "Encapsulated cells as therapy," *Scientific American*, **280**, April, p. 58.
264. Herman, "Gene therapy."
265. Ibid.
266. R. Herman (1991), "Tinkering with essence of humanity," *Washington Post Health Magazine*, 8 Oct., p. 6.
267. Ibid.
268. Ibid.
269. Ibid.
270. Dreyfus and Nelkin, "Jurisprudence of genetics," p. 314. For an historical overview of early state mandated PKU testing between 1963 and 1968 and the state legislative citations to the 43 states where such genetic testing is required, See P. Reilly (1997), *Genetics, Law and Social Policy*, pp. 37, *passim*, 49–52 and Ch. 4 (1977).
271. Dreyfus and Nelkin, "Jurisprudence of genetics," pp. 320, 321. See O. Jones (1992), "Sex selection: regulating technology enabling the predetermination of a child's gender," *Harvard Journal of Law and Technology*, **6**, pp. 1, 21, where the principal justification of sex selection is that its use serves to reduce or eliminate certain sex-linked diseases such as hemophilia, Cooley's anemia, Down syndrome and more than 400 others that increase aggregate social anxiety and tax society's medical and financial resources.
272. Dr. James Watson, Director of the Human Genome Initiative, said, "Our fate is in our genes." L. Jaroff (1989), "The gene hunt," *Time*, 20 Mar., pp. 62, 67.
273. J. Fletcher and D. Wertz (1990), "After the human genome is mapped," *Emory Law Journal*, **39**, pp. 747, 757. See Nobles, "Birthright," p. 2097; Fletcher and Wertz, "After the human genome is mapped," pp. 758, 763, 787–8; L. Andrews (1987), "The future of confidentiality of genetic information", *in Medical Genetics: A Legal Frontier*, p. 209.
274. Nobles, "Birthright," p. 2094. This author notes that state constitutional provisions protecting the right of privacy are found in Alaska, Arizona, California, Florida,

Hawaii, Illinois, Louisiana, Montana, South Carolina and Washington. California in particular prohibits reasonable searches and seizures by private and public employers. Cal. Const. art. I §13.

275. Loving v. Virginia, 388 U.S. 1, 12 (1967) (marriage); Prince v. Massachusetts, 321 U.S. 158, 166 (1944) (contraception); Skinner v. Oklahoma, 316 U.S. 535, 541–2 (1942) (procreation); Pierce v. Society of Sisters, 268 U.S. 510, 535 (1925) (child rearing and education).

276. Griswold v. Connecticut, 381 U.S. 479 (1964).

277. Roe v. Wade, 410 U.S. 113, 153 (1973). See Smith and Iraola, "Sexuality, privacy." See generally G.P. Smith, II (1988), "Limitations on reproductive autonomy for the mentally handicapped," *Journal of Contemporary. Health Law and Policy*, **4**, p. 71.

278. Lawrence v. Texas, 539 U.S. 558 (2003), with the right of privacy being rooted in the Due Process clause.

279. United States v. Miller, 425 U.S. 435 (1976). The Patient's Bill of Rights Plus Act (Senate Bill 300) of 1999 also sought to forbid discrimination in group health insurance premiums based on predictive genetic information.

280. Fisher v. United States, 425 U.S. 391, 399 (1976).

281. H.R. 5612, 101st Cong., 2nd Sess. (1990).

282. S. 1416, 104th Cong., 1st Sess. (1995).

283. G. Annas, L. Glantz and P. Roche (1995), *The Genetic Privacy Act and Commentary*, Feb., p. vi. See generally, Laurie, *Genetic Privacy*, Chs. 3, 4; G. Annas (1993), "Privacy rules for DNA databanks: protecting coded future diaries," *Journal of the American Medical Association*, **270**, p. 2346.

284. See for example H.R. 304, H.R. 341, H.R. 3178.

285. 110 Stat. 1936, 42 U.S.C. §201 *et seq.* (1997), 26 U.S.C. §62 *et seq.* (1997), 29 U.S.C. §1181 et seq. (1997).

286. 29 U.S.C. §1181 (1997).

287. S. 382. But cf. S. 1053. H. Devar (2003), "Senate backs safeguards for genetic data," *Washington Post*, 15 Oct., p. A10.

288. See 151 Congressional Record D156 (*Daily Digest*, 1 Mar. 2006). The bill was reintroduced as S. 358 on 22 Jan. 2007. For an analysis of this proposed legislation, See Hudson, "Prohibiting genetic discrimination."

289. J. Stone (1973), "Knowledge, survival, and the duties of science," *American University Law Review*, **23**, pp. 231.

290. See generally R. Delgado and D. Millen (1982), "God, Galileo and government: toward constitutional protection or scientific inquiry," in G.P. Smith, II (ed.), *Ethical, Legal and Social Challenges to a Brave New World*, p. 231

291. See Nelkin, "Threats and promises."

292. See R. Edwards and D. Sharpe (1971), "Social values and research in human embryology," *Nature*, **231**, pp. 87, 90.

293. Executive Order 12975. *Weekly Compilation of Presidential Documents*, **31**, 3 Oct. 1995, p. 1759. See A. Dzur and D. Levin (2004), "The 'Nation's Conscience': Assessing Bioethics Commissions as Public Forums," *Kennedy Institute of Ethics Journal*, **14**, p. 333.

294. R. Weiss (2001), "From the cutting edge to the end of the road: Bioethics Commission set to expire today," *Washington Post*, 3 Oct., p. A29.

295. See G. Stolberg (2002), "Bush's bioethics advisory panel recommends a moratorium," *New York Times*, 11 July, p. A21 (reporting on the Panel(s recommendation for a temporary moratorium, not a ban, on human cloning). At its August 2002 meeting, the House of Delegates of the American Bar Association approved a resolution opposing governmental actions that would prohibit scientific research conducted for therapeutic purposes or penalize individuals or research entities that participate in such research. Report No. 117B. See A. D'Andrea (2005), "Federalizing bioethics," *Texas Law Review*, **83**, p. 1663, note.

296. R. Weiss (2002), "Bush unveils bioethics council," *Washington Post*, 17 Jan., p. A21.

297. R. Weiss (2004), "Bioethics panel calls for bans on radical reproductive procedures," *Washington Post*, 16 Jan., p. A2; L. Turner (2004), "Science, politics and the President's

Council on Bioethics," *Nature Biotechnology*, **22**, p. 509. See R. Weiss (2004), "Greater regulations of fertility encouraged: Bioethics Council seeking changes," *Washington Post*, 2 Apr., p. A8 (suggesting an official congressional policy be set which follows embryo research only up to 14 days of development).
298. See note 297.
299. 42 U.S.C.A. §263a-1 (1992).
300. L. Jones (2003), "Multiple Births: How Are We Doing?," *Fertility and Sterility*, **79**, p. 17.
301. Ibid.
302. J. Robertson (2003–04), "IVF after 25 years: challenges for a maturing technology," *Lab Rpt*, **3**, Winter, pp. 8, 9, Institute for Bioethics, Health Policy and Law, University of Louisville.
303. Ibid.
304. Ibid.
305. W. Burger (1982), "Reflections on law and experimental medicine," in Smith, *Ethical, Legal and Social Challenges to a Brave New World*, **1**, p. 211, M. Shapiro (1987), "Introduction to the issue: some dilemmas of biotechnological research," *Southern California Law Review*, **51**, p. 987; Posner, *Catastrophe*, pp. 93, *passim*.
306. See B. Commoner (2002), "Unraveling the DNA myth," *Harper's*, Feb., p. 39.
307. See generally M.A. Rothstein (ed.) (1997), *Genetic Secrets: Protecting Privacy and Confidentiality in the Genetic Era*; Lillquist and Sullivan, "*Law and Genetics of Racial Profiling*," p. 391.
308. See generally S. Korbin (1983), "Confidentiality of genetic information," *UCLA Law Review*, **30**, p. 1283; M. Rothstein (1996), "Preventing the discovery of plaintiff genetic profiles by defendants seeking to limit damages in personal injury litigation," *Indiana Law Journal*, **71**, p. 877.
309. 42 U.S.C. §§12011–12213 (1994).
310. 5 U.S.C. §552a (1988).
311. S. Jasanoff (1990), "Biology and the Bill of Rights: can science reframe the Constitution?," *American Journal of Law and Medicine*, **13**, pp. 249, 288.
312. Ibid., p. 287. See Smith, "Procreational autonomy."
313. L. Andrews (1990), "Genetics and the law," *Emory Law Journal*, **39**, pp. 619, 620; E. Branscomb (2001), "It's a genome, not a cure all," *Washington Post*, 2 July, p. A1.
314. A. Capron (1990), "Which ills to bear? Reevaluating the 'threat' of modern genetics," *Emory Law Journal*, **39**, pp. 665, 694.
315. Ibid., p. 695. See generally M. Shapiro (1990), "Biotechnology and the design of regulation," *Ecology Law Quarterly*, **17**, p. 1. See also L. Altman (2000), "Genomics chief has high hopes and great fears, for genetic testing," *New York Times*, 27 June, p. D6.
316. J. Fletcher and D. Wertz, "After the human genome is mapped," p. 759. See generally P. Kim (2002), "Genetic discrimination, genetic privacy: rethinking employee protection from a brave new workplace," *Northwestern University Law Review*, **96**, p. 1497 (arguing the central issue of employer use of genetic information is grounded in privacy and thus privacy protections need to be in place in order to protect individual autonomy).
317. Fletcher and Wertz, "After the human genome is mapped."
318. Ibid.
319. Burger, "Reflections on law and experimental medicine." See generally Posner, *Catastrophe*; J.F. Kilner, R.D. Pentz and F.E. Young (eds.) (1997), *Genetic Ethics*, Chs. 15, 19.
320. See A. Caplan (2004), "Bioethics: is biomedical research too dangerous to pursue?," *Science*, **303**, 20 Feb., p. 1142.
321. C.S. Lewis (1965), *The Abolition of Man*, p. 71.

4.　Human experimentation: conflicts and confluences

INTRODUCTION

Medical research has been central to America's vision of a good society—for, through its use, biological knowledge is enhanced which, in turn, allows for its application to the development of various technologies to cure disease.[1] Indeed, the abiding goal of medicine has always been to relieve pain and suffering; and medical research aims to implement that very goal[2] by not only promoting health, but, whenever possible, preventing disease in the first instance from ever occurring.[3]

The size and complexity of contemporary medical research is seen dramatically when it is realized that approximately 16 000 to 20 000 investigations are conducted annually. It is estimated, further, that more than 19 million individuals have enrolled in medical experiments—with more than 2 million participating each year.[4] Within each investigation undertaken, a significant risk of pain, disability and death is ever present for the experimental subjects.[5] This proliferation of biomedical research studies has led to significant concerns regarding the adequacy of present federal regulatory schemes to ensure safety for study participants.[6] Recent litigation against institutional review boards (IRBs) and IRB members as defendants may indicate new levels of responsibility will be imposed in order to safeguard those who participate.[7]

Fundamental to the whole research process and the human experimentation component of it is the need to assure that subject-participants have a level of information which, in turn, allows them to understand fully both the level of potential benefits and the risks to them as a consequence of their participation. Informed consent, then, becomes the linchpin necessary to foster a positive level of continuity between the goal of advancing medical technology safely and humanely by and through human experimentation. At the same time, the doctrine of informed consent is forever a source of conflict because of its fluidity and its fact-sensitive character. Inevitably, it is but a relative, as opposed to absolute, term dependent upon numerous variables including, foremost, the nature, reliability and integrity of the source for its completeness.[8]

Because of the breadth of research undertaken in the genetic sciences, unique issues are confronted—starting, as such, with investigations into the human genome, progressing to research into the genetic mechanisms involved with disease, then proceeding to study of the genetic bases of behavioral traits and, ultimately, testing the effectiveness of various genetic therapies in clinical trials—and inconclusiveness of results is guaranteed.[9] Inevitably, this situation, in turn, gives rise to an acceptance of the fact that incomplete or inadequate information is one very significant way to undermine the whole consent process.[10]

Before exploring the principles governing informed consent to research, a foundational examination of those principles governing informed consent to medical care must be undertaken—this, simply because, as these two notions of informed consent have developed, each has been "informed" by the other. Accordingly, the doctrine of informed consent to medical care is the predicate to understanding the applications of informed consent to research.[11]

INFORMED DECISION MAKING

Within the phrase "informed consent" are to be found both manipulative and coercive vectors of force. First, the health care provider

> must gain the "consent" of the patient to prove that she was not physically or psychologically forced into a procedure. We then insist that this consent be "informed," recognizing that if a patient readily agrees to one thing about which she understands little or about which she has a false understanding, we have somehow or other abrogated or sidestepped her autonomous decision-making rights.[12]

The patient–physician relationship is central to the foundations of medical morality. From it emerge normative guidelines that effectuate ideally the end of medicine—namely, to render "a right and good healing action in the interests of a particular patient."[13] Technical competence, then, is shaped by this goal and—indeed—the very act of medical profession is to be considered as unauthentic if it neglects to fulfill the real expectation of technical competence.[14] It is upon both the patient–physician relationship and acknowledged technical competence that a "participatory moral agency" builds that forces a disclosure of all those levels of information necessary for the patient to make a valid choice and genuine consent to surgically invasive or non-invasive medical treatments.[15]

While the desire for obtaining information may be seen as stronger than the one for actually making the determinative health care decision itself, not every patient wants information.[16] Indeed, realizing the fact that most individuals make decisions rather badly forces many to choose to delegate medical decision making to others.[17] It is, quite simply, for those declining to make their own decisions, "psychologically attractive to pass responsibility for hard choices to others."[18] When these delegations occur, it might be wise to consider developing a "full social impact calculus" which in turn considers the complete number of persons affected by them[19]—for example, the immediate family members, close friends and social workers as well as spiritual and health care providers. This calculus could, as well, be taken when the initial decision for sustaining treatments or accessing them is made—with some cases even arising where the sum of the social, economic and medical consequences "on others may outweigh the impact on the person most affected."[20]

Patient information deficits must be remedied by the physician to the fullest extent possible.[21] The information disclosed must be complete, clear and understandable in the patient's own language so that he is thereby allowed to know not only the nature of his illness, its prognosis and the alternative modes of treatment together with their cost and probable effectiveness, but the levels of discomfort and side effects on the ultimate quality of life. This duty of disclosure cannot be excused by the physician on the grounds of patient ignorance or harm. To do so would underscore the inequality in information between patient and doctor and obstruct the goal of a morally valid consent that in turn is the memorialization of the patient's individual moral agency.[22]

The physician must always guard against manipulating patient choice and consent in order simply to accommodate his own personal or social philosophy. Setting valid limits on the degree to which manipulated consent is morally permissible is difficult. Two major situations are recognized commonly where a physician can—and indeed should—exert moral agency for the patient and make the value choice on his behalf. The most common case is where the patient and/or family request him to act accordingly—this, because of their emotional unwillingness or intellectual instability to deal with the immediate situation. In cases of this nature, it would be a failure of the authenticity of his act of profession for the physician not to assume moral agency and decide what course of action should be undertaken. When dealing with surrogate decision makers, it is doubly important for the physician to determine with certainty that the surrogate is being guided by the best interests of the patient.[23]

The second situation where a physician should exert moral agency for the patient is to be found in those emergency cases—in an intensive care or coronary care unit or in an operating or emergency room—where, because of the urgency of the situation, it is impossible for the physician to consult the patient, his immediate family or designated surrogate decision maker. In both of these situations, the physician's Golden Rule should be to act in such a manner as to "accord the patient the same opportunity to express or actualize his own view of what he considers worthwhile" as would be desired by the physician himself.[24] This rule, then, reinforces the mandate not only to bring compassion to the patient's illness, but to exhibit it as a "conscious advertence" in the act of profession and the act of medicine as well.[25]

The other side of the equation in informed decision making is obviously the patient himself. Thus, the ethics of the good patient require that he be truthful in the information that he gives to his physician; avoid manipulating him; follow faithfully mutually agreed-upon recommendations; educate himself so that he may comprehend the facts disclosed to him by the physician; promise not to consult another physician (unless he suspects either dishonesty or malpractice); and realize his partial obligation to participate in those reasonable therapeutic experiments designed to promote a healing of his disease or those directed toward the discovery of possible cures for his own disease for others (non-therapeutic), provided the other rules for professional behavior are followed.[26] What is seen in totality, then, between the patient and the physician is a set of mutually binding obligations that, if met, assure informed decision making in health care services.[27]

The ongoing debate regarding the efficacy and integrity of the doctrine of informed consent and its application has been termed "oblique and inconclusive,"[28] and—indeed—little more than a "fairy tale."[29] The reason for this state of affairs is laid to a structural weakness reflecting, as such, not only a rapacious health care delivery system that is increasingly cost-conscious,[30] complex and sophisticated[31] but—as well—by constraints imposed by the tort law system, human psychology and the physician–patient relationship,[32] all of which are largely intractable.[33] Coupled with these foundational issues is recognition that the level of both empirical research and analysis, together with comparative risk evaluation necessary to resolve the uncertainties, is not being pursued.[34]

Yet, for all of the weaknesses, the doctrine of informed consent serves a significant purpose in contemporary society: namely, as both a construct and often a template for establishing an interdependent relationship, if not therapeutic partnership, between the patient and his physician where truth-telling becomes the crux of the doctrine and a true moral relationship between both parties is recognized.[35] Although the doctrine has yet to become an integral part of the ethos of medicine,[36] it nonetheless provides an important mechanism for maintaining a purposeful discourse between physician and patient and, as such, nurturing and preserving their essential partnership of healing and of trust.[37]

MALPRACTICE AND INFORMED CONSENT (PROFESSIONAL OR LAY STANDARDS)

A claim for malpractice is recognized essentially when a patient, as a direct result of a physician's failure to render that level of care consistent with what would have been given by other practicing physicians in the community in question, is injured.[38] Thus, it is seen that the standard of conduct against which the defending physician's conduct is measured is tied to the conduct that other similar situated professionals in the field would have followed under the same or similar circumstances—with the end result being that the objective standard of reasonableness is thereby excluded totally from the evaluation.[39]

As to the elements of a cause of action for failure to obtain informed consent to either a medical treatment or procedure, there is less uniformity of view.[40] Indeed, under older case law, the duty to obtain an informed consent to a medical intervention was inherent in the essential idea that nonconsensual touching was (and is) a legal battery.[41] Modern case law, however, now takes one of two approaches to the duty to obtain informed consent,[42] yet treats the central issue as one of negligence.[43]

Some states require a professional standard to be followed that in turn imposes a duty upon all physicians to inform their patients of not only the same risks[44] but the alternatives to any proposed medical treatment in the same manner as other physicians would practicing in the community. Accordingly, it was held in a 1981 case in Illinois[45] that applying the reasonable medical practitioner standard of informed consent meant that there must indeed be specific expert medical testimony "of the necessity to inform patients of possible alternatives."[46] Consequently, even though a separate cause of action may well arise in a case of this nature for failure to obtain informed consent apart from one in malpractice as well, with regard to the defending doctor's behavior *vis-à-vis* the specific prosecuting patient, the *same* standard of conduct will apply—namely, adherence to that level of care given in the relevant community by other practitioners.[47]

Other states choose to apply what is regarded as a "lay" or "prudent patient" standard of informed consent—thereby requiring a physician to inform his patient of *all* sources and degrees of information which an average, ordinary reasonable patient should and would require in order to make an informed decision regarding the need to submit to a proposed treatment therapy.[48] Under this standard of informed consent,

> a physician is liable to his or her patient if (1) the physician fails to disclose any risk in the recommended treatment, or the existence of any alternative methods of treatment, that a reasonable person would deem material in deciding whether to undergo the recommended treatment; (2) the patient would have foregone the

recommended treatment had he or she known of the undisclosed information; and (3) as a result of the recommended treatment, the patient actually suffers an injury the risk of which was disclosed, or the patient actually suffers an injury that would not have occurred had the patient opted for one of the undisclosed methods of treatment.[49]

THE FOUNDATIONAL PARADIGM

The 1972 case of *Canterbury v. Spence*[50] presents a modern, comprehensive or focal paradigm of the legal concept of informed consent in application. There, a young boy complaining of back pain submitted to a myelogram which revealed a filling defect. The boy's mother was contacted after the test and an operation was recommended by Dr. William T. Spence—the attending physician—stating that such an operation was "not anymore [serious] than any other operation."[51] The boy submitted to the operation without being informed that the risk carried with it was one of paralysis. Mrs. Canterbury arrived at the hospital *after* the operation and signed a consent form. The boy fell from his bed a day after the operation while, without assistance, he attempted to void. He thereupon became paralyzed and required to undergo surgery yet another time. This time, Mrs. Canterbury signed a consent form *before* the operation. Years later, the youth hobbled about on crutches, "a victim of paralysis of the bowels and urinary incontinence."[52] At trial, Dr. Spence testified that paralysis was to be expected in the neighborhood of 1 percent of the cases of operations of the type performed here. The central issue of the case was the scope and application of the doctrine of informed consent.

Because there is a duty to disclose, the scope of that duty should be known. Any standard set in terms of what is done in the profession will be at odds with the patient's prerogative to decide on prospective therapy. This right of self-decision shapes the boundary of the duty to reveal.[53] In order that the patient's interest in achieving his own determination of treatment is fulfilled, it is the law which must set the standard for adequate disclosure.[54] The test enunciated in *Canterbury*, then, is "[a] risk is thus material when a reasonable person, in what the physician knows or should know to be the patient's position, would be likely to attach significance to the risks or clusters of risk in deciding whether or not to forego the proposed therapy."[55] This includes a discussion of the inherent and potential dangers of the proposed treatment, the alternatives to that treatment and the results likely if the patient remains untreated.

The courts have noted two exceptions to the general rule of disclosure. The first is where the person is unconscious or otherwise incapable of consenting and there is imminent harm which would result from failure to treat which in turn outweighs any harm threatened by the proposed treatment.[56] If possible, consent of relatives should then be obtained. The second exception arises when the disclosure threatens the patient so as to become unfeasible from a medical point of view. The critical inquiry, then, would be whether the physician was guided by sound medical judgment.[57] This privilege does not carry with it the paternalistic notion that the physician may remain silent simply because diligence might prompt the patient to forgo therapy the physician maintains the patient needs.[58]

There is always a danger in this area of consideration that a subjective, hindsight test might be employed. *Canterbury* speaks to this concern and resolves it by requiring a determination of whether a prudent person in the patient's position would have decided to undergo treatment if informed of all perils bearing significance.[59] This affords opportunity for medical testimony regarding the relevance of certain risks as will other testimony by anyone having sufficient knowledge and capacity to testify. The courts thus assume a determinative role in assessing liability.[60]

In the pre-*Canterbury* period, courts sought to enforce a narrower objective test for materiality (reasonable doctor) and a broad-based test for causation (subjective patient). With *Canterbury*, a broad test for materiality is advanced (reasonable patient) and a narrower objective test for causation (what a reasonable patient would have chosen) preferred.[61] Although criticism has been maintained that with *Canterbury* the courts are incorrectly treating informed consent as but another branch of negligent medical practice instead of recognizing the patient's interest in autonomy and his right to make an informed choice about medical care as the key interest protected by the informed consent doctrine, these criticisms are muted when hard questions are raised regarding how to value the protected interest and determine damages for interference thereto.[62]

A discernible trend has been seen to expand the thrust of *Canterbury* by holding physicians to a new level of disclosure.[63] Accordingly, in several jurisdictions, disclosures made by a physician must include his own "comparative lack of experience or lack of certain professional credentials."[64] In other words, the full scope of the physician's professional limitations must be revealed.[65] If this trend becomes a movement, it will serve to not only deepen the foundational purpose of the doctrine of informed consent but, indeed, bring a new vitality to it.

ALTERNATIVE TREATMENT

Utilizing either the professional standard or the lay standard to informed consent, a physician is under a duty not only to inform his patient of appropriate alternative treatments—in addition to the alternative of no treatment at all—but to describe and evaluate the benefits and the risks of those treatments to his at-risk patient.[66] Not every conceivable alternative to every detail of treatment need be provided, however.[67] Setting the limits of a physician's duty to inform of alternative treatments continues to be a struggle for the courts. If a professional standard of informed consent is adhered to, much difficulty in application is alleviated, since a jury panel will seek to decide the issue in conflict by comparing the testimony of competing medical experts.[68] If, however, the lay standard is followed, the jury determination is more complex—this, owing to the fact that an evaluation must be made of what an average, ordinary reasonable patient would both want and need to know under similar circumstances.[69] Obviously, a decision reached according to this standard requires considerable and complex analysis of the credibility of opinions of opposing experts on varying community standards. Of additional complexity is the court's need to comprehensively instruct a jury on the elements of a medically acceptable alternative before the jury can then be allowed to decide whether the average reasonable patient would, indeed, have wanted to know of the alternative.[70]

Medical acceptability is the criterion by which a determination is made to disclose alternative treatment options.[71] The obvious difficulty here is in coming to grips with those components or elements of a particular treatment—especially a new one—that thereby qualify it as acceptable and, furthermore, determining to whom it must be found acceptable.[72]

> In terms of a doctor's duty to disclose, this issue can be broken down into two parts. First, what criteria, objective or subjective, make a particular treatment acceptable? Second, are there additional factors which create (or excuse) the particular physician's duty to know about the treatment?[73]

The etiology of every new medical treatment—whether it be surgery, drug, therapy or an exotic technique—shows an initial evaluation or classification of it as experimental.[74]

In those cases where a "lay" approach to informed consent is followed, it must be recognized straight away that it cannot be extended effectively in order to determine what specific alternative treatments are medically acceptable although it may well indeed be used as a mechanism through which acceptable treatments are revealed.[75] The consequence of applying the "lay" standard or approach in order to enable a jury to determine whether a reasonable patient would have given due consideration to the treatment and accepted it as valid medically would lead to an interesting quandary for the concerned physician, for he would never be in a position to know actually what alternatives he might have to describe. This in turn could drive him to even describe "quack" treatments for fear that some future jury could find that some reasonable patient might have wished to be informed of such treatments.[76]

The wiser approach to develop here would be to acknowledge the standard for medical acceptability as being based solely on the perception of the reasonable practitioner.[77] In this way, the pivotal inquiry would not necessarily be whether a reasonable practitioner would inform a patient of the particular alternative. Rather, the question to be raised would be simply whether an average, ordinary reasonable practitioner would believe the treatment was a viable "medically acceptable" alternative or, stated otherwise, whether it was recognized as an appropriate modality of treatment by a significant number of acknowledged experts in the field.[78] The role of expert testimony then would be to essentially explore both the number and the respectability of those accepting the treatment.[79] Developing and following this standard would allow a physician to "avoid the danger of having to describe the theories of quacks or to explain treatments too new to have a track record, but could still be held to have a duty to keep up with the relevant literature and other sources of information, and to inform of new treatments as they met the criteria of acceptance."[80]

FUTURE TREATMENT

It is often maintained that, if a particular medical treatment were to be classified as futile, an attending physician is under no obligation to provide it to his patient. Indeed, the assertion goes even further: namely, that the physician need not even advise his patient of the existence of such treatment.[81] Judging the futility of any treatment is, arguably and correctly, a medical matter. No input from the patient is thus required. Since a futile treatment offers no benefit to the patient, it can be argued that a physician does not have an obligation to render treatment of a non-beneficent nature and neither—for that matter—does a patient have a right to demand it.[82]

Without knowledge of medical or surgical alternatives and without having access to information regarding the pros and cons of each, a patient obviously has few if any tools with which to form a therapeutic alliance with his physician or even enter into a meaningful treatment dialogue with him.[83] While the doctor avoids conflicts with his patient, this veil of silence often robs the patient of his right of self-determination—all under the guise of medical paternalism.[84] Whenever a treatment is labeled futile, it is exempted from the requirement of discussion. Thus, the label itself "becomes a very powerful tool for relieving physicians of the requirement to talk with their patient. The label marks off a realm in which it is argued that the requirement does not apply."[85]

DEVELOPING NORMATIVE STANDARDS

The Nuremberg Code of 1947 and the Declaration of Helsinki in 1964 served as catalysts for shaping a new international concern for safeguarding the treatment of human subjects in scientific experimentations. The Code evolved from the aftermath of the military trials of Nazi leaders and prominent physicians who performed non-therapeutic and nonconsenual experiments on wartime prisoners. It is, essentially, a set of ten principles requiring the protection of the rights and welfare of all research subjects. It mandates human experimentations embody, within their protocols for use, fundamental concepts which embrace the adherence to voluntary, informed consent and the avoidance of unnecessary risk, validate the feasibility of the study undertaken and balance participant risk with the perceived benefits of the study itself.[86] To a significant extent, the principles of the Code provide the foundation for all modern codes of research ethics.[87]

The World Medical Association produced the Declaration of Helsinki to provide guidance to physicians in medical research involving human subjects. Criticized as vague and indeterminate and thus making it less informative as an ethical guide, the Declaration nonetheless shares some of the central normative values of the Nuremberg Code—namely, informed consent guarantees, risk/benefit assessability and the minimization of participant-subject risk.[88]

These two documents spurred United States congressional interest in the 1970s into human testing. After hearings, the then Department of Health, Education, and Welfare (DHEW) issued a series of regulations on the subject and established a National Commission for the Protection of Human Subjects of Biomedical Research to oversee further study of this area of concern.[89] In 1979, the Commission published a report which has come to be known as the Belmont Report. This report, unlike others purporting to provide ethical guidance, declines to make specific recommendations for administrative action; rather it is a statement of policy.[90]

The Belmont Report recognizes three basic ethical principles as the foundation upon which all rule making for human testing should rest: respect for persons, beneficence and justice.[91] As applied in a specific research context, the principle dictating respect for personhood requires that research subjects give informed consent to participate in a study and that consent is not adequate unless the subject is given sufficient information upon which to evaluate whether or not to participate, fully comprehends the import of the decision to participate, and makes the decision free from coercion and undue influence.[92] The principle of beneficence requires all research be justified on the basis of a favorable risk/benefit assessment, which entails an assessment of alternatives to human testing and how adequately the subjects can be protected from risk of harm.[93] Finally, the principle of justice requires fairness in the selection of subjects and that vulnerable populations, such as children and the mentally disabled, should not participate in studies unless there are adequate protections in place.[94]

The simplistic approach and all-encompassing nature of the report have subjected it to charges that its focus is too diffuse because the guidance provided by the principles is not only at times unclear and indeterminate, but is even outdated because it fails to address the necessity of initial and continued oversight together with ever present conflicts of interest.[95] Even with this concern, the Report was essential to the development of the Common Rule.

The central concern in the Belmont Report of 1979 was ensuring fairness in risk distribution. New concerns were raised in 1994 and focused on the need to assure a reasonable distribution of benefits to wide vulnerable populations.[96] Subsequent protections were given—specifically—to children.[97] As well, legislative schemes were adopted requiring the manufacturers of certain new drugs and biological products which seek to protect children by adequate pediatric labeling[98] also be provided with economic incentives[99] for conducting these pediatric studies in the first instance.[100]

THE COMMON RULE

In the 1980s, in an attempt to standardize the regulation of human testing across the federal agencies, the White House established a committee which developed a set of regulations that came to be known as the "Common Rule." The standardization process took nearly ten years to complete, but in 1991 the Common Rule was published in the *Federal Register* and adopted simultaneously by approximately 15 different federal agencies.[101]

The Common Rule applies to all federally funded or sponsored research and any research conducted by an agency that chooses to abide by it.[102] The Rule requires each agency to develop and promise to follow a "statement of principles" designed to protect the rights and welfare of human research subjects either at or sponsored by the institution in question—regardless of whether the particular research in question is subject to federal regulations. Accordingly, in exchange for receiving federal funds for all or part of its research, an institution agrees to be in compliance with the ethical requirements of the Belmont Report or similar set of ethical principles acceptable to the Office of Human Research Protections for all of its research—whether, as noted, it is funded privately or federally.[103]

The key requirements of the Common Rule are that all proposals involving human research be reviewed independently by a separate body, designated as an institutional review board or IRB, in order to establish its ethical acceptability and to determine, as well, the requirements necessary for valid informed consents to be obtained by all research participants. The responsibilities of the board include: classifying the risks involved as either minimal or greater than minimal in order to determine the extent of review it will give to the proposal in the first instance; ensuring that risks to subject-participants are not only minimized but are reasonable in relation to anticipated benefits derived from the experimentation; ensuring subject selection is equitable and that when informed consent is obtained that it be documented; and lastly, obtaining assurances that the monitoring of participants is adequate to guarantee privacy protections and that, if vulnerable groups such as children are used, additional levels of protection be extended to them.[104]

Since the inception of the Common Rule, medical research has become not only more complex, but decentralized as well. No longer typically is a single researcher at a single institution involved. Rather, not only are research protocols conducted at numerous locations simultaneously, involving large numbers of researchers and subject-participants, but clinical trials are often done at global multi-centers. Simply put, the IRBs are ill equipped to handle multi-site trials. Excessive workloads and inadequate resources plague the whole review process.[105]

INSTITUTIONAL REVIEW BOARDS

Considered to be the backbone of the federal regulatory system, IRBs perform important functions, for they have the responsibility for not only reviewing, approving and monitoring research involving human subjects, but—when appropriate—terminating such research.[106] Since research involving human subjects is not regulated directly by the federal administrative system, the delegated authority and responsibility of the IRBs for this supervision are significant.

Before the approval and commencement of any human subject research, an IRB must determine that the selection of subjects is equitable and that risks will be minimized; that the risks associated with the research are reasonable relative to the expected benefits; that material facts will be disclosed which, in turn, will enable the subjects to give an informed, voluntary consent; that risk/benefit analysis will be ongoing during the research itself; that the privacy of the subjects will be maintained; and that "vulnerable" subject safeguards will be in place.[107]

Under current regulations, each IRB is mandated to have at least five members "with varying backgrounds to promote complete and adequate review of research activities commonly conducted by the institution."[108] As well, racial and ethnic diversity must be considered in the membership composition.[109] For research involving vulnerable populations, representation on the IRBs should include someone with knowledge about those populations.[110] Membership on the board must also include one person with a primary area of concern in science and one who has not.[111] There must also be one member of the particular board who has no affiliation with the institution.[112] Predictably, because of the flexibility of these guidelines, not only the composition but the internal workings of the IRBs vary considerably from institution to institution.[113]

The Office of Human Research Protections (OHRP) of the Department of Health and Human Services is the small agency responsible for overseeing the work of IRBs and assuring the implementation, specifically, of the Common Rule.[114] The Food and Drug Administration itself also acts in partnership with this office in sharing responsibility for overall IRB oversight.[115]

Although not viewed as a direct counterpart to OHRP, the Food and Drug Administration has created an office called the Office for Good Clinical Practice whose responsibility is to ensure that all human research studies regulated by it are conducted according to good clinical practice. This standard of review is seen as a total research process standard designed to assure not only that the data and results from investigations are credible and accurate, but that those participating in research studies have their rights, safety and well-being protected as well.[116]

AN INEFFECTIVE SYSTEM

In assessing the effectiveness of the nationwide system for protecting the rights and welfare of human research subjects, a pervasive sense of crisis is found.[117] Government studies show conclusively that IRBs review far too many protocols within an accelerated time frame, lack adequate resources to conduct careful reviews, and do not have sufficient levels of expertise within their membership ranks in order to complete their evaluations.[118] The whole review process has been found to be too tilted in favor of the researcher and the institutional interests over those of human subject protection.[119] No doubt because of the sheer volume and expanded mission or scope of the IRB workloads which have increased with the pace of scientific advancement, IRBs have changed their philosophical character from their peer review body predecessors of the 1950s and 1960s under the U.S. Department of Health, Education, and Welfare.[120]

The early peer review bodies—coming as they did in the wake of the conclusion of World War II and the development of the Nuremberg Code and the Declaration of Helsinki—sought to set new normative standards for conducting human experimentation. These new standards not only emphasized the individual rights of research subjects, but—as well—the significance of informed consent together with the need for disclosing to all subjects a balanced view of the benefits and the risks associated with the particular experimentation.[121] The principal investigators, then, were charged with the sole responsibility for conducting the trials.[122]

Because of concerns over the objectivity of the investigators and the manner by which "normal healthy research subjects" were oftentimes referred, without benefit of a regular treating physician to advise or counsel them on the propriety of the experiment, efforts were first undertaken by the federal government—through the National Institutes of Health in 1953—to safeguard the vulnerable. This goal was to be achieved by a set of federal guidelines which established a procedure for peer review of all studies by the professional colleagues of the medical (scientific) investigators.[123]

Over the years , "mission creep" set in which, in turn, had the effect of expanding the limited scope of the review to include accounting for ethical concerns and certifying compliance with relevant federal laws. Committee reviews were extended, as well, to all institutions receiving any research funds from the federal government.[124] Because vaguely written policies proliferated without specific mandates for the reviewing bodies to follow, "even as their potential functions expanded, the reviewing bodies were left without clearly defined standards to implement, leading to potential accountability and performance evaluation problems."[125]

THE ETHICS OF HUMAN SUBJECT RESEARCH (CONSENT IN HUMAN EXPERIMENTATION)

There are two forms of human experimentation: therapeutic and non-therapeutic. When experimentation is undertaken on a person solely in order to obtain information which will be useful to others—thus in no way treating illnesses the experimental subject may have—it is considered as non-therapeutic in nature. Contrariwise, when a therapy is used with the primary view of ascertaining the best form of treatment for a particular patient, it is therapeutic.[126]

In non-therapeutic research, the doctor confronts the subject of his research as a scientist. The doctor in such cases has no patient—only a *subject* of investigation. It can be argued, therefore, that the usual privileges accorded to a doctor's work and those doctrines to which the liabilities of doctors are judged should *not* be applicable here.[127] This is the situation simply because those privileges and liability doctrines "proceed from the premise that the doctor must be given considerable latitude as he works in the personal interests of his *patient*.[128]

A strict duty of disclosure is nevertheless imposed by the law wherever one is exposed to a risk or asked to abridge certain fundamental rights by someone who possesses expertise.[129] Without too much difficulty, an argument could be made that, under the developing doctrines of strict liability, liability should be imposed without fault—irrespective of disclosures for harm occasioned during the course of non-therapeutic experimentation.[130]

All hypothetical or experimental remedies being conducted by various researchers do not come within the ambit of a physician's obligation to advise a patient of alternative therapies.[131] Yet, where the particular therapy which is being used is itself of an experimental nature, this fact and the very existence of either alternatives or professional doubts become material facts. Consequently, as such, these facts should be disclosed.[132]

The most vexatious type of medical experimentation to the lawyer, ethicist and physician is commonly referred to as mixed therapeutic and non-therapeutic experimentation. Although a patient may be undergoing valid treatment for a particular illness, the treatment may not have been chosen with the sole view of curing that particular patient of his own illness. Treatment, then, is administered as part of an experiment or as a research program either to test new procedures or—as the case may be—to compare the efficacy of previously established procedures. Patients are assigned to various treatment categories not as a consequence of a careful consideration of the patient's needs but in measure to the specific needs of the research design.[133]

Randomized clinical trial (RCT) is a procedure under which patients are placed in categories of treatment by a randomizing device; hence, experimenter bias can be eliminated statistically.[134] There is a mixed reaction in cases of this nature to the need for disclosure to the patient that his treatment will not be determined by an independent judgment made by the physician but, rather, by a random procedure.[135] There are no decided cases which resolve the conundrum of whether it is necessary to disclose to the patient that an experiment is being conducted and the very nature of the experiment itself.[136]

The legal status of mixed therapeutic and non-therapeutic experimentation is, in part, unquestioned and predictable. The general obligation to obtain patient consent to a therapy which will be used on the patient adheres. With this also goes the need by the physician to make full disclosure of expected benefits and possible hazards.[137]

The inherent tension between clinical research and the medical interests of subjects can never be eliminated. For the law to require researchers to follow the same therapeutic obligations as treating physicians will result in a cultural prohibition of clinical trials altogether.[138] Managing the tension to the maximum extent possible then becomes the direct challenge to the whole enterprise of medical experimentation.

FETAL CONSENT

The issue of fetal consent is fraught with more ambiguities and uncertainties than the general area of consent.[139] Here, a determination must be made whether consent should be required before fetal research may be commenced and, if so, from whom such consent must be obtained. It has been maintained that, since meaningful life outside the uterus may be sustained by a viable fetus, it should therefore be regarded—for purpose of consent—as a premature infant.[140] Although consistent with *Roe v. Wade* in the determination that the fetus is not to be regarded as a person, it is proper "to procure consent for experimentation on a viable fetus in a manner similar to that in which it is procured in the case of any other premature infant."[141]

Usually, with cases of premature infants, the parents exercise their judgment with the best interest of the fetus in mind. When—because of danger to her health—a mother seeks an abortion of a viable fetus it would be both humane and equitable for the court to appoint a guardian for the fetus to the abortion. Such an appointment would hopefully allow procedures to be structured to save the life of the fetus and prevent experimentation which would endanger its health.[142]

The extent of the state's interest in a nonviable fetus is unclear. If, for purposes of consent, a nonviable aborted fetus is treated as but a collection of the mother's tissue, then experimentation on a nonviable fetus *in utero* would likely be considered an experimentation on the mother.[143] Although medically sound, this is regarded by some as both morally and psychologically repugnant. Nonviable fetuses should, it is argued, be distinguished from other human tissue. Yet the mother herself should have no particular concern with experimentations performed on disorganized fetal tissue and, hence, need not be requested to give her consent to such acts.[144] An exception must, of course, be allowed and maternal consent sought when a woman desiring an abortion is, for moral reasons, opposed to experimentation on an intact or disorganized aborted fetus.[145]

So it is seen, then, in the final analysis, that the wishes and directives of parents make abortion moral. It is also the parents who determine whether the particular fetal research is moral—so long as the experimenters respect the range of the parental decision or, as in many cases in modern society, a single woman's decision.[146] Particularly in matters of fetal research and generally as to human experimentation, the contemporary medical practitioner not only needs to do that which is considered professionally right but, in addition, must be viewed by others as doing that which is correct.[147]

PROXY CONSENT

The doctrine of informed consent is applied through the mechanism of proxy or substituted consent given by a parent or guardian to only two groups: children and those adjudicated individually as legally incompetent.[148] For all other categories—such as, for example, mental competence (without a declaration of legal incompetence)—the subject or individual patient's capacity to consent is controlling in and of itself. For minors, their personal capacity to understand is in cases largely irrelevant. The adolescent is considered incompetent and subject, technically, to the same protections as neonates. In all cases, the emancipated minor may consent to his own medical treatment and no permission from a parent is required.[149] So long as there is no discernible risk of harm, there is considerable professional support that parents should be allowed to consent to non-therapeutic research on a child. The law remains unsettled and without a definite point of direction here, however. Obviously, where research is undertaken for the unquestioned benefit of a particular child, there can be no question that the parent may consent to standard therapy—and arguably should, particularly in a life-threatening situation where no standard therapy exists.[150]

Generally, there are three approaches to proxy decision making: one allows a competent patient's original health care advance directive or decision—made in a state of competence—to be respected during a subsequent incompetency; second, if there is a friend or relative sufficiently close to the incompetent to surmise what course of action would have been taken if the distressed individual were in fact competent to make a decision, the court may allow a "substituted judgment" to be made by the friend or surrogate; third, if there are no bases for determining what an incompetent patient would have wished regarding a particular health care treatment matter, a final or dispositive decision will be made by the patient's family or court appointed guardian in the "best interests" of the patient.[151]

The inherent weakness of utilizing the best interests standard is that there is no societal consensus regarding how the inherent value of life is affected by—for example—higher brain functions, severe physical deterioration or unrelievable pain. It has been suggested that using a best interest approach for making health care decisions imposes highly contested societal values very paternistically on the individual in extremis.[152] Yet, for an incompetent or incapacitated person, subjective proofs of intent or disposition are not otherwise available and the best interests standard is perhaps the more appropriate mechanism by which a cost–benefit analysis or balancing test can be posited—opposed, as such, to utilizing a substituted judgment test.

INFORMED REFUSAL

The phrase "informed consent" is an unfortunate construct because it implies that medical decision-making processes *should* eventuate in a *consent* to treatment.[153] As a consequence of this, all too often physicians engage in *post hoc* reasoning or rationalizing that concludes, since a patient is going to undergo treatment in any event, it is unnecessary to inform him of this preordained outcome.[154] Recommended treatment is not always consented to by patients, however. In fact, patients should be able to secure a guarantee that a decision not to consent—or to give an informed refusal—should be as informed as in a decision to consent.[155]

The first such case of informed refusal was decided in 1980 by the California Supreme Court.[156] Here, an action in medical malpractice was maintained by two children whose mother, it was asserted, was denied material information by her long-standing personal physician that, if given, might have reasonably led to her making a life-saving decision regarding a diagnostic test. Told by her physician that she should take a Pap test for cervical cancer, the decedent mother declined on at least two occasions, citing cost as her reason for not proceeding. She died subsequently from cervical cancer—that would have in all likelihood been discovered if the Pap test had been administered. The physician did inform his patient, the children's mother, of the possible negative consequences of declining the test: namely, there was a significant statistical probability she might have cancer that would remain undetected until it became nontreatable.

Here, the court concluded, properly, the physician breached his duty to disclose material information which he knew or should have known would be regarded as significant by a reasonable person in his particular patient's position—given the patient's unique concerns or lack of familiarity with medical procedures—when deciding to either accept or reject a recommended medical procedure.[157] The court mandated this duty of disclosure to include not merely diagnostic tests, but treatment as well or those procedures allegedly designed to detect illness that could in turn lead to death or serious complications if not treated timely.[158] When recommending a risk-free procedure, however, a physician may safely forgo discussion beyond that necessary to conform to competent medical practice as well as to obtain the patient's consent.[159]

This case provides a clear framework for decision making, a legal framework as well as an ethical one, that—adopted by the legal and medical professions—would require physicians to inform their patients of the options and consequences of a refusal of recommended interventions. If it were adopted widely by the courts, what would be seen would be virtually a mandated *process* (rather than a mere reaffirmation of a duty to warn) whereby physicians would treat their patients as collaborators in a mutual medical decision-making process.[160] Sadly, with but a few case exceptions,[161] and one notable one before the New Jersey Supreme Court in 1987, where it was held that a right of informed refusal was but a logical correlative to the right to make an informed consent,[162] the doctrine of informed refusal is still in its infancy. It should be the wave of the future, however.

RELIGIOUSLY MOTIVATED REFUSALS (PARENTAL ACTIONS)

In 1944, the United States Supreme Court held that the state could protect children from burdensome and exploitative labor even though such was condoned and, indeed, encouraged by religious motives on the part of parents or guardians.[163] Having decreed this, it was relatively easy for the Court to decide summarily that a parent could not withhold a blood transfusion from its child who required it in order to sustain life even though religious beliefs of the parents precluded such an act being administered.[164] Many lower courts have followed this posture and found little, if any, difficulty in concluding that parents cannot prevent their children—on whatever religious grounds—from receiving treatment without which the health of their children would be called into serious question.[165] In fact, some courts have even gone so far as to hold that parents who have minor children dependent upon them "are not even free to risk their own lives in a religious case"—not out of paternalistic concern for the parents, but out of concern for the welfare of the children.[166]

ADULT DECISIONS

The recognition of the right to refuse medical treatment based upon a religious belief or otherwise has nonetheless been upheld—and with growing regularity.[167] In 1976, the New York Supreme Court held that members of the Jehovah's Witnesses religious sect could, indeed, refuse to submit to blood transfusions.[168] An application by a hospital was made for an order authorizing a qualified physician from a hospital to perform a blood transfusion on a 23-year-old married patient—fully competent, not pregnant and with no children. A dilation and curettage had been performed on her on 3 December 1976. Some 24 hours after the operation she developed a uterine hemorrhage which resulted in lowering her hemoglobin count dramatically. She, in turn, developed anemia. The patient and her husband, as members of the Jehovah's Witness sect, had both signed documents which refused to permit blood transfusions. The application sought permission to perform—given a favorable opinion for such action by a qualified physician— a blood transfusion or undertake any other surgery considered necessary to save the life or protect the patient's health.

The Court denied the application, stating in part:

> As a general rule, every human being of adult years and sound mind has a right to determine what shall be done with his own body and cannot be subjected to medical treatment without his consent . . . specially where there is no compelling state interest which justifies overriding an adult patient's decision not to receive blood transfusions because of religious beliefs, such transfusions should not be ordered. . . . Such an order would constitute a violation of the First Amendment's freedom of exercise clause. . . . However, judicial power to order compulsory medical treatment over an adult patient's objection exists in some situations. . . . It may be the duty of the court to assume the responsibility of guardianship for a patient who is *non compos mentis* to the extent of authorizing treatment necessary to save his life even though the medical treatment authorized may be contrary to the patient's religious belief. . . . Here the patient is fully competent, is not pregnant and has no children. Her refusal must be upheld, even if the procedure is necessary to save her life.[169]

VULNERABLE POPULATIONS (COERCIVE ENVIRONMENTS AND FORCED MEDICATIONS)

While the Common Law has been used as a major source of protection for the rights of individuals with mental illness[170] and their right to refuse unwanted treatments,[171] over the years more and more the extent to which the *parens patriae* power of the state is exerted or imposed upon its incompetent citizens has been balanced with the rights of autonomy of the incompetent themselves.[172] The threat of malpractice liability being sought and imposed for unwanted medication upon mentally ill individuals provides only limited additional protection to individual autonomy, the reason for this being that, before malpractice injury will be recognized, the aggrieved patient must show normally how he suffered a physical harm as a consequence of the forced medical therapy. Damages for the common associated injuries of insult to dignity and emotional pain and suffering in cases of this nature are simply not available except in the most egregious cases.[173]

In modern medical facilities, antipsychotic medications are used widely because they are so effective in reducing and eliminating psychotic symptoms but can also be used to alter a mental patient's moods, thought processes and behavior. There are, to be sure, side effects to these medications such as blurred vision, skin rashes, decreased blood pressure, constipation and movement disorders. Generally, these inconveniences are within the realm of reasonable toleration.[174]

In 1982, the United States Supreme Court ruled in *Mills v. Rogers*[175] and its companion case, *Youngberg v. Romeo*,[176] that a state, exercising its substantive and procedural statutory powers, is the best forum for protection of the rights of involuntarily committed mental patients, who in turn would be entitled to federal due process protection. In these two cases, the High Court declined to weigh the rights of involuntarily committed mental patients to refuse unwanted medications against state interests and thereby deferred to professional judgments made regarding the use of restraint. There is no question that the right to refuse psychotropic drugs has decreased greatly—particularly since the Youngberg case.

THE PRISON SETTING

In February 1990, the United States Supreme Court issued a 6-to-3 decision granting broad powers to prison officials to force mentally ill inmates to take antipsychotic drugs against their will on the grounds that a permissible constitutional accommodation must be sought "between an inmate's liberty interest in avoiding the forced administration of antipsychotic drugs and the State's interest in providing appropriate medical treatment to reduce the danger that an inmate suffering from a serious mental disorder represents to himself or others."[177]

Walter Harper was convicted of robbery in 1976 and was incarcerated from 1976 to 1980 at the Washington State Penitentiary, where—for most of the time—he was placed in the prison's mental health unit and consented to the administration of antipsychotic drugs for his manic-depressive and later diagnosed schizophrenic condition. He was paroled subsequently in 1980 on the express condition that he participate in psychiatric treatment. His parole was revoked in December 1981, after he assaulted two nurses at Seattle hospital, and upon his return to prison he was sent to a special offender center where convicted felons with serious mental disorders are treated. After again giving his voluntary consent to the administration of antipsychotic medications, Mr. Harper subsequently, in November 1982, refused to continue taking his prescribed medications. Prison officials upheld the decision of Mr. Harper's physician to force him to take the medication under a prison regulation that made provision for the involuntary treatment of inmates suffering from mental disorders and who were "gravely disordered" or posed a "likelihood of serious harm" to themselves, others or their property.

The controlling regulation grants the inmates the right to a hearing before a committee composed of the associate superintendent, together with a psychologist and psychiatrist having no involvement with the pertinent case. The prisoner has a complete right, under the regulation, to present evidence and—consistent with the adversarial nature of the hearing—cross-examine witnesses at the hearing itself, as well as the additional right to appeal the committee's determination to the superintendent of the prison. In 1985, after his appeals were rejected, Harper initiated suit before the Washington Supreme Court asserting the involuntary medication violated his constitutional rights; and the state court agreed with him.[178] The prison policy was supported by the American Psychiatric Association, who asserted that the antipsychotic drugs were very effective treatment, and challenged by the American Psychological Association on the grounds that drugs of this nature have grave effects and have been used indiscriminately by the psychiatric profession.[179]

Writing for the majority of the United Supreme Court, Justice Anthony M. Kennedy found adequate procedural safeguards to Mr. Harper's liberty or due process interests in the fact that the procedures set forth for reviewing the involuntary medication order were adequate as well as being substantively sound and rational.[180] Especially noteworthy for Justice Kennedy was the fact that the questioned procedures provided for review by officials not directly involved in the inmate's treatment.

Interestingly, the day before the Harper decision was issued, the Court ruled 5-to-4 in *Zinermon v. Burch* that Darrell Burch had stated a sufficient cause of action under the federal Civil Rights Law[181] to establish a violation of his procedural due process rights because of his admission to the Florida State Hospital in Chattahoochee as a "voluntary" mental patient when he was unable, because of his incompetence, to give an informed consent to the admission.[182] What the Court concerned itself with here was meeting the constitutional requirement that some kind of notice and some kind of hearing must be allowed *before* the state deprives a citizen of liberty or property.

Pre-deprivation procedural safeguards were necessarily absent here in the admissions process—perhaps the most predictable point in the whole process where a deprivation might well occur. In *Harper*, the necessary safeguards were in place and operating throughout all phases of the deliberative process. With both cases—*Harper* and *Zinermon*—what is seen is the Court's determination to balance individual constitutional guarantees within an admittedly restricted penal environment against the needs of the institutional environment to exercise its expertise and undertake its social mandate to give care and treatment to mentally handicapped inmates who might not always be mindful of the degree to which they need such treatment and thus restricted in their ability to give a full and voluntary consent to it.

PRISON RESEARCH

Any research institution seeking federal funds for experimentation with prisoners must comply with two sets of regulations to ensure safety and informed consent are met. The Department of Health and Human Services regulations require a minimum of one institutional review board to review the research protocol[183]—and additionally perform a risk–benefit analysis of the proposed research, allowing as such only certain types of experiments to be performed on the subjects.[184] An integral part of the protocol directs the basic content of the necessary informed consent required of each prisoner subject. The eight required elements of a valid consent are: a description of any reasonably foreseeable risks or discomforts; the benefits to the subject expected from the research; a disclosure of appropriate alternative procedures or courses of treatment; a statement of the extent to which confidentiality of the records identifying the subject will be maintained; an explanation in cases where there is more than minimal risk as to the extent medical treatments will be available if injury occurs; a statement of whether any compensation will be paid for the participation under these risks; an explanation of with whom contact can be made should questions arise concerning the research; and, finally, a statement that participation in the experiment is not only voluntary but involves no penalty of any nature or loss of benefits for refusal to participate or discontinue participation once commenced.[185]

The Food and Drug Administration has also structured similar regulations regarding prisoner safety and consent to experimentation protocols.[186] Interestingly, these regulations are presently unenforceable and thus serve only as a guideline for institutional action. The practical effect, however, of both sets of regulations is—because of their stringency—to bar biomedical research in prisons[187] and—since 1987—eliminate all experimental testing of federal prisoners as well.[188]

PHARMACEUTICAL STRATEGIES

In 2000, it was estimated that between $88 billion and $95 billion was invested in biomedical research—with the federal government spending approximately $25 billion, private foundations approximately $8 billion to $10 billion and private industry anywhere from $55 billion to $60 billion.[189] For the year 2003, the pharmaceutical industry claimed an investment in biomedical research of $33.2 billion.[190] These figures have been challenged as being vastly inflated and not a true level of expenditure since they are exceeded vastly by industry-wide profits.[191] These profits, however, may take anywhere from 10 to 15 years to be realized since this is the time frame for a drug to move from a laboratory to FDA approval[192]—with the cost of development ranging from $300 million to $600 million.[193]

Medical research and product development have become predominantly reliant on clinical trials conducted on vulnerable populations.[194] Indeed, medical research and development have, historically, been funded by the public sector—though, as seen in more recent years, the majority of funding has been provided by the private sector, such as pharmaceutical manufacturers.[195] The implementation of stricter regulations for drug approval by the federal Food and Drug Administration (FDA), along with increased product liability, has created financial obstacles for pharmaceutical companies funding the development of new drug treatments.[196] In addition to financial concerns, the restrictions present in the United States, such as the requirement of double-blind studies, have created the need to explore less regulated arenas in order to perform necessary trials and research before the drug can be mass-marketed.[197] Medical trials on vulnerable populations, with important safeguards, can provide the necessary data to allow mass-marketing of helpful and potentially life-saving drugs.[198]

Owing to the higher availability of test subjects and the greater ease in conducting clinical trials, developing Third World countries are becoming increasingly desirable for conducting clinical trials. Clinical trials are performed with less obstacles owing to the prevalence of extreme poverty, widespread diseases and the lack of adequate health care. Because of the lack of available health care, experimental trials are often viewed as medical care and perceived to be better than no care at all. The trials are often for drugs which target conditions that afflict many people within the Third World country. Furthermore, there is less risk of litigation, more compliance within the community for participation in the trials and less strictly enforced ethical review board oversight of clinical trials.[199]

When experimentation occurs in developing countries, there is the concern of balancing the benefits of the experimental trials, on the *macro* level as well as to the immediate test subject, along with ensuring informed consent and proper minimization of risk to the test subjects.[200] The ability to strike a balance between personal autonomy and the greater good of society is largely debated when the testing and research are performed on vulnerable populations that may not be deemed capable of giving informed consent.[201] Additionally, the issue of drug accessibility for these developing countries has to be balanced against the manufacturer's patent protections.[202]

When proper protections are provided for vulnerable populations and measures have been made to create easier accessibility for the test subjects to the newly developed drugs, the experiment benefits people on both a *macro* and a *micro* level.[203] The test subjects benefit from the development of the needed drugs and the experiments can provide the data needed for the application approval to mass-market the drug.[204] Creating greater access to the newly developed drug has to be instituted carefully so as not to infringe on the manufacturer's patent rights.[205] Patent rights help compose the bulk of the financial incentive to develop and research new products.[206] Within the context of the immense financial and regulatory restrictions the private sector faces, the use of experimental testing on vulnerable populations can be viewed as a necessity to advance science and allow for the development of life-saving drugs and treatment.[207]

A novel, yet practical, approach to medical research was taken in 2004 by the federal government when the Medicare program began to allow payments for new expensive treatments as well as diagnostic treatments conditioned on agreement by pharmaceutical companies and other groups to underwrite studies designed to determine whether these new procedures work on those who receive them. Patients availing themselves of this practice must agree to participate in supervised follow-up studies if they are to receive medical aid. It is thought that, if the treatments are ineffective, then they are not necessary medically and—thus—*not* within Medicare coverage. This policy is transforming, fundamentally, the scope of coverage and reimbursement by making a bold effort to make medical research and medical care more cost-effective.[208]

When dealing with vulnerable populations, special safeguards need to be in place in order to ensure the truly "informed" nature of informed consent.[209] The use of foreign experimental trials often deals with populations deemed vulnerable because of poverty, lack of medical resources, and less stringent regulation.[210] The lagging regulation and more relaxed ethical oversight of foreign drug trials make the foreign market appealing to many large pharmaceutical companies.[211] Some foreign countries even encourage experimental drug testing on their shores and work with the drug companies in arranging the trials.[212] A benefit of the trials is that they can bring medical drugs and science to places where people could not otherwise afford them. The concern is that test subjects are not being duly informed about the experimental nature of the trials and the potential risks involved.[213] There is also the issue as to whether the informed consent has been improperly induced by the threat of medical care being withheld.[214] This facet of the problem arises in many poorer nations where test subjects would probably not have access to medical care without participating in the trials.[215] The debate is whether this experimental care is better than no care at all for the test subjects or an unfair abuse of their potential vulnerability.[216]

In many foreign countries, then, experimental drug trials are seen as a resource of hope for impoverished test subjects who are suffering from various conditions.[217] Though some of these trials do offer positive benefits, there are potential risks to participate in such experiments, and test subjects need to be adequately informed as to what to expect when consenting to such trials. The need to explain to the subjects the nature of the experiment along with the right to withdraw at any time is important. This is especially of concern in countries where medical care is a luxury few can afford and experimental trials are often offered with other medical services that come as an alluring packaged deal. With properly informed and consenting test subjects, experimental drug trials can bring medical services to people who otherwise might never receive medical care.[218] Furthermore, these trials are often needed for the drug to be approved for marketing to the public.[219]

COMMONALITIES OF CONCERN

There are, essentially, two over-arching concerns when dealing with all vulnerable populations—pregnant women, human fetuses and neonates, children, prisoners, the terminally ill, elderly individuals and the incompetent: namely, a recognition and maintenance of the intrinsic human dignity of the research subjects by the surrogate decision maker[220] and the need to factor this value into decisions which, while considering the feelings of the incompetents in arriving at what is in their best interest, also balance this need with an appreciation of wider family interests in allowing or, as the case may be, disallowing participation in medical experimentations.[221] While the best-interests standard gets applied normally when a court or governmental agency is the responsible decision maker, when a parent or other surrogate is the primary decision maker, "so long as it is a plausible medical option and is not so antithetical to the patient's interests that it constitutes neglect or abuse," the medical course chosen does not have to be the *best* choice.[222]

In those cases where a never-competent patient's interests are in issue, the interests of third parties are always a "looming omnipresence" which inevitably intrude into surrogate decision making—especially when such an incompetent's interests are either diffuse and murky "or in equipoise and the potential impact on third parties is extreme."[223]

Without continuing investigation and research into the aging process and the disease etiologies associated with it, there could be no real expectation of scientific advancement in the field of geriatrics.[224] The ongoing challenge is how to accommodate a reasonable and human balance of the private rights of personal dignity and privacy for elderly research participants with the *macro* goals of research which stress the wide potential future benefits to the elderly as a societal group.[225]

NEW DIRECTIONS—NEW DILEMMAS (THE CALIFORNIA PRECEDENT)

In a case of great national moment, a first instance in the American judicial system, the Supreme Court of California decided in 1990 that an individual must first give an informed consent to a surgical intervention that would in turn yield tissues that would be transformed subsequently, through genetic engineering, into commercial products.[226]

John Moore sought treatment at the Medical Center of the University of California, Los Angeles (UCLA) for leukemia. As a necessary part of the treatment for this disease, it was determined by Dr. David W. Golde, Moore's physician, that his spleen had to be removed through an intervention called a splenectomy. After the routine surgery in 1976, and upon consultation with Shirley G. Quan, a medical researcher and employee at UCLA, it was determined that Mr. Moore's spleen cells were quite unique in their composition and of considerable commercial value—especially since the properties could be altered through genetic engineering and used as a basis for cancer therapy and a potential treatment for AIDS and in speeding the recovery of bone marrow transplant patients.

Thereupon, Golde and Quan used genetic engineering to develop a cell line in August 1979, with an estimated commercial value of $3 billion and sold it to the Genetics Institute. On 30 January 1981, the Regents of the University of California proceeded to apply for a patent on the cell line, listing Golde and Quan as the inventors. It was alleged by Moore that Golde and Quan had indeed "formed the intent" to undertake their project before the actual surgery was performed on him. He was not informed by Golde or Quan of their research plans and neither was his permission for their actions sought.[227]

In 1984, Mr. Moore maintained a law suit wherein he argued not only that he should have been informed of the fact that some portion of his tissues had been used to create a commercial product, but also that he had a right to receive some portion of the money paid for the products that were based on his cells. The trial court determined he had no cause of action.[228] The California Court of Appeals held that Mr. Moore's spleen was his own personal property and he therefore had "an unrestricted right to . . . use, enjoyment and disposition" of it; and furthermore that the defendant Medical Center had converted his tissue inasmuch as Moore could not be held to have abandoned the organ.[229]

When the case was heard by the Supreme Court of California, however, it reversed in part the decision of the Appeals Court by holding that, while Moore should have been informed of the actions that were taken with the cell line from his spleen in order to allow him the opportunity of entering into negotiations for payment thereof, once the cells left his diseased spleen and his body he ceased to own them.[230] The Court cited strong precedent holding that, in soliciting a patient's consent to a medical intervention, a physician is under a fiduciary duty to disclose all pertinent information (for example, personal interests unrelated to the patient's health whether research or economic in nature that might affect the doctor's professional judgment) to enable the patient to make an informed decision regarding the proposed intervention.[231] A failure to disclose freely this information could, as it was found here, result in an action for breach of fiduciary duty or lack of informed consent.

> A physician who treats a patient in whom he also has a research interest has potentially conflicting loyalties. This is because medical treatment decisions are made on the basis of proportionality weighing the benefits to the patients against the risks to the patient.[232]

The Court continued by acknowledging that competing interest of such disclosures, stating:

> To require disclosure of research and economic interests may corrupt the patient's own judgment by distracting him from the requirements of his health. But California law does not grant physicians unlimited discretion to decide what to disclose. Instead, it is the prerogative of the patient, not the physician, to determine for himself the direction in which he believes his interest lie.[233]

CONCLUSIONS

Perhaps it is a correct assessment that no meaningful collaboration or hoped-for therapeutic alliance can be achieved between doctor and patient until physicians themselves treat patients as adults and not children; learn that there is a real distinction between their ideas of best treatment and those which are seen as *best* by their patients; learn how to acknowledge their own ignorance in diagnosis, as well as treatment and prognosis; and thereby explain to their patients the inherent uncertainties in both the art and the science of medicine which, in turn, give rise to valid differences of belief based upon clinical experience.[234] Sadly, all too often, the quest for diagnosis and cure, or what has been termed "the Riddle," seduces many physicians and forces them to ignore the realities of pathological processes.[235] The sense of a patient's participation in the direction of his medical treatment, hopefully with a greater sense of trust and confidence, will allow the "ethics of intimacy rather than the ethics of strangers [to] take root and flourish."[236]

Seen as a normative value rather than an empirical constant,[237] perhaps—in reality—the doctrine of informed consent has consequences that are of less importance than the values it seeks to promote.[238] To be sure, the doctrine needs to be contextualized both procedurally and substantively in legal doctrine.[239] Setting new dialogic responsibilities for physicians, however, may not succeed in strengthening the process.[240] Indeed, in the present cost-conscious health care environment, such an imposition may only serve to further complicate its simple and direct mandate: namely, to provide a knowledgeable atmosphere for a therapeutic partnership or moral agency between physician and patient to occur.[241] As well, without the doctrine of informed consent, then, there would be little opportunity to create an atmosphere in which—in health care delivery systems—both interdependence and interrelationship are acknowledged—professionally and legally—as practical normative values.[242]

Without IRB decisions being open to greater public scrutiny, which in turn would have the effect of promoting a culture or process of "mutual learning through the development of something akin to a common law of research ethics,"[243] conflicts in purpose and administration of the review will continue. At the core of the conflicts is the dual role of physicians as patient health care advocates and research investigators—a role which gives rise, as seen, to a moral dilemma inherent within every research encounter.[244] Not only do these conflicts have to be lessened and managed—if not resolved—but new ways need to be found which serve to insulate the IRB members and staffs from various institutional pressures.

In order to strengthen the force of the Common Rule, and thereby begin to address the patterns of weakness in the IRB system, the Rule—itself—

needs to be made more inclusive and bring in, particularly, the FDA.[245] Such a step would serve to establish a much needed level of consistency among all regulatory bodies—this, because a considerable number of research applications which discourage openness in the researcher–subject relationship are in study proposals within the jurisdiction of the FDA itself.[246] The establishment by Congress of a national board to review and to interpret all the regulations on federal research would also be a positive step toward reformation.[247]

In an attempt to lower research costs, pharmaceutical companies are employing contract research organizations, rather than university medical centers, thereby making use of private physician-investigators who—in many cases—are regarded as but "marketers" or "salespeople."[248] Delivery of a high number of patients for clinical trials is the primary goal. Any disclosures to the patients that their physicians have been offered a wide array of "incentives" in order to bring them into the trial and assure that they complete it are regarded as irrelevant information that need not be disclosed.[249] Such actions show, sadly, a slide from medical professionalism into venture capitalism and similarly cast physicians in the role of little more than "self-interested marketers."[250]

Although the doctrine of informed consent will always remain a relative term, then, "with the degree of completeness resting on so many variables including of course the nature and reliability of the source," it should be seen as more than an aspirational goal.[251] Rather, it can—and indeed should—serve as a useful construct for embedding the doctrine as an integral part of the ethos of medicine[252]—an ethos tied to a recognition of patient trust and partnership with the physician as the cornerstone of the healing enterprise[253] which must always seek to provide "a right and good healing action in the interests of a particular patient."[254]

In the final analysis, however, it remains for the profession of medicine—not the legal profession—to formulate, and then effect, a truly contemporary doctrine of informed consent—one, to be sure, that is responsive to the "proddings of the law," but, more importantly, one that is cognizant of the very complex and nuanced interactions between patients and their physicians.[255]

Informed consent—in order to be considered effective within the context of medical research—is best viewed conceptually as an evolving process instead of a static "one-time disclosure event and/or signing of a consent form."[256] Rather, it is a process whereby a structured conversation between the research participant and a member of the research team occurs before the actual consent is executed.[257] While the ideal for informed consent in medical research has always been securing an informed and voluntary consent from capable research subjects, directed and fortified by an interactive set of federal regulations together with related multinational documents, this norm has been challenged and redirected, even "trampled," by the medical research power structure.[258] Indeed, the very idea of a sharing of information with and education of the research participant

> has fallen prey to the idea of informed consent as a document to be signed by the participant, constructed by the research sponsor or site to comply with the regulations. In medical treatment and clinical research, these documents typically include lengthy descriptions of diagnoses, prognoses, treatment alternatives, risks and benefits of the alternative treatments, the risk of non treatment, the right to refuse, the commitment to provide care even in the face of refusal, and the injury compensation policy of the sponsoring institution.[259]

The research participant, instead of being educated to a level of understanding, is simply overwhelmed and even coerced by documents of this format.[260] If the model for informed consent can somehow be redirected toward an engagement or ongoing conversation which, in turn, allows for reinforcement of information disclosed previously and the introduction of new information when advisable, as well as an acknowledged respect for autonomous participant decision making, the written consent then becomes merely tangential to the process of informed consent.[261]

NOTES

1. D. Callahan (2003), *What Price Better Health? Hazards of the Research Imperative*, p. 256. See generally A. Cribb (2005), *Health and the Good Society*.
2. Callahan, *What Price Better Health?*, p. 51.
3. Ibid., p. 253. See G.P. Smith, II (2005), "Human rights and bioethics: formulating a universal right to health, health care or health protections," *Vanderbilt Journal of Transnational Law*, **38**, p. 1205.
4. R. Saver (2006), "Medical research and intangible harm," *University of Cincinnati Law Review*, **74**, pp. 941, 944.
5. Ibid., p. 946.
6. S. Hoffman and J. Berg (2005), "The suitability of IRB liability," *Pittsburgh Law Review*, **67**, p. 365. See J. Merz, D. Magnus, D. Choo and A. Caplan (2002), "Protecting subjects' interests in genetic research," *American Journal of Human Genetics*, **70**, p. 965.
7. See for example Grimes v. Kennedy Krieger Institute, Inc., 782 A.2d 807 (Md. 2001); Robertson v. McGee, No. 01-CV-60-C. 2002 U.S. Dist. Lexis 4072 (N.D. Okla., 28 Jan. 2002). See also Saver, "Medical research," pp. 961–81 (surveying various legal theories for recovery including claims for emotional distress, common law fraud, break of fiduciary duty, negligent design and implementation of the research protocol and intangible harm for dignitary injury). See generally D. Resnik (2004), "Liability for institutional review boards: from regulation to litigation," *Journal of Legal Medicine*, **25**, p. 131.
8. J. Tobias (2001), "Contemporary challenges in clinical research," Ch. 32 in L. Doyal and J.S. Tobias (eds), *Informed Consent in Medical Research*.
9. M. Chadwick (2001), "Informed consent and genetic research," in Doyal and Tobias, *Informed Consent*, pp. 203–208.

10. Ibid.
11. See C.H. Coleman, J.A. Menikoff, J.A. Goldner and N.N. Dubler (eds) (2005), *The Ethics and Regulation of Research with Human Subjects*, Ch. 7.
12. W. Gaylin and B. Jennings (1996), *The Perversion of Autonomy*, p. 55. See generally E. Pellegrino (1994), "Patient–physician autonomy: conflicting rights and obligations in the physician–patient relationship," *Journal of Contemporary Health Law and Policy*, **10**, p. 47; E. Pellegrino (1995), "The human person, the physician and the physician's ethics," *Linacre Quarterly*, **62**, p. 74.
13. E. Pellegrino (1979), "Toward a reconstruction of medical morality: the primacy of the act of profession and the fact of illness," *Journal of Medicine and Philosophy*, **4**, pp. 32, 47.
14. Ibid., p. 49.
15. Ibid. See generally D.P. Sulmasy (1997), *The Healer's Choice: A Spirituality for Physicians and Other Health Care Professionals*.
16. C.E. Schneider (1998), *The Practice of Autonomy, Patients, Doctors and Medical Decisions*, p. 110. See T. McConnell (2000), *Inalienable Rights: The Limits of Consent in Medicine and the Law*, pp. 77, 78 (maintaining the position that physicians are *not* obligated to comply with such patient wishes because such a waiver is valid only if it is both voluntary and informed).
17. Schneider, *Practice of Autonomy*, p. 99. See also M.A. Hall, M.A. Bobinski and D. Orientlicher (2003), *Health Care Law and Ethics*, 6th edn., p. 208.
18. Schneider *Practice of Autonomy*, p. 175.
19. R. Dworkin (1993), "Medical law and ethics in the post-autonomy age," *Indiana Law Journal*, **68**, pp. 727, 737.
20. Ibid. See generally R. Dworkin (1996), *Limits: The Role of the Law in Bioethical Decision Making*, Ch. 7.
21. Pellegrino, "Toward a reconstruction," p. 50. But see R.M. Veatch (1997), *Medical Ethics*, 2nd edn., pp. 203, 204, discussing the therapeutic privilege to withhold information.
22. Pellegrino, "Toward a reconstruction," p. 50.
23. Ibid., p. 51.
24. Ibid.
25. Ibid.
26. Ibid., pp. 52, 54–5. See L. Doyal (2001), "The moral importance of informed consent in medical research: concluding reflections," in Doyal and Tobias, *Informed Consent*, p. 313 (arguing that certain types of medical research—epidemiological, for example—should be exempted from the informed consent requirement and, further, that in certain other cases where the research subject is incompetent, as with children having the consent of their parents, or in trauma cases where there is an acceptable risk–benefit ratio the exemption should apply as well). See D. Callahan (2003), *What Price Better Health*? (arguing that the therapeutic/non-therapeutic distinction gives rise to "therapeutic misconception" which arises when "a clinician researcher carries out research of no expected or intended benefit to a patient but which the patient believes will offer a chance of benefit"). See also G. Calabresi (1964), "Reflections on medical experimentations in humans," *Daedalus*, **98**, pp. 387, 401 (advocating some form of consent should always be required which seeks to strike a balance between present and future lives). See generally J. Montgomery (2001), "Informed consent in clinical research with children," in Doyal and Tobias, *Informed Consent*, p. 173.
27. See D.W. Brock (1991), "The ideal of shared decision making between physicians and patients" *Kennedy Institute of Ethics Journal*, **1**, p. 28.
28. P. Schuck (1994), "Rethinking informed consent," *Yale Law Journal*, **103**, pp. 900, 904–905.
29. J. Katz (1994), "Informed consent—must it remain a fairy tale?," *Journal of Contemporary Health Law and Policy*, **10**, p. 69.
30. See generally T.S. Jost (2003), *Disentitlement? The Threats Facing our Public Healthcare Programs and Rights-Based Response*.

31. See generally Schneider, *Practice of Autonomy*.
32. See both Pellegrino, references at note 12; Schneider, *Practice of Autonomy*, p. 205.
33. Schuck, "Rethinking informed consent."
34. Ibid.
35. Gaylin and Jennings, *Perversion of Autonomy*, p. 55.
36. Katz, "Informed consent," p. 91.
37. See generally both Pellegrino references at note 12; E. Pellegrino (1986), "Rationing health care: the ethics of medical gatekeeping," *Journal of Contemporary Health Law and Policy*, **2**, p. 23. See also M. Hall (2002), "Law, medicine and trust," *Stanford Law Review*, **55**, pp. 463, 478 (maintaining that, without a minimal level of trust, patients will neither disclose information to the physician nor follow medical recommendations made to them).
38. D. Dietz (1981), Annotation, "Physicians, surgeons and other healers," *American Jurisprudence*, 2d, **61**, §202. See also Hall et al., *Health Care Law and Ethics*, pp. 201, 203, 210.
39. Annotation, Dietz, "Physicians, surgeons," §202.
40. Ibid. See A. Twerski and N. Cohen (1988), "Informed decision making and the law of torts: the myth of justiciable causation," *Illinois Law Forum*, p. 607.
41. Annotation, Dietz, " Physicians, surgeons," §197. See F.V. Harper, F. James and O.S. Gray (1986), *The Law of Torts*, **1**, §3.2, p. 268.
42. H. Prillaman (1990), "A physician's duty to inform of newly developed therapy," *Journal of Contemporary Health Law and Policy*, **6**, pp. 43, 44.
43. Dworkin, "Medical law and ethics," p. 729. Since the decision in Salgo v. Leland Stanford Jr. University Board of Trustees in 1957, the courts have been emphasizing and developing a negligence of "failure to use due care" theory of liability. 154 Cal. App. 560, 578, 317 P. 2d 170, 181 (1957). This theory in turn places the physician in default for failing to educate adequately his patient to the *collateral* risks involved in the treatment. Indeed, *Salgo* provided the groundwork for the explosion of cases dealing with informed consent. There, as now, the physician is confronted with a perplexing problem: namely, how to balance the patient's need to know the risks and alternatives to treatment in order to give an informed consent with the individual patient's mental and emotional condition to accept and understand the medical information. See also D. Thomasma and E. Pellegrino (1998), "Medicine, science, self-interest: value sets in conflict in human experimentation," in D.N. Weisstub (ed.), *Research on Human Subjects: Ethics, Law and Social Policy*, pp. xvii, *passim*. Under *Salgo*, then, a physician owes a duty to his patient to disclose facts necessary to the formation of an intelligent consent and, further, subjects himself to liability for violation of that duty.
44. Hondroulis v. Schuhmacher, 553 So. 2d 398 (La. 1989).
45. See for example Ziegert v. South Chicago Community Hospital, 99 Ill. App. 3d 83, 425 N.E. 2d 450 (1981).
46. Prillaman, "Physician's duty," p. 45.
47. Ibid.
48. Ibid. See generally D.D. Federman, K.E. Hanna and L. Lyman Rodriguez (eds.) (2003), *Responsible Research: A Systems Approach to Protecting Research Patients*; K. Getz and D. Borfitz (2002), *Informed Consent: A Guide to the Risks and Benefits of Volunteering for Clinical Trials*; 45 C.F.R. §46.01, Federal Policy for the Protection of Human Subjects; 21 C.F.R. §50.1, Protection of Human Subjects, Federal Regulations for Industry-Sponsored Trials, Appendix B—History of Regulations Affecting Patient Protection in Clinical Research, pp. 178–90.
49. Neal v. Lee, 365 Pa. Super. 464, 478, 530 A.2d 103, 111 (1987). See also Festa v. Greenberg, 354 Pa. Super. 346, 511 A.2d 1371 (1986), *app. denied*, 515 Pa. 580, 527 A.2d 541 (1987).
50. 464 F.2d 772 (D.C. Cir. 1972), *cert. denied*, 409 U.S. 1064 (1972). See also Nathanson v. Kline, 186 Kan. 393, 350 P.2d 1093, clarified, 187 Kan. 186, 354 P.2d 670 (1960); Schloendorff v. Society of New York Hospital, 211 N.Y. 125, 105 N.E. 92 (1914), overruled on other grounds by Bing v. Thunig, 2 N.Y.2d 656, 143 N.E.2d 3, 163 N.Y.S.2d 1 (1957).

51. Canterbury v. Spence, 464 F.2d 772 (D.C. Cir. 1972), p. 777.
52. Ibid., p. 776.
53. Ibid., p. 786.
54. See M. Myers (1967), "Informed consent in medical malpractice," *California Law Review*, **55**, pp. 1396, 1407–10.
55. Canterbury v. Spence, 464 F.2d 722, p. 787.
56. See Dunham v. Wright, 423 F.2d 940, 941-942 (3rd Cir. 1970).
57. See Roberts v. Wood, 206 F. Supp. 579, 583 (S.D. Ala. 1962). See also T. Beauchamp and J. Childress (1979), *Principles of Biomedical Ethics*, Ch. 3. There is a therapeutic privilege to withhold information from a patient if it is either considered potentially harmful or it would cause any counter-therapeutic deterioration—no matter how slight—in the patient's physical, psychological or emotional well-being. Veatch, *Medical Ethics*, pp. 203, 204. The "urgency of the situation" justifies this exception to the doctrine of informed consent. J. Katz (1972), *Experimentation with Human Beings*, pp. 37, 84. See also K. Boozang (2002), "The therapeutic placebo: the case for patient deception," *Florida Law Review*, **54**, p. 687 (arguing, for example, that, if viewed as effective treatment, with a therapeutic effect being achieved by its prescription and use, the representation that placebo use is therapy or medicine is neither untrue nor unethical); G. Annas (1996), "Questing for goals: duplicity betrayal and self-deception in postmodern medical research," *Journal of Contemporary Health Law and Policy*, **12**, pp. 297, 300, 314 (asserting that the very concept of therapeutic research should be eliminated altogether since it confuses the ideology of medicine with the ideology of science).
58. *Myers*, "Informed consent," pp. 1409–10. See generally A. Meisel (1979), "The "exceptions" to the informed consent doctrine: striking a balance between competing values in medical decisionmaking," *Wisconsin Law Review*, p. 413.
59. Canterbury v. Spence, 464 F.2d 722, p. 791.
60. Landmark examples of the way in which courts have treated the application of informed consent include: DiRosse v. Wein, 261 N.Y.S. 2d 623, 24 App. Div. 2d 510 (1965) (failure to tell of the danger of exfoliative dermatitis from "gold" treatment for rheumatoid arthritis, resulting in exfoliative dermatitis, imposed liability on the physician); Corn v. French, 71 N.W. 280 289 P.2d 173 (1955) (physician held liable where mastectomy was performed with a signed consent form, but patient had told physician that she did not want anything removed).
61. Twerski and Cohen, "Informed decision making," p. 615, n. 30.
62. Ibid., p. 620, n. 47.
63. J. Dolgin (2005), "The evolution of the patient: shifts in attitudes about consent, genetic information and commercialization in health care," *Hofstra Law Review*, **34**, p. 137.
64. Ibid., pp. 163, 164.
65. See Howard v. University of Medicine and Dentistry of New Jersey, 800 A.2d 73 (N.J. 2002).
66. Prillaman, "Physician's duty," p. 47.
67. Ibid.
68. Ibid., p. 48.
69. Ibid.
70. Ibid.
71. Ibid., p. 52.
72. Ibid.
73. Ibid.
74. Ibid. In a landmark case in California, in 1990, it was determined that an individual patient must first give an informed consent to a surgical procedure that would in turn yield tissues which would be transformed, subsequently, through genetic engineering, into commercial products of considerable value. John Moore v. The Regents of the University of California et al., 51 Cal. 3d 120, 763 P.2d 749, 271 Cal. Rptr. 146 (1990). See C. Harrison (2002), "Neither Moore nor the market: alternative models for compensating contributors of human tissue," *American Journal of Law and Medicine*, **28**, p. 77.
75. Prillaman, "Physician's duty," p. 57.

76. Ibid.
77. Ibid.
78. Ibid.
79. Ibid., p. 58.
80. Ibid.
81. S. Wolf (1988), "Conflict between doctor and patient," *Law, Medicine and Health Care*, **16**, pp. 197, 198.
82. Ibid.
83. Ibid., p. 198. See generally J.M. Jacob (1988), *Doctors and Rules*.
84. See generally A.E. Buchanan and D.W. Brock(1989), *Deciding for Others: The Ethics of Surrogate Decision Making*.
85. Wolf, "Conflict between doctor and patient," p. 199. See generally G.P. Smith, II (1996), "Utility and the principle of medical futility," *Journal of Contemporary Health Law and Policy*, **12**.
86. G. Annas (1991), "Mengelés Birthmarks: the Nuremberg Code in the United States courts," *Journal of Contemporary Health Law and Policy*, **7**, p. 17.
87. See G. Annas and M.A. Grodin (1992), *The Nazi Doctors and the Nuremberg Code: Human Rights in Human Experimentation*.
88. G. Annas (1992), "The changing landscape of human experimentation: Nuremberg, Helsinki and beyond," *Health Matrix*, 2, p. 119.
89. The National Commission for the Protection of Human Subjects of Biomedical Research, Department of Health, Education, and Welfare (1979), *The Belmont Report: Ethical Principles and Guidelines for the Protection of Human Subjects of Research*, 44 Fed. Reg. 23, 192. The first regulations on human subject protections were issued by the then Department of Health and Human Services in 1974, 39 Fed. Reg. 18914 (30 May 1974) (codified as amended at 45 C.F.R. §46 (2002)).
90. National Commission, *Belmont Report*.
91. Ibid., B1, B2, B3.
92. Ibid., B1.
93. Ibid., B2.
94. Ibid., B3.
95. See generally Coleman et al., *Ethics and Regulation*, Ch. 2.
96. L. Ross and C. Walsh (2003), "Minority children in pediatric research," *American Journal of Law and Medicine*, **29**, p. 319.
97. Protections of Human Subjects, 45 C.F.R. §46 (2001)—with Additional Protections for Children Involved as Subjects in Research, §46, Subpart D.
98. 21 C.F.R. §§201, 312, 314, 601 (1998).
99. Food and Drug Administration Modernization Act of 1997. Pub. L. 105–115, nat. 21, 1997, III Stat. 2296, 214. S.C.A. §335a et seq. (1997).
100. See the Children's Health Act of 2000; the Pediatric Research Initiative Act of 1999.
101. Federal Policy for the Protection of Human Subjects, 56 Fed. Reg. 28001, 28002-32, (18 June 1991) (codified in scattered sections of the CFR). Each agency adopted the Common Rule separately. See for example 45 C.F.R. §46.101-124 (2005) (Dept. HHS). See "Who's watching the watchdogs? Responding to the erosion of research ethics by enforcing promises," *Columbia Law Review*, **103** (2003), p. 893, ns 43, 44, p. 899 (commenting that 16 agencies have adopted the Rule and that the FDA declined to adopt the Common Rule, but passed a similar set of regulations at 21 C.F.R. §50 (2002)).
102. 40 C.F.R. §26.10(a) (2005). See 45 C.F.R. §46 (2002).
103. See Coleman et al., *Ethics and Regulation*, p. 137.
104. See "Who's watching the watchdogs?," pp. 900–903; M. Malinowski (2003), "Choosing the genetic makeup of children: our eugenic past—present and future?," *Connecticut Law Review*, 36, pp. 125, 165–8.
105. "Who's watching the watchdogs?," pp. 904–905.
106. See 45 C.F.R. §§46.101–46.124 (1998). D. Addicott (1999), "Regulating research on the terminally ill: a proposal for heightened safeguards," *Journal of Contemporary Health*

Law and Policy, **15**, pp. 479, 483. See generally J. Robertson (1979), "The law of institutional review boards," *UCLA Law Review*, **26**, p. 484.

107. 45 C.F.R. §46.111 (1998).
108. 45 C.F.R. §46.107(a) (1998).
109. 45 C.F.R. §46.107(a), §46.107(b).
110. 45 C.F.R. §46.107(a).
111. See 45 C.F.R. §46.107(c).
112. 45 C.F.R. §46.107(d).
113. Addicott, "Regulating research," p. 484.
114. Coleman et al., *Ethics and Regulation*, p. 137.
115. Ibid., p. 170.
116. Ibid., p. 161.
117. R. Saver (2004), "Medical research oversight from the corporate governance perspective: comparing institutional review boards and corporate boards," *William and Mary Law Review*, **46**, p. 619, n. 21, p. 626.
118. Ibid., p. 622. See generally Symposium (2007), " Censorship and Institutional Bonds," *Northwestern University Law Review*, **101**, p. 399.
119. Saver, "Medical research oversight from the corporate governance perspective,"
120. Ibid., pp. 633, *passim*.
121. Ibid., p. 634.
122. Ibid.
123. Ibid.
124. Ibid., p. 635.
125. Ibid., p. 635. See also note 101.
126. C. Fried (1974), *Medical Experimentation: Personal Integrity and Social Policy*, p. 25.
127. Ibid., p. 26.
128. Ibid.
129. Ibid., p. 27. See J. Katz and A. Capron (1975), *Catastrophic Diseases: Who Decides What?*, Ch. 8.
130. Fried, *Medical Experimentation*, p. 27.
131. Ibid., p. 29.
132. Ibid.
133. Ibid., p. 30.
134. Ibid., p. 31.
135. Ibid., p. 32.
136. Ibid., p. 31. See note 86, Annas.
137. See note 130.
138. C. Coleman (2005), "Duties to subjects in clinical research," *Vanderbilt Law Review*, **58**, pp. 387, 449.
139. G. Reback (1974), "Fetal experimentation: moral, legal and medical implications," *Stanford Law Review*, **26**, pp. 1191, 1201.
140. Ibid.
141. Ibid., p. 1202.
142. Ibid.
143. Ibid.
144. Ibid.
145. Above 20 to 30 percent of conceptuses, embryos and fetuses "die" by spontaneous or natural abortion. Almost all such abortions are defective—genetically or congenitally. "Nature takes the same way medicine does: it closes the book on failures." J. Fletcher (1974), *The Ethics of Genetic Control*, p. 51.
146. P. Ramsey (1975), *The Ethics of Fetal Research*, p. 39.
147. Ibid., p. xix. See H. Tiefel (1976), "The costs of fetal research: ethical considerations," *New England Journal of Medicine*, **294**, p. 85.
148. L. Tribe (1988), *American Constitutional Law*, 2nd edn., p. 1369. See generally M. Freeman (ed.) (2005), *Children, Medicine and the Law*.

149. J. Lantos and J. Miles (1989), "Autonomy in adolescent medicine: a framework for decisions about life sustaining treatment," *Journal of Adolescent Health Care*, **10**, pp. 460, 461.
150. R. McCormick (1976), "Experimental subjects—who should they be?," *Journal of the American Medical Association*, **235**, p. 2197; M. Shaw (1976), "Dilemmas of informed consent in children," *New England Journal of Medicine*, **289**, p. 885.
151. Tribe, *American Constitutional Law*, pp. 1368–9.
152. Ibid., p. 1369.
153. J. Katz (1984), *The Silent World of Doctor and Patient*, pp. 60–62, J. Katz, "Informed consent," p. 138.
154. A. Meisel (1988), "A dignitary tort as a bridge: the idea of informed consent and the law of informed consent," *Law, Medicine and Health Care*, **16**, pp. 210, 215.
155. Ibid.
156. Truman v. Thomas, 27 Cal. 3d 285, 165 Cal. Rptr. 308, 611 p. 2d 902 (1980).
157. 611 P. 2d, pp. 905, 906.
158. Ibid., p. 910.
159. Ibid., p. 906.
160. Meisel, "Dignitary tort," p. 216.
161. See for example Moore v. Preventive Medicine Medical Group, Inc., 178 Cal. App. 3d 728, 223 Cal. Rptr. 859 (1986).
162. In re Farrell, 108 N.J. 335, 529 A.2d 404, 410 (1987).
163. Prince v. Massachusetts, 321 U.S. 158 (1944).
164. Jehovah's Witness v. King County Hospital, 390 U.S. 598 (1968) (per curiam), aff'd 278 F. Supp. 488 (W.D. Wash. 1967).
165. See Tribe, *American Constitutional Law*, Ch. 14. In Commonwealth v. Twitchell (No. 89-210, Mass. Super. Ct., 23 May 1989), a married Christian Science couple were convicted of manslaughter and given ten years of probation in the death of their two-year-old son. They refused the child any medical treatment and relied solely upon prayer for his treatment. See Note, "Commonwealth v. Twitchell: who owns the child?, *Journal of Contemporary Health Law and Policy*, **7** (1991), p. 413.
166. The leading case here, which relied upon a theory of *parens patriae* to sustain government intervention, was Application of President and Directors of Georgetown College, Inc. 331 F.2d 1000 (D.C. Cir.), rehearing en banc den., 331 F.2d 1010 (D.C. Cir.), cert. den. 337 U.S. 978 (1964). Here, the order of the trial judge authorizing a hospital to administer blood transfusions was upheld. The patient and her husband had refused to consent to the transfusions for religious reasons. Their objections were found insufficient to override the *parens patriae* interest of the sovereign. See also Powell v. Columbia Presbyterian Medical Center, 49 Misc. 2d 215, 267 N.Y.S. 2d 450 (Sup. Ct. 1968).
167. In re Osborne, 294 A.2d 37 (D.C. Ct. App. 1972); Erickson v. Dilgard, 44 Misc. 2d 27, 252 N.Y.S. 2d 705 (Sup. Ct. 1962).
168. Matter of Melideo, 390 N.Y.S. 2d 523 (Sup. Ct. 1976).
169. Ibid., p. 524.
170. Comment, "A common law remedy for medication of the institutionalized mentally ill," *Columbia Law Review*, **82** (1982), p. 1720.
171. Rogers v. Commissioner of the Department of Mental Health, 458 N.E. 2d 308, 314 (Mass. 1983). In June 2003, the Supreme Court decided the case of Sell v. United States, 123 S. Ct. 1274 (2003), and sought to resolve the issue of forcibly medicating a defendant too mentally ill to stand trial. See 123 S. Ct., 2178. Writing for the majority, Justice Stephen G. Breyer found involuntary medication, by use of antipsychotic drugs, to be valid constitutionally if it furthered significantly an "important" government objective. Ibid., 2185. Specifically, the drugs must be "substantially likely" to render the defendant competent and "substantially unlikely" to produce effects that interfere with a defendant's ability to receive a fair trial. Ibid., 2184–5. These rules would apply to trial-competency determinations "whether the offense is a serious crime against the person or a serious crime against property." Ibid. Procedures for balancing the new criteria are

notably absent in the Court's decision. See G.P. Smith, II (2004), "Just say no! The right to refuse psychotropic medication in long-term care facilities," *Annals of Health Care*, **13**, p. 1. See generally Stephan Beyer (1982), "Madness and medicine: the forcible administration of psychotropic drugs," Ch. 7 in George P. Smith, II (ed.), *Ethical, Legal and Social Challenges to a Brave New World*.

172. See for example Rivers v. Katz, 67 N.Y. 2d 485, 495 N.E. 2d 337, 504 N.Y.S. 2d 74 (1986).
173. E. Clayton (1987), "From Rogers to Rivers: the rights of the mentally ill to refuse medication," *American Journal of Law and Medicine*, **13**, pp. 1, 50.
174. See generally M. Swartz (1987), "What constitutes a psychiatric emergency: clinical and legal dimensions," *Bulletin of the American Academy of Psychiatry and the Law*, **15**, p. 57.
175. 457 U.S. 291 (1982).
176. 457 U.S. 307 (1982).
177. Washington et al. v. Walter Harper, 494 U.S. 210 (1990).
178. 110 Wash. 2d 873, 759 P. 2d 358 (1988).
179. R. Marcus (1990), "Mentally ill prisoners can be medicated involuntarily, justices rule 6–3," *Washington Post*, 28 Feb., p. A6.
180. Washington et al. v. Walter Harper.
181. 42 U.S.C. §1983 (1982).
182. Zinermon et al. v. Burch, 494 U.S. 113 (1990). See generally Daniels v. Williams, 474 U.S. 327 (1986); Hudson v. Palmer, 468 U.S. 517 (1984); Parrott v. Taylor, 451 U.S. 527 (1981).
183. See 45 C.F.R. §46.103(b) (1989).
184. 45 C.F.R. §§46.305, 306 (1989).
185. See also 45 C.F.R. §46.116(b)(1)–(8) (1989), for additional elements of informed consent where appropriate.
186. See C.F.R. §§50.23, 50.25, 56.105, 56.107 (1990).
187. D. Maloney (1984), *Protection of Human Research Subjects*, pp. 343, 348. See R. Schwartz (1985), "Informed consent to participating in medical research employing elderly human subjects," *Journal of Contemporary Health Law and Policy*, **1**, p. 115.
188. See "Experimentation on prisoners: the inadequacy of voluntary consent," *New England Journal on Criminal and Civil Confinement*, **15** (1989), pp. 55, 70. See also J. Overholser (1987), "Ethical issues in prison research: a risk/benefit analysis," *Behavioral Sciences and Law*, **5**, p. 187. For a current web-based online resource, prepared by T. Howard Stone, which evaluates the state of clinical research involving prisoners see http://www.louisville.edu/medschool/ibhpl/ Reference_guide.htm.
189. Coleman et al., *Ethics and Regulation*, pp. 63, *passim*.
190. Ibid., pp. 64, 76.
191. Ibid., p. 64.
192. Ibid., p. 76.
193. Ibid., p. 208.
194. A. Golszek (2003), *In the Name of Science*.
195. Ibid. See Symposium, "The Pharmaceutical Industry and Its Relationship with Government, Academia, Physicians and Consumers", *Hofstra Law Review*, **35** (2006), p. 681.
196. Comment, "Regulating experimental AIDS drugs: a comparison of the United States and France," *Loyola of Los Angeles International and Comparative Law Journal*, **13** (1990), p. 393.
197. Ibid.
198. Fitzgerald and A. Wasunna (2005), "Away from exploitation and towards engagement: an ethical compass for medical researchers working in resource poor countries," *Journal of Law, Medicine and Ethics*, **33**, p. 559.
199. Ibid. See M. Santro and T. Gorrie (eds) (2005), *Ethics and the Pharmaceutical Industry* (Ch. 2).
200. Ibid., See note 199.
201. Ibid.

202. Joanne Mariner, "Profit margins, death rates, drug patents and HIV/AIDS," http://news.findlaw.com/mariner/20031124.htm (accessed 1 Feb. 2007).
203. "Access to medical care in under-served markets," http://www.dfidhealthrc.org/publications/atm/DFID_synthesis_aw.pdf (accessed 1 Feb. 2007).
204. Ibid.
205. Mariner, "Profit margins."
206. Ibid.
207. Zulfiger Ahmed Bhutta, "Ethics in international health research: a perspective from the developing world," CMH working paper series, Paper No. WG2:4, http://www.cmhealth.org/docs /wg 2_papers 4.pdf. See also Council for International Organizations of Medical Science (CIOMS) (2002), "International ethical guidelines for biomedical research involving human subjects," www.cioms.ch/guidelines_nov_2002_about.htm (last visited 15 November 2007).
208. G. Kolata (2004), "Medicare covers new treatments with a catch," *New York Times*, 5 Nov., p. A1.
209. Peter Wehrwein, "AIDS vaccine trials debated," http://www.hsph.harvard.edu/review/aids. shtnl (accessed 4 Feb. 2007).
210. Fitzgerald and Wasunna, "Away from exploitation".
211. R. Simons (2005), "Meds and miracles: China's medical system is straining to accommodate a flood of Western firms testing new medicines, *Newsweek*, 11 Apr., p. 85.
212. Ibid.
213. Ibid.
214. Ibid.
215. Ibid.
216. Fitzgerald and Wasunna, "Away from exploitation."
217. Ibid.
218. Ibid.
219. 21 C.F.R. Pact 312 (2007). See L. Karki (2005), "Review of FDA law related to pharamaceuticals: the Hatch–Waxman Act, regulating amendments and implications for drug patent enforcement," *Journal of the Patent and Trademark Office Society*, **87**, pp. 602, 605.
220. N.L. Cantor (2005), *Making Medical Decisions for the Profoundly Mentally Disabled*, Ch. 4. Federal regulatory protection is extended only to the following vulnerable populations: pregnant women, human fetuses and neonates, prisoners and children. 45 C.F.R. §46.111(b), and Part 46, Subparts B, C, D.
221. Cantor, *Making Medical Decisions*.
222. Ibid., p. 148.
223. Ibid. See C. Coleman (2005), "Duties to subjects in clinical research," *Vanderbilt Law Review*, **58**, pp. 387, 425–6.
224. See generally M. Knapp and A. Biegot (1985), *Research with Older Subjects: Geriatrics and the Law*.
225. C. Swift (1988), "Ethical aspects of clinical research in the elderly," *British Journal of Hospital Medicine*, **40**, Nov., p. 370. See also Schwartz, "Informed consent".
226. John Moore v. The Regents of the University of California et al. See Comment, "Spleen for sale: Moore v. Regents of the University of California and the right to sell parts of your body", *Ohio State Law Journal*, **51** (1990), p. 499.
227. See generally M. Danforth (1988), "Cells, sales and royalties: the patient's rights to a portion of the profits," *Yale Law and Policy Review*, **6**, p. 179.
228. John Moore v. The Regents of the University of California, No. C513755 (Super. Ct. L.A. Co. 1988). See Note, "Source Compensation for tissues and cells used in biotechnical research: why a source shouldn't share in the profits," *Notre Dame Law Journal*, **64**, p. 628.
229. 202 Cal. App. 3d 1230, 1245, 249 Cal. Rptr. 494, 504 (Cal. Ct. App.), *cert. granted*, 252 Rptr. 816, 763 P.2d 479 (1988).
230. See generally R. Scott (1981), *The Body as Property*; Note, "Regulating the sale of human organs," *Virginia Law Review*, **71** (1985), p. 1015.

231. Cobbs v. Grant, 8 Cal. 3d 229, 242, 104 Cal. Rptr. 505, 502 P. 2d 1 (1972). But see R. Weiss (2006), "Most cancer patients unconcerned about doctors' ties to drug firms," *Washington Post*, 30 Nov., p. A11; N. Goldstein (2006), "Financial conflicts of interest in biomedical human subject research," *Biolaw*, **9**, p. 26 (urging disclosure of financial interests within the provisions of all informed consent authorization forms).

232. Moore, 763 P.2d at 484. See Note, "Conflict and interest: financial incentives and informed consent in human subject research," *Notre Dame Journal of Law, Ethics and Public Policy*, **17** (2003), p. 181.

233. Moore, 763 P.2d, 484, 485. See Greenberg v. Miami Children's Hospital Research Institute, Inc., 264 F. Supp. 2d 164 (S.D. Fla. 2003) (holding a researcher who is not a tissue source's physician has no duty to disclose the researcher's commercial interests in tissue-based research when obtaining informed consent from tissue sources). See also K. Oberdorfer (2004), "The lessons of Greenberg: informed consent and the protection of tissue sources" research interests," *Georgetown Law Journal*, **93**, p. 365. In Washington University v. Catalona, 490 F. 3d 667 18th (in 2007), Missouri law was affirmed by recognizing that biological materials are considered donated by research participants for research purposes as an *inter vivos* gift, with the University being accepted as donee.

234. Katz, *Silent World of Doctor and Patient*, p. xi.

235. S.B. Nuland (1994), *How We Die*, pp. 249, 265.

236. H. Moody (1988), "From informed consent to negotiated consent," *Gerontologist*, **28**, Supp., pp. 64, 70.

237. Shuck, "Rethinking informed consent," pp. 932, 956.

238. Ibid., pp. 937, 939.

239. Ibid., p. 951.

240. Ibid., p. 935.

241. Pellegrino, "The human person."

242. Gaylin and Jennings, *Perversion of Autonomy*, p. 243.

243. A. Capron (2006), "Experimentation with human beings: light or only shadows?," *Yale Journal of Health Policy, Law, and Ethics*, **6**, p. 431.

244. Ibid., p. 431.

245. Ibid., p. 448. See note 101 regarding the FDA's position on the Common Rule.

246. Capron, "Experimentation with human beings."

247. Ibid., pp. 447.

248. Ibid., p. 448.

249. Ibid., p. 448, 449.

250. Ibid., p. 449.

251. J. Tobias (2001), "Contemporary challenges in clinical research: paying lip service to informed consent, or a genuine shift of gear?," in Doyal and Tobias, *Informed Consent*, pp. 318, 319.

252. Katz, "Informed consent," p. 91 (arguing that, until the doctrine becomes an integral aspect of the ethos of medicine, it is condemned to remain a fairy tale).

253. See generally E. Pellegrino and J. Harvey (2001), "Whom should the patient trust?," *America*, 1 Oct., p. 19.

254. Pellegrino, "Toward a reconstruction," p. 47.

255. Katz, "Informed consent," p. 71. See Merz et al., "Protecting subjects' interests."

256. Coleman et al., *Ethics and Regulation*, p. 356.

257. Ibid.

258. Ibid., p. 345.

259. Ibid.

260. Ibid. See H. Gert (2002), "Avoiding surprises: a model for informing patients," *Hastings Center Report*, **32**, p. 23 (discussing information overload under present informed consent practices).

261. Callahan, *What Price Better Health?*, p. 346.

5. Organ and tissue transplantation: a case study in distributive justice

INTRODUCTION

Produced in 1906, George Bernard Shaw's play *The Doctor's Dilemma* is as fresh a statement of the current medical issue of resource allocation as it was when first produced. The dilemma for Shaw's principal character, Dr. Sir Colenso Ridgeon, was to decide—between two patients—which was so deserving as to receive a new wonder drug, designed to cure consumption, that he had developed.

One patient was an artist and "dishonest scoundrel" but married to a most attractive woman named Jennifer. The other patient was an honest doctor working with the poor. Initially, Ridgeon decided to give the treatment to the physician, but changed his mind, subsequently, because he was smitten by Jennifer and hoped to curry "favor" with her by assisting her husband. Reversing himself largely because three of his colleagues determined her husband to be a dishonest sociopath, Ridgeon treated the honest doctor and referred the artist-husband of Jennifer to another colleague—condemning him, as such, to death. He rationalized his choice by concluding, "having patients die is a rational part of being a doctor."[1]

Today, a similar rationalization is made for those Americans who must die prematurely simply because no organ transplants are available to them. On 3 December 2007, there were over 97 800 candidates for organ transplants—with a new name being added every 10 minutes.[2] From January 2007 to 30 November 2007, 21 401 transplants were performed from 10 847 donors.[3]

These statistics are indeed quite sobering for they confirm what has become an accepted fact of life in modern society: namely, because of the critical shortage of organs for transplantation, dying prematurely is accepted as a "rational" course of medical and social action.

CONTEMPORARY ISSUES

It is within organ and tissue transplantation that—today—complex ethical dilemmas arise concerning the allocation and rationing of a resource for which there is a severe shortage which has been growing for over three decades.[4] It has been suggested that the real cause for this shortage in organs is not tied ultimately to any insufficiency in numbers of cadaveric organs, but—rather—is owing to public policies which prohibit the purchase and sale of organs.[5] A significant point of aggravation compounding the shortage is the fact that many recipients require multiple transplants and, further, within the transplant community there is a recorded failure in dealing with the issue of chronic rejection which results in nearly half of donor organs from cadavers wearing out after a decade or more.[6]

Research efforts continue to be used successfully in experimenting with ways to grow, autologously, patients' cells into replacement organs.[7] In less than a decade, possibly even within but a few years, it is speculated that transplants from animals to humans, termed xenotransplantation, will occur.[8] Yet, even with the present limited success of biotechnology and its expected improvements with transplantations over time, the present crisis over organ and tissue shortage will continue to deepen.

What is needed to change course and confront and ease, if not resolve, current ethical concerns with organ and tissue transplantation is a realization that, if economic theory is embraced, the present shortage can be resolved by accepting policies which would allow cadaveric organ markets to form. These markets would, in turn, allow "cadaveric organ prices to rise and fall as necessary to equilibrate supply and demand and thereby to eliminate the shortage."[9] This is, of course, but one solid approach, which—together with other options—will be explored more fully later in this chapter.

Current policies regarding organ and tissue transplantation have evolved more or less as a result of both historical accident and inertia where— when shaped initially—the policies were concerned with essentially living-donor-only kidney transplants. In that formative period, few, if any, shortages existed: there was no backlog of patients awaiting cadaveric donors, and payments to donors were unnecessary. A policy of altruistic (uncompensated) supply made sense. Without careful analysis, this original policy has been carried forward by a state of inertia where, today, it makes no sense—for there are, as seen, chaotic shortages.[10]

AN HISTORICAL OVERVIEW: ORGAN TRANSPLANTS

Today, there are 11 United Network for Organ Sharing (UNOS) regions encompassing 51 organ procurement organizations (OPOs) for organ retrieval and distribution. Together, they serve 868 organ-specific transplant programs at 261 transplant centers.[11]

Organ allocations—not tissue transplants—were the center of focus in 1988 when the Organ Procurement and Transplant Network (OPTN) was established. The newly established regional organ procurement organizations were regarded as being capable of providing services for organs and tissues alike—thus eliminating the need for additional administrative agencies.[12] Even though independent tissue and eye banks continued their efforts in tissue recovery, the OPO began to compete for donors. And it was estimated that by 2001 the OPOs were responsible for facilitating approximately 40 percent of all tissue donations.[13]

Largely unregulated until 1985, individual organ procurement organizations made their own policies and resolved ethical issues themselves within this informed, self-directed system.[14] Under its operation, organ allocations were shaped solely by clinical outcomes. Accordingly, the prototypical allocative model was one that guaranteed organs went only to those patients considered most likely to have a longer graft survival rate. Debates simply never focused on issues such as access, equity or statistical uncertainty.[15]

By the early 1980s, the demand for transplants had begun to grow faster than supply; and more interest groups wished to be heard. The media raised the issue of fairness in the whole allocative system—and especially demanded justifications for wide regional variation.[16] As the absolute number of transplantations increased, managing the allocation centers themselves became more complex.[17] Advancing technological changes in immunosuppression and non-renal transplantation were also vectors of force in setting a new climate for re-evaluation if not change.

In order for non-renal transplants to grow, insurance funding and a regular supply of organs had to be found. And, in order to obtain insurance coverage, there had to be an authoritative approach of the invitations. In efforts to advance the supply of organs, not only were changes in the procurement system needed, but shared rules for allocation had to be shaped and set.[18]

Acting in response to these issues, a federal Task Force in Organ Transplantation was formed in 1985.[19] Supported by the transplant community itself, the Task Force sought to set policies to meet the changes occurring in immunosuppression and non-renal transplantation. Among the notable outcomes of the work of the Task Force was a determination that the cost of immunosuppressive drugs would be paid out of public monies—this, because non-renal transplants were seen as clinical, rather than experimental, procedures. As well, in a conscientious effort to oversee both the procurement and the allocation of organs, a new organization was structured at government expense, the Organ Procurement and Transplantation Network (OPTN), and control of it was given to the proposed community instead of a government bureaucracy.[20]

In order to facilitate the stronger tissue donor recovery rates seen in the early 1990s, new Health and Human Services regulations, termed Conditions of Participation (COP), were promulgated in 1997 which required Medicare and Medicaid-supported hospitals to report to the OPO—or its duly delegated agency—all hospital deaths. Not only do hospitals now have the ability to determine donor suitability, but the responsibility to approach every appropriate family member about organ, eye or tissue donations.[21] While the rates of organ donation have not been increased markedly by these regulations, tissue banks have witnessed impressive increases.[22]

Improprieties within the tissue banking industry in 2000 and 2001, largely over issues of improper uses of informed consent, focused new public concerns and governmental interest in policing the industry itself. As well as new guidelines for OPOs when considering tissue processing partnerships, new laws have been passed in parts of the country requiring OPOs to accept an individual's official, stated interest to donate through use of a driver's license designation or donor registry and disallow any effort by a donor's next of kin to override that original decision.[23] Donor registries allow people to record, formally, their desire to donate and exist already in over half of the states.[24]

FEDERAL OVERSIGHT

The Public Health Service of the U.S. Department of Health and Human Services regulations on allocation of organs[25] do not allow distributions to be based exclusively on a candidate's place of residence.[26] Rather, they mandate "sound medical judgment" which, in turn, seeks the "best use of donated organs" and avoids wasting them or engaging in "futile transplants"—all in order to "achieve equitable allocation of organs."[27] Yet, in practice, patients are still given a priority for any organs procured within the local OPO.[28]

Exceptions to local priority rules are, in fact, allowed for those patients having highly sensitive immune systems in kidney transplantations—this, because of the importance of organ/recipient immunological compatibility for graft survival. Since 1999, for liver transplantations for patients within the "acutely urgent category" (or those likely to die within a week without a transplant), an exception is made, as well, to local priority.[29] Organs are shared across a region when local recipients are not found. And, when none are found within a region, then—within the time constraints of effective organ survival—they are made available nationally.[30]

TISSUES

While records of musculoskeletal transplantation go back to *circa* AD287, it was not until 1878 that successful documented transplants of tissue of this nature were reported.[31] In 1942, in Cuba, a surgical bone bank was established and—in 1949—the establishment of the US Navy Tissue Bank in Bethesda, Maryland, is seen as the beginning of the modern tissue bank.[32] For most of the following 30 years, this Navy Bank not only recovered and preserved tissues to treat injured servicemen in battle and domestically, but also led the science of tissue banking by funding cutting-edge programs.[33]

The central purpose of tissue banks has been, clearly, to provide surgeons and clinicians those tissues which can best meet particular medical needs. Yet, interestingly, in responses to changes in surgical practice, which have led to new and different demands for donated tissue over the last several decades, both organizational and operational foci of tissue banks have been changed as well.[34]

Throughout the 1960s and 1970s, many hospitals maintained their own discard bone banks in order to meet the demands of growing orthopedic surgeries. In the 1980s, hospitals, universities and private entrepreneurs all began to intensify their efforts to develop tissue and blood banks.[35] As older patients began to increase in numbers during the 1980s and 1990s, joint replacement and limb-salvage surgeries attained a new level of prominence which, in turn, required new types of tissue for these successes,[36] while autografts harvested as such from a patient's own bone remain the "gold standard" for orthopedic surgeries when a patient's bone is insufficient, unsuitable or unavailable.[37]

Building upon its record of modest regulation of the tissue industry begun in 1993, and tightened in 1997,[38] the US Food and Drug Administration (FDA) in 2005 finalized three new rules[39] giving itself more authority and oversight over a broader range of human cells and tissues as well as cellular and tissue-based products or HCT/Ps.[40] Additionally, these rules expand the range of communicable disease checked when donations are received and they strengthen procedural and record-keeping requirements for facilities that handle tissues and thereby set a "good tissues practice."[41] These new rules do not cover bone marrow or whole organs for transplant—for they are managed separately by the Health Resources and Services Administration under the Department of Health and Human Services.

In order to strengthen the enforcement of these rules, the FDA is permitted to inspect the manufacture of HCT/Ps—this, in order to ensure the highest level of compliance with safety criteria and to recall or even destroy tissue not meeting the criteria.[42] The good tissue practice (GTP) rule also requires reports from the transplant facilities when adverse reactions occur and product deviations are found. This rule sets a high level of overall quality control from the point of tissue recovery through processing, storage, labeling, packaging and distribution.[43]

Tissue safety does not, in the final analysis, rest solely with the FDA. Rather, cooperative support must also come from the Centers for Disease Control, state health departments and the tissue industry itself—especially through the American Association of Tissue Banks (AATB) and the Eye Bank Association of America. Interestingly, from 80 to 90 percent of all tissue transplanted in the US comes from a bank accredited by the AATB. The Eye Bank Association, similarly, accredits 95 percent of the eye banks in the US charged with receiving these donations. The Joint Commission on Accreditation of Healthcare Organizations (JCAHO) tissue standards[44] will also serve to strengthen an overall strategy in upgrading protections for tissue collection.[45]

THE FLOW OF COMMERCE

The fiftieth anniversary of the first ever successful organ transplant, a kidney transplant from a living donor, was marked on 23 December 2004.[46] Overall, in 2004, more than 27 000 human organs were transplanted—then, a new all-time record driven by a significant 11 percent increase from cadaveric donations.[47] There were 7153 deceased donors in 2004, with an average of three organs being harvested from each.[48] Donations from living donors in 2004 increased only slightly by 2 percent and were mostly in the form of one kidney or a slice of liver or lung (which can regenerate into a full organ).[49] These overall increases in donations, in turn, led to a 6 percent increase in transplantations.[50]

UNOS estimates that, since 1982, at least 416 457 Americans have received new kidneys, hearts, livers, lungs, pancreases and intestines which had the effect of extending their lives and relieving discomfort.[51] The American Association of Tissue Banks reports bone, tendons and cartilage nearly doubled in 2001 to 875 000 from a previous figure in 1996 by 475 000.[52]

Although no commerce in organs for transplantation is allowed, interestingly, not only do transplant surgeons and hospitals continue to make solid profits from "organ-trading business," but even procurement agencies and not-for-profit transplant registries continue to prosper.[53] In fact, mounting personal online internet searches to obtain transplant organs is becoming quite common—from personal websites to making pleas in electronic chat rooms, internet marketing has become a lucrative way to obtain private matchings for organ sale.[54] Because of an inconsistent federal policy on the sale of organs, which allows for sales of human eggs, sperm or blood, some women obtain upwards of $75,000 in the open market for their eggs to be used, as such, for *in vitro* fertilization procedures.[55]

In the transnational community, markets already exist for organs.[56] From India, where living donors sell—openly—kidneys, skin and eyes,[57] to China, where executed prisoners routinely have their organs and skin removed without prior consent of either themselves or their families,[58] organ marketing is commonplace.[59] Thousands of "black market" transplants have occurred as a consequence of the voluntary sale of purchased donor kidneys alone.[60] When it is realized that, in the United Kingdom alone, 8000 people need a transplant of one or more organs, each year, and fewer than 3000 transplantation procedures are undertaken, it is easy to understand the desperate mood of the putative recipients and the lengths taken in order to obtain a life-giving and renewing organ.[61]

The need for a market for human organs can be analysed at three levels of inquiry: economic, libertarian or moralistic. For the economist, embracing a utilitarian ethic results in efforts to find a way to save lives which is both efficient and economical. The libertarian—being autonomistic—places a high burden of proof on those imposing limits on the personal freedoms to use one's body in any way desired. The moralist seeks to defend the vulnerable by asserting sales of organs promote mutilation and thus not only degrade, but exploit.[62]

Whichever analytical frame is chosen, inevitable questions arise regarding restrictions on buying and selling or inalienability. If markets are assessed, then does this require of all opponents thereto that they defend non-sale as the proverbial "exception"? Or is some level of human decency always in place which demands a coordinate response designed to enhance human freedom and welfare which, in turn, refuses to reduce everything to its market price? Or is principled argumentation to be forsaken altogether in favor of *ad hoc* decision making tied to real successes, costs and public pressures?[63]

By focusing on non-utilitarian principles of voluntary consent and of free donation,[64] the American society has refused to embrace simple utilitarian calculations designed to yield the most organs necessary for transplantation.[65] Ideas of commercializing the human body and essentially treating it as personal property[66] are found to be degrading—ethically and spiritually[67]—and, furthermore, seen as direct steps in the coarsening of the very fabric of social sensibilities and attitudes.[68]

THE COMMON LAW APPROACH

The Common Law, as interpreted in 1765 by Blackstone's *Commentaries*, was clear: no one could have property rights in a human corpse.[69] Since the law of theft operated only to protect rights of property and ownership, a corpse was incapable of being stolen. Thus, body snatchers worked regularly to obtain cadavers for anatomists for subsequent use in medical schools.[70] Interestingly, however, property rights could be held in coffins or shrouds and their theft was an imprisonable act.[71]

While stealing a corpse was a mere indecency, and not a felony, consecrated burial grounds were protected and disruption of them carried a penalty as a misdemeanor. This was used as a basis by the Common Law judges to eventually develop new criminal laws prohibiting the disinterment of corpses without authority. At first, these new criminal offenses applied to body snatchers instead of to their customers. Executors and close family members could assert a right of burial, but could still not assert ownership of a corpse. Accordingly, in cases where cadavers were discovered being used in anatomy or surgical dissection classes, there was no clear way of forcing their surrender unless they could be first identified (which, depending upon the extent of the dissection could be difficult) and then made the subject of a legal claim by the family or the descendant's executor. The only right possessed by the family was to have the body retrieved for burial and nothing more.[72]

In 1828, with parliamentary study being undertaken of this area, the courts seized the initiative and expanded the criminal law of body snatchers—as applied to cemeteries—to reach to the points of common delivery: the medical school anatomy classes.[73] And, in 1832, Parliament passed the Anatomy Act which destroyed the trade of body snatchers altogether by essentially introducing a strict licensing procedure upon anatomy schools as well as upon instructors and students themselves who wished to perform anatomical examinations. Government inspection, fines and imprisonment were set in place for violations of the Act.[74]

Today, efforts to stop the illegal trafficking of cadaveric body parts have taken a dramatic turn. In 2006, it was reported by the national press that a business operating in the state of New Jersey—Biomedical Tissue Services—was actually a body harvesting operation and was in collusion with several Brooklyn, New York, funeral home directors—taking, as such, nonconsensual dissections of corpses and obtaining exactions of bone, tendons and skin and then proceeding to ship them to various hospitals in Florida, Nebraska and Texas for transplantation.[75]

The Food and Drug Administration forbids body harvesting firms from cutting up cancerous and diseased corpses without first obtaining family consent from the appropriate parties and a careful screening by these firms of the cadavers based on their age and cause of death. In a business where a dead body is worth tens of thousands of dollars for its parts, safety is a less important issue of concern, it would seem, than advancing the entrepreneurial spirit.[76]

LEGISLATIVE INITIATIVES AND DISAPPOINTMENTS

With the promulgation of the Uniform Anatomical Gift Act (UAGA) in 1968 and its subsequent adoption in some form by the 50 states and the District of Columbia in 1973,[77] a statutory right was conferred upon all individuals allowing them—prior to death—to designate either their complete bodies or organs from them for donated transplants. When a descendant's wishes are not communicated prior to death, the Act provides a right of disposition to the next of kin allowing him the right to decide whether to donate his relative's organs.[78] The UAGA was silent on the subject of sales.[79] Thus, the Common Law position was largely controlling and provided no one was acknowledged as having a definitive property interest or right in a human corpse.[80] This meant no one was granted any form of authority to enter into a sale or to make a gift of a cadaver or any of its parts.[81] It is important to note that this did not mean sales or gifts of this were illegal; rather, only contracts for sales or deeds of gifts were, at law, not enforceable.[82]

For a period of time in the late 1960s and early 1970s—specifically, from 1968 to 1973—some five jurisdictions[83] prohibited the sale of human bodies and organs[84] yet permitted contingent sales to be made by decedents as well as sales by their next of kin.[85] With the promulgation, adoption and universal interpretation of UAGA, all states' statutes permitting such sales—save one, Mississippi[86]—were abolished effectively.[87]

In order to redirect national thinking from a purely voluntary behavior basis *vis-à-vis* organ donation, the UAGA was built upon a principle of "encouraged voluntarism."[88] In order to advance this principle, the whole process of consent was simplified. This was accomplished by the introduction of donor cards designed to allow individuals, carrying them as such, to indicate their consent to donate their organs upon death.[89] Wishing, if possible, to enhance the voluntary principle of altruism implicit in the UAGA for transplantable organs, yet faced with the realities of the failure of UAGA's "encouraged voluntarism" to produce enough donors,[90] the United States Congress acted in 1984 by passing the National Organ Transplant Act (NOTA).[91] In addition to underwriting financial support for the development and maintenance of local nonprofit organ procurement organizations and additionally a National Organ Procurement and Transplantation

Network to assist in matching organ donors with those needing transplants, the Act criminalizes the intestate acquisition, receipt or transfer of all transplant tissue (for example, organs)—with the exception of blood.[92] Since the legislation is directed toward imposing a prohibition on sales affecting interstate commerce, some doubt has been raised about the validity of suppression of intra-state organ sales.[93] Interestingly, NOTA has been strengthened specifically on this issue of intra-state sales by the enactment of specific statutes prohibiting either the purchase or the sale of human organs.[94]

Again, in a national effort to educate the public to the communal values associated with organ transplantation and thereby encourage and, hopefully, enhance opportunities for more organ harvesting, in 1986 a provision was added to the Omnibus Budget Reconciliation Act that was passed into law in 1987, mandating all Medicare and Medicaid affiliated hospitals to establish "written protocols for the identification of potential organ donors."[95] This means that requests be made for organs and tissues whenever a death occurs in a hospital setting. Options to donate organs are to be presented in a discreet and sensitive manner to all families of potential donors enrolled as Medicare or Medicaid patients.[96]

Hospital compliance with required request provisions of the federal law or complementary state-enacted legislative schemes is very uneven: characterized in fact as poor to grudging in some states.[97] It is said that a number of physicians view the law here as an intrusion into their professional autonomy.[98] Still others are angered over perceived inequities in the distribution of the organs and tissues.[99] These attitudes translate into a lukewarm enthusiasm, if that, as the physicians seek to comply with required request provisions[100] by phrasing their requests for permission to harvest the organs of a family member "in a way that encourages a positive response and does not impose distress on the survivors."[101] With no set of rules designed to achieve this delicate balance, how can such a legal requirement as this be met?[102] As one organ transplant coordinator observed, "the consent rate when someone asks who does not want to ask, or does not know how to ask, is zero."[103] Thus, the reality of the situation is that, unless negative incentives can be structured and then imposed on doctors or hospitals, the net enforcement effect of required request laws will be viewed as little more than excessive hortatory language[104]—typical of so many congressional enactments.[105]

NOTA AMBIGUITIES

Although body parts are prohibited from being sold under NOTA, the law recognizes that, if transplantations are in fact to occur, intermediaries must receive compensation—or "reasonable payments"—for recovering tissues from altruistic individuals who donate cadaveric tissue to the tissue banks.[106] These nonprofit organizations then, in turn, transfer the raw tissue to other entities which process it into implantable materials called allografts. A considerable number of these businesses are for profit while others are organized as nonprofits.[107]

It has been argued that "reasonable payments" allow the intermediary to recoup some of its actual expenses and thereby earn "normal" profits.[108] Yet, when intermediaries receive unreasonable or "super-normal" profits, they are enabled to earn more than their expenses and opportunity costs since they are paid actually for the tissue itself.[109]

Interestingly, the government takes no steps under NOTA to enforce it by preventing intermediaries from selling tissue or earning super-normal profits.[110] The true burdens of non-enforcement, then, fall more directly upon donors and recipients. Since tissue markets are imperfect in that some processors have greater access to the raw tissues available than others and use uniquely patented technologies to produce allografts, these and other marketing strategies allow super-normal profits to be earned by advantaged processors.[111]

Presently under NOTA, what is seen is that charitable resources—here, cadaveric tissues—are exploited by their commodification. Put simply, they are but materials that can be bought and sold.[112] NOTA would be strengthened considerably if it were enforced at the level it was intended by preventing intermediaries from earning excessive profits or by authorizing nonprofit tissue banks to sell donated tissues to for-profit processors.[113] This would have the effect of redistributing the tissue's economic value from the latter to the former.[114] The controlling question is, in the final analysis, not whether human tissue should be sold, but rather who should capture its value: nonprofit entities or for-profit businesses?[115]

ADVANCING PUBLIC AWARENESS (THE FEDERAL EFFORT)

The first federal legislation since 1990 amending the NOTA was enacted in 2004 at the Organ Donation and Recovery Improvement Act.[116] Instead of addressing the disagreements over the establishment of fair and equitable policies for organ allocation, the Act focuses solely on strengthening efforts to increase donation rates, including ways to make live donation an easier and more financially appealing option. Essentially, under the Act, the Department of Health and Human Services is the dispersing agent for $15 million to assist those entitled with developing strategies to increase organ donation through public education programs at organ procurement organizations and hospitals and assistance with travel and other expenses for those who make living donations.[117]

STATE ACTION

In July 2006, the National Conference of Commissioners on Uniform State Laws approved and recommended for enactment in all the states the Revised Uniform Anatomical Gift Act of 2006.[118] While designed to encourage the making of anatomical gifts, it is also designed to honor and to respect the autonomy interest of individuals to make or to decline to make an anatomical gift of their body or its parts.[119] The current gift system founded upon altruism is preserved within the revision by requiring a positive affirmation of an intent to make a gift and prohibiting the sale and purchase of organs.[120] The Act does not cover donations by living donors but, instead, is limited in scope to donations from deceased donors as a consequence of gifts made before or after their deaths.[121] By encouraging and establishing standards for donor registers, the Act takes a positive step toward achieving a wider opportunity for popular education on the societal benefits of making anatomical gifts.[122]

The 2006 revision retains the basic policy of both previous anatomical gift Acts in 1968 and 1987 by strengthening the "opt-in" system which honors the free choice of an individual to donate his organs.[123] As well, the revision preserves the right of other individuals (for example, the person acting as the decedent's agent under a power of attorney for health care, the decedent's adult grandchildren and an adult who exhibited special care and concern for the decedent) to make an anatomical gift of a decedent's organs even if the decedent had not made a gift during life.[124]

Section 8 prevents families from making or revoking anatomical gifts in contravention of a donor's wishes. Accordingly, when a donor makes an anatomical gift, there is no reason to seek consent from the donor's family as they have no right to give it legally.

Section 11(b) provides that, in those cases where an anatomical gift of the body parts of a decedent do not pass to a named person, it then passes to a procurement organization for, normally, transplantation or therapy and possibly for research or education. In such cases, the organ procurement organization for the service area in which the donor dies proceeds to allocate the organs locally, regionally or nationally in accordance with those allocation policies established by the OPTN.

No doubt one of the most controversial provisions of the Act allows for donor cards to trump living wills if a conflict should arise.[125] In a case where, for example, a living will or other documents state no ventilator or medical care be administered under the Act, this direction may be disregarded[126] simply because ventilator assistance is required in order to maintain organ viability prior to a transplantation. Accordingly, organ procurement organizations are empowered to keep potential donors on life support during the time an assessment is made of their organs' suitability for transplantation.[127]

LIVING DONORS

Since World War II in the United States, as seen, live donors have been used as sources for organ and tissue transplantation running the gamut from blood and bone marrow to kidneys.[128] Interestingly, while no adult can be forced—without giving a mature, informed consent—to donate any organ, a minor, mental incompetent or prisoner has traditionally not been accorded this option.[129] The case law in the United States—although lacking in any unified rationale—does evidence three bases for testing the validity of the application for a compulsory, nonconsensual donation.[130]

Under one test, the court inquires whether the donation would be in the best interests of the donor—with no relevance being given to any measure of sympathy for the proposed recipient or the family.[131] The second test is one of substituted judgment, where the court speculates how the minor (if mature or competent) would decide relative to the request to donate.[132] But this act of speculation is not flippant or inconsequential; rather, the court seeks to make a decision utilizing the same motive and considerations as would move the incompetent himself. In this regard, then, the test of substituted judgment does not deviate from adherence to the ethical principle of respect for persons. Indeed, it has been suggested that this very principle recognizes that one's welfare—rightly understood—may well depend upon an act that helps others.[133] An absolutist approach to this principle of respect, however, would allow for no compromise of any nature.[134] The third test utilizes a judicial review of whatever parental decision has been made here, with the court accepting in principle the importance of the parental position yet—without accepting any correlative duty to the donor—weighing the entire family dilemma, making an ultimate decision based on achieving a balance of family interests.[135]

Some argue ethically and morally that all intra-familial donations should be prohibited simply because of the coercive forces operating within the family unit which, hypothetically, could justify the need for requiring an incompetent healthy sibling to make a forced organ donation to a competent, unhealthy brother or sister.[136] If such a scenario were in fact to be written, no destructive harm to the particular family unit would occur. Indeed, just the opposite would happen—for the unit would be preserved and strengthened by such a donation. At a minimum, the factors that constitute a valid consent should be defined with as much precision as possible—recognizing as such that there is an enormous factual difference between a family member authorizing tissue removal from the body of a deceased relative and, on the other hand, from a living relative.[137]

There are other ethical and social considerations raised regarding organ transplants from living donors. One simply finds such actions to be inherently immoral.[138] This idea builds on the belief in the general ethical principle that life should always be preserved and, further, that one should never seek his own destruction nor endanger in any way his own life except as an expression of love for another.[139] Commerce in human body parts—it is maintained—also acts to restrict free will and individual autonomy. This, in turn, is buttressed by the view that, in harming oneself by deliberately undergoing tissue removal, one may well indeed harm society by later becoming sick or enfeebled and thus a burden upon it.[140] Abstract moral principles and concerns of this nature must give way to the realities and the needs of contemporary society[141] and not stand as roadblocks to the maintenance of actual life.

The counter-utilitarian argument to these moral-ethical concerns states that any absolute prohibition on the use of organs from minors or incompetents is unjustified—this,[142] in light of the simple fact that donations from such classes restore health and renew life to others and are done without jeopardizing or ending the lives of the donors. Where the risks from the donation to the minor, incompetent or incarcerated prisoner are minimal, or even if substantial yet much less than the harm that would occur to an individual donee deprived of the benefits of sustained living, organ transplantations should be undertaken.[143]

AN EXTRA-FAMILIAL ALTERNATIVE

Paired exchanges or swaps—already done in a small number of US hospitals—are also an option.[144] Essentially, this program involves patients who need transplants and have either friends or relatives willing to donate a kidney, for example, but whose kidneys are not a match. In order to allow reciprocal transplants nationwide, each donor–patient pair is matched with another pair.[145] It is estimated that this type of "priced kidney exchange," if implemented fully, would in turn allow transplants for approximately half of the 6000 US patients who have willing donors with incompatible kidneys because of different blood types or other reasons. With over 60 000

US patients awaiting kidney transplants—and with 3718 on the waiting list who died in 2004 alone because of the failure to find suitable organs—an activated program of this type would be a true lifesaver.[146]

For any such exchange program of this nature to become successful at a national level, since UNOS is not contracted to allocate organs for living donors, governmental involvement would most likely be required. As well, two other concerns would then have to be addressed: namely, the development of safeguards which assure no coercion be extended on donors to participate and—furthermore—the development and implementation of a support network designed to deal with the emotional difficulties most normally associated with donors not being related closely to one another or who live a distance from the actual recipients.[147]

OTHER SCHEMES AND PROCEDURES

Presently in the United States, the prevailing system for organ donation is one of presumed non-consent; or, in other words, a person is presumed "unwilling" to be an organ donor at death unless he or his family gives permission.[148] As noted, this scheme is failing to generate sufficient resources for transplantation; thus new approaches must be evaluated and then implemented.

One such approach was first proposed in 1968 and simply calls for compulsory *post mortem* examinations to determine the salvageability of cadaveric organs.[149] As such, autopsies would be done routinely and not, as now, used only when requested by the decedent's family or as a consequence of violent death under suspicious circumstances. The *post mortem* examinations and autopsies would be carried out in all cases so long as they did not interfere with homicide investigations; and the dying person or his next of kin would be allowed to object to such procedures and give contra instructions, thereby opting out.[150]

A more contemporaneous suggestion has been to design and implement a system wherein persons who object to forced donations of this type could refuse to participate in a manner wholly consistent with individual patient and/or family sensitivities. This is both efficient and cost-effective and also meets the plethora of religious, ethical and legal requirements of informed consent.[151] This suggestion, as engrafted on to the basic approach, is very sensitive and seeks to balance personal attitudes with the demands of a market society. Perhaps, in fact, the suggestion is too broad in its focus and seeks too wide an accommodation of personal interests. In any event, considerable more research must be undertaken in order to test its practical feasibility.[152]

A more expanded version of the compulsory *post mortem* examination and autopsy retrieval approach is seen in escheatage.[153] Although viewed as immoral by some authorities in the United States, as a system promoting recognition of the state's inherent right of ownership in the bodies of all its citizens unless otherwise specified by the citizen or its family,[154] escheatage is being utilized by a number of European countries as a means of combating the shortage of donor organs.[155] In practice, the state simply delegates its ownership rights to licensed physicians who are thereby authorized to harvest and allocate salvageable organs to compatible donees.[156] Here is an example of utilitarianism at its highest order. Yet, the practice has been analogized to both slavery and totalitarianism.[157]

The social policy against escheatage in America is found rather simply in a recognition of the sacredness of the body of life and of death which in turn advances the idea that one's body should not be seen as a form of collective personal property disposable at will by the state upon death. As dead bodies are recognized more and more as valuable sources of life, through the harvesting of their organs for the living, perhaps—with time—a definition of their status as property will of necessity be forced upon all sophisticated societies in the world community.[158] Yet, even in countries where escheatage is in place, there is a natural reluctance among medical personnel to dismember their former patients' bodies, for which they heretofore had worked to sustain life, without an actual consent from the next of kin: this, even though the state, through escheatage, has adopted a policy of presumed consent.[159] This attitude then, together with the high level of emotionalism, rather than rationalism, being exhibited on this issue in the United States, means that it is doubtful whether the system would have a real potential for successful adoption.

MANDATED CHOICE

All competent adults would, under a system employing mandated choice, be required to decide and record whether or not they wished to become organ donors upon their death. This election could be accomplished by asking that their choice be placed on driver license applications, tax returns or official state identifications. Provision for a change of mind would be allowed by written directive at any time.[160] The key factor under this system is that an individual's decision would be taken as binding—and not overridden by subsequent family wishes.[161]

Adopted by the Council on Ethical and Judicial Affairs of the American Medical Association as a mechanism to enhance opportunities for organ donations, this system seeks to return the issue to the putative donor instead of his family.[162] Even though there is provision within the Uniform Anatomical Gift Act which requires the wishes of a decedent be honored, the law is ignored routinely by organ procurement organizations when they seek a consultation with the family before proceeding with the harvesting. And, all too often, the family refuses the transplantation.[163] Ideally, under this scheme, it would be easier—psychologically—for the family to discuss with the prospective donor the anticipated consequences of his act well before the triggering event.[164]

In various surveys of public opinion in the United States on the validity of a mandated choice scheme, 90 percent of those surveyed recorded their support—with 93 percent acknowledging they would honor the wishes of family members to make organ donations if these decisions were made known to them.[165] Interestingly, in Scandinavia since 1996, Swedish mandated choice requires all citizens to choose between donating and not donating; and this law has given rise to an increase in organ donations.[166] Similarly, in France and Austria where presumed consent laws allow the harvesting of a decedent's organs for clinical use unless an "opt-out" decision is made, similar successes to those in Sweden have been recorded.[167]

ADDITIONAL MECHANISMS

Two other mechanisms are also available for consideration: the development of a futures market;[168] and a standard death benefit payment.[169] The two central obstacles to implementation of these mechanisms are present state and federal laws that prohibit the sale or purchase of human organs,[170] and a pervasive reluctance among physicians to seize the initiative at the appropriate moment and make timely inquiries regarding consent to undertake harvesting.[171] In order to resolve this second obstacle, it has been suggested that tort law be re-shaped in such a way as to acknowledge a new standard of care with regard to a patient's body. Accordingly, should physicians fail to determine whether a patient has signified an organ sales contract, to preserve a cadaver for subsequent harvesting, or to inform the proper organ procurement agency of its status, liability would be imposed upon the physicians to the estate of the deceased for the value of his organs.[172] Amending or repealing present legislation would be required to meet the first obstacle.

Under a futures market, an individual would enter into a prospective contingent sale—before death—of his own organs.[173] Proposed as such, a futures market would be only a small modification of the current system of contingent organ donation. Accordingly, individuals could be presented with an opportunity to execute a contract for the sale of their organs when they received a driver's license, bought insurance, answered a specific solicitation for organ donation through the mail or—for that matter—stood on a street corner.[174] Future markets contracts could, thus, be sold and purchased on a secondary market—with the owner of the contract being allowed to sell the organs to those in need of them. Some countries, as seen, presently allow kidneys to be obtained through *inter vivos* sales.[175] The main difference with this proposal from the present system would be that the seller-donor would be promised remuneration—primarily at death. The system would function along the lines of the National Organ Procurement and Transplantation Network, and pertinent donor information, including any limitations imposed on which organs were harvestable, would be fed into a computer and accessed by telephone.[176]

While payment at death for these organs harvested successfully would be the most efficient, two other payment systems would be available: under one, at the time of execution of the organ sales contract, a vendor could be paid a fee for all of his organs made available at death; or, under another scheme, an executory contract could be entered into by both parties—vendor and vendee—specifying that the vendor's estate or designated person would be paid a set fee for the cadaver whether or not upon examination at death the organs were determined harvestable.[177] Of central concern regarding the second scheme—payment at the time of contracting—would be the necessity to develop a monitoring system whereby individual sellers were not able to enter into multiple contracts for the sale of their body parts.[178] It has been suggested that the donor fee could be set at $5000 for each major organ (for example, liver, kidney, heart), with lower amounts for blood, skin, bone marrow, corneas and pituitary glands.[179] If—for example—married male donors could be educated to the fact that the contract for the sale of their organs at death had the effect of being a form of supplemental life insurance policy with a payoff as high as $30 000, it is thought many such men would sign on as donors.[180]

The final economic mechanism for obtaining organs for transplantation has been a standard death benefit payment of $1000.[181] This would be paid by presently operating organ procurement organizations to the families of the organ donors and ideally would not be viewed as coercive in any way—but rather only motivational.[182] The amount and the source of the benefit would be controlled strictly by law, thereby hopefully continuing the prohibition on bartering for organs.[183] Under this proposal, any organ obtained—regardless of whether the donor family accepted the death benefit payment—would enter the national organ allocation system where all donee-recipients are registered and treated alike and where allocations are made, in turn, on matching medical need and period of time waiting.[184]

Of course for this proposal to be adopted without any real or implied complications—as with the future market itself—the illegality of such payments presently set forth in the National Organ Transplant Act and the Uniform Anatomical Gift Act of 1987 would have to be amended to allow administration of this one-time death benefit to a donor family.[185] Since these present laws allow reasonable payments to be made to those who participate in the actual harvesting of the human organs for transplantation (for example, surgeons, hospital staff involved in donor care), it may be asked why a similar reasonable payment should not be allowed to the family members of the donor—who, next to the donor himself, are the most important participants in the process of harvesting and transplantation.[186]

If death benefits (that is, payments to defray funeral costs) were made to relatives agreeing to donate, then incentives would shift clearly from *quid pro quo* to cash. Interestingly, in 2002, the Ethics Committee of the American Society of Transplant Surgeons endorsed a pilot program under which the family of someone who dies could be offered small sums of money—not exceeding several hundred dollars—for agreeing to donate their relative's organs. This money would not be viewed as an exchange of money for cadaver organs, but rather as a reimbursement for funeral expenses or as a charitable contribution.[187] Since, as observed, there is a federal prohibition on the sale of organs, new legislation would have to be passed in order for this program to go forward. Past congressional efforts, which failed, were undertaken in 2001 and 2002 to not only authorize this particular program but authorize tax credits for cadaver donations as well.[188]

CADAVERIC ORGAN MARKETS: FURTHER CONSIDERATIONS

One proposal calls for a system to be created where "agents of for-profit firms offer a market-determined price for either *pre mortem* or *post mortem* agreements to allow firms to collect cadaveric organs for resale to transplant centers."[189] Compensation would, accordingly, be given to those making a *pre mortem* commitment to have their organs harvested at death or, alternatively, to family members when *post mortem* permission is given to remove organs.[190] Some proposals set the payment at $1000 while others at a level of compensation equal to the donor's burial expenses.[191] Compensation and organ markets should not be seen as equivalent options,[192] for there are real distinctions to be drawn between the way in which prices, or compensation, are determined and the various incentives drawn from those prices.[193]

Inasmuch as a free market in cadaveric human organs for transplantation has never been created, it is difficult to draw upon direct evidence to test expectations regarding market performance.[194] Yet, it is nonetheless speculated that the living-donor market would be supplanted by the formation of markets in cadaveric organs and, furthermore, these would yield more lower-cost organs than would be seen with a simple compensation policy.[195] It has been shown repeatedly that, when markets are allowed to function freely, enduring shortages are not recorded.[196]

The market base for obtaining organs becomes even more fragile and volatile when it is realized that the shortage of cadaveric organs is tied to the very suitability of the cadavers themselves. Thus, to be a suitable cadaveric candidate for organ transplantation, the cadaver must have died as a result of either a cerebral hemorrhage or injury to the head and be maintained with respirator and ventilator assistance before its relatively healthy major organs are harvested.[197]

CLINICAL OPTIONS (THE PITTSBURGH PROTOCOL)

Brain-dead patients, termed heart-beating cadaver donors (HBCDs), exhibit no brain function, but their hearts are kept beating in order to maintain perfusion of their vital organs.[198] The *in situ* preservation (or preservative infusion) of fluids is designed to keep the vital organs viable for an adequate period of time—long enough to allow discussion with the family and formal consent for organ donation.[199] At least three states have passed legislation allowing this type of preservation without first obtaining consent from the family of the dead person.[200] These donors are typically victims of automobile accidents or gunshot wounds to the head. Ironically, as the demand for transplantable organs increases, the pool of HBCDs is decreasing as a result of the implementation of strict automobile safety and gun control legislation.[201] As the availability of organs from HBCDs dwindles, physicians—as noted—have begun to look to other groups for the needed organs.

In an attempt to satisfy the growing demand for donor organs, or at least contain the growing crisis, the University of Pittsburgh Medical Center approved a protocol which allows patients who would not otherwise qualify as HBCDs, because they have some brain function, to nevertheless donate their organs if they or their surrogates so choose.[202] These patients, known as non-heart-beating cadaver donors (NHBCDs), are taken off life-support equipment at a predetermined time in an operating room.[203] The donors are declared dead at the "irreversible cessation of cardiopulmonary function," and after two minutes their organs are then immediately harvested.[204]

The protocol is applicable where the prospective donors cannot otherwise qualify as organ donors by the now traditional neurological criteria.

These patients range from those who have full use of their mental faculties, but suffer from various degenerative neurological or cardiopulmonary diseases that leave them respirator dependent, to others who are terminally brain injured, but nevertheless have sufficient neurological function to disqualify them as HBCD candidates.[205] After the patients or their surrogates (who are entrusted to act in the best interest of the patient) make known their desire to forgo further life-sustaining treatment, and that they desire to donate their organs, the attending physician may discuss the possibility of withdrawing treatment within the controlled environment of an operating room.[206] Two minutes after the heart stops beating, the patient is declared dead and the organs are harvested.[207] NHBCD organs acquired in this manner are without perfusion for only a short period of time. Warm ischemia time is greatly reduced, and the available evidence indicates that organs thus obtained are as viable as those from HBCDs.[208]

A fundamental question in determining whether the Pittsburgh protocol may be maintained as an ethical means of increasing the pool of organ donors is whether the patients or their surrogates knowingly submitted to the procedure. Was consent given as part of an informed decision-making process, or was it obtained through coercion or the withholding of necessary information?

The protocol provides numerous measures to ensure patient autonomy.[209] Foremost is that the physician cannot initiate discussion about the removal of life-sustaining equipment.[210] He may only discuss the steps outlined in the protocol after the patient manifests a desire to be free of artificial life support in conjunction with a desire to become an organ donor.[211] Moreover, the protocol provides that decisions involving patient management are to be made prior to and separate from discussion of the procedure.[212]

The protocol mandates full disclosure of all information regarding the decision to forgo artificial life support.[213] The physician must inform all involved parties regarding the procedures for removing life-sustaining therapies and specifically the organ procurement process for non-heart-beating donors, acknowledge that organs will not be harvested until the patient is pronounced dead and—further—advise the concerned patients that consent for the procedure itself may be withdrawn at any time.[214]

Furthermore, the Pittsburgh protocol minimizes the perception that patients may have been coerced in their decision by providing that the physician responsible for the withdrawal of life support cannot be involved in the harvesting or transplant procedure.[215] Similarly, physicians involved with the transplant procedure may not be involved in patient management prior to the death of the donor.[216] Finally, in addition to the conceptual separation of patient management from the transplant procedure, the protocol goes so far as to recommend the physical separation of the treating physician from the transplant team: that the transplant surgeon not be present in the operating room until after the patient is declared dead.[217] The personal interests of the physicians, as well as any institutional bias resulting from a perceived need to maintain a reputation or increase revenue, are thus effectively nullified.

CARDIAC DEATH

In a surprising number of cases, many hospitals have never had the occasion to receive an organ donation from one whose death was declared consistent with cardiopulmonary criteria.[218] Organ donations from this source are nowhere near as widely accepted as those obtained from brain death.[219] New rules issued by OPTN/UNOS in March 2007 are designed to encourage cardiac donations[220] but will surely raise the same level of ethical concern that has been raised over the years when this standard for organ retrieval has been advocated.[221]

The principal concern today, as in the past, with this standard is that potential donors are actually not dead when life-sustaining measures cease. Intervals between withdrawing those measures, pronouncing death and subsequently recovering needed organs are very short. In fact, the time frame can be anywhere from two minutes to five minutes between the onset of sufficient cardiac activity to generate a pulse and the declaration of death.[222] In order to retrieve, for example, a liver or a kidney and pancreas, recovery from a donor must be initiated within a 30- to 60-minute time frame.[223] Accordingly, potential donors are normally brought into the operating theater while technically still "alive" even though life support has been withdrawn.[224] Heparin is subsequently administered—with explicit consent—to maintain organ function and is, in fact, considered to meet the current standard of care for organ recovery.[225] If thrombosis occurs, oxygen to the organ source is threatened, which often means in turn an otherwise successful retrieval is aborted.[226]

Although there is justifiable ethical concern over the propriety of the cardiac death standard for organ retrieval, this concern may be seen as perhaps too sensitive to the immediate and irreversible situation: imminent death. The process of death has begun before the subsequent organ retrieval is initiated. If it were otherwise, then this uneasiness would—indeed—be appropriate. Under present policies and practice, however, any concern regarding a two- to five-minute interval before a declaration of death is made is both misplaced and unreasonable—especially since the benefit of a timely organ retrieval can redound to the benefit of extended life to one or more donees. Simply put, then, the sustaining benefits of prompt organ recovery far outweigh any ethical reservations or "costs" regarding what is viewed by some as an unduly expedited process. To be efficacious, it cannot be otherwise.

ETHICAL, MORAL AND RELIGIOUS CONCERNS

As might be expected, various ethical, moral and religious concerns have been raised to these market mechanisms designed to increase the supply of harvestable organs for purposes of transplantation.[227] Chief and foremost has been the financial vulnerability of the poor to being pressured into becoming "forced" donors—forced as such by their own circumstances and coerced by the enticement of affluent buyers.[228] Other concerns are whether a commercial market would enhance opportunities for suicides and murders[229] and promote harvesting of the organs of anencephalic infants before actual death.[230] Those religious views and traditions that regard the body as a gift of God and man's rights in it as merely those of a steward, with no correlative rights of ownership, would include a prohibition on the sale of body parts and would thus be in direct conflict with these market mechanisms.[231]

These fears of the slippery slope are understandable. Yet, while it is recognized that commercial profit making with non-related donors may have a tendency to promote an exploitation of those who are financially vulnerable, and may lead to progressive abuses and self-degradations, it is argued here that death payments benefits cannot be properly viewed as morally objectionable. This is simply because the verifiable benefits of sustained life that accrue to participating donees of non-commercial organ sales outweigh the moral fears or costs of using this mechanism as an inducement for stimulating the market for transplantable organs.[232]

UTILITARIAN v. EGALITARIAN ALLOCATIVE STANDARDS

The search for rational and principled standards of apportionment of scarce resources is and will remain a vexatious problem for decades to come. Informal "rules of thumb" cannot be countenanced. Of course, one way to avoid totally the problem of distribution is to avoid using the scarce medical resource altogether. But, here, this would mean certain death to the countless thousands of transplant hopefuls.

Both in the formation of the transplantation waiting list and in the actual distribution of donated organs, there is, however, a consensus that the primary criterion operable at both stages should be medical: that is, medical need and probability of success. Intense debate focuses rather upon whether these medical criteria should be defined broadly or narrowly (that is, the relevance of factors such as age, life-style and probability of success measured by a qualitative survival).[233] Rehabilitation or salvageability—consistent with basic principles of *triage*—is also of relevance.[234]

Since the law provides at present no uniformly agreed-upon principles that may be applied in order to regulate the allocation of scarce medical resources (for example, cadaveric and human organs), current medical practice draws upon a structure for decision making evolved as such from a number of philosophical and ethical constructs. There are five utilitarian principles of application that are operative in the hierarchy of *triage*: the principles of medical success, immediate usefulness, conservation, parental role and general social value.[235]

Translated as such into decisional operatives, there emerges a recognition that priority of selection for use of a scarce medical resource should be accorded to those for whom treatment has the highest probability of medical success or would be most useful under the immediate circumstances, to those who require proportionally smaller amounts of a particular resource, to those having the largest responsibilities to dependents or to those believed to have the greater actual or potential general social worth. The utilitarian goal is, simply stated, to achieve the highest possible amount of some good or resource. Thus, utilitarian principles are also commonly referred to as "good maximizing strategies."[236]

Egalitarian alternatives, on the contrary, seek either a basic maintenance or a restoration of equality for persons in need of a particular scarce resource. There are five basic principles utilized here: (1) the principle of saving no one—thus priority is given to no one because, simply, none should be saved if not all can be saved; (2) the principle of medical neediness under which priority is accorded to those determined to be the medically neediest; (3) the principle of general neediness which allows priority to be given to the most helpless or generally neediest; (4) the principle of queuing, where priority is given to those individuals who arrive first; and (5) the principle of random selection, where priority of selection is given to those selected by pure chance.[237]

To the utilitarian, maximizing utility, and hence what is diffusely referred to as the "general welfare," is both the primary ground and subject to all judgments. That which is required in order to maximize utility overall may thus infringe upon an individual's own entitlement of rights to particular goods. Accordingly, moral rights are either rejected generally or recognized as certainly not absolute.[238]

RULES OF EXCLUSION AND FINAL SELECTION

Perhaps utilization of a rule of exclusion might go far to eliminate what may be viewed as the harshness of *triage*. Under such a rule, some individuals would be simply eliminated from "competition" for the particular scarce modality of treatment or care facilities even if the resource(s) were in unlimited supply. Thus, applying this rule, the scarcity of the resource(s) in question would never even be considered.[239]

Rules of exclusion are preferable, in certain definite ways, to rules of final selection when implementing the principles of *triage*. With rules of exclusion, it is generally unnecessary to make comparisons between specific individuals, for either the patient meets the minimum medical criteria or he does not. When operable, these rules have the appearance of greater objectivity and less arbitrariness than a final selection rule that states simply: "First come, first served." If the standard of exclusion is structured in such a manner and at a level high enough to achieve the purpose of initially reducing the applicant group to that specific treatment number, the very selection process will turn on the decision of exclusion and obviate the need to even be forced to apply additional rules of ultimate or final selection.[240] There are, essentially, two approaches to structuring and applying rules of final selection: utilization of a comparative analysis of the social utility of curing various patients in a selection pool, or no comparison but rather application of an arbitrary yet egalitarian formula, normally first come, first served (regardless of whether the first served might be a socially irresponsible derelict).[241]

As observed, medical providers themselves failed in the past to articulate precise rules to guide them in determining patient social utility *vis-à-vis* use of a scarce resource or, for that matter, to structure a list of exceptions to the first-come rule of final selection. These rules of final selection based, it is seen, on value judgments and value judgments alone are not arguably within a special area of competence for a physician to make. Contrariwise, rules of exclusion are based on and, indeed, formulated from professional evaluations and considerations and are regarded as less subjective and arbitrary and more acceptable to patients and doctors alike than the rules of final selection.[242]

No principle of preference is clearly correct, humane or totally just. Other suggestions include selection of a patient user by chance or randomization and queuing,[243] the establishment of separate waiting lists for patients in different age groups and for those with or without families[244] and—perhaps most ideally—widespread support and development of a program calling for the total utilization of artificial organs which would alleviate the scarcity of natural organs.[245] To one degree or other, all of these suggestions are attractive. Obviously no definite solutions can be submitted here. If, however, health care providers seek to pursue their decision-making responsibilities in a rational manner and guided by a spirit of humanism which minimizes human suffering and maximizes the social good of each situation, a humane standard of justice will be achieved. Defining the extent and application of the social good will obviously vary with the situation of each case.[246]

CONCLUSIONS

Thus far, it has been seen that voluntary donations of cadaveric organs have been an ineffective means of tackling the crisis in organ transplantation, and the same is true of the required request provisions of the federal legislation in 1987. Under current federal and state legislative directives, sale of human organs is prohibited. Compulsory *post mortem* examinations and retrievals bear a close resemblance to recognizing a new collective property right by the government, through escheatage, in all the dead bodies of its citizens. Strong anti-government sentiments against intrusiveness into issues of privacy and autonomy—when combined with equally strong moral, religious and ethical attitudes about the sacredness of the body—will preclude these two mechanisms from ever being adopted successfully in America.

The development of a futures market, although fraught with two major obstacles as observed, nonetheless bears further study and testing. Perhaps the most attractive of all the suggested mechanisms is the standard death benefit—this, simply because of its non-commercial focus. But—as with the futures market option—present laws in the United States would surely have to be rewritten or amended regarding present prohibitions against the sale of organs to make certain such one-time death payments would be allowed. As well, harvesting physicians will have to be educated to the needs allowed and, furthermore, educated to the needs (or legal "rights") of their living patients to "prosper" from dead ones. Education on a massive scale in both public and private sectors is called for here.

There are mixed indications that the goal of educating the public on the market realities for organ and tissue transplantation is being achieved. A public opinion survey commissioned by the Coalition for Donation in 2005 found that nine out of ten Americans support organ and tissue donation, but only 34 percent are informed sufficiently of the steps which must be taken in order to effect a *pre mortem* donation.[247] Only 10 percent of those surveyed were actually opposed to or reluctant about making a donation, 56 percent indicated a willingness to donate their own organs and tissue, 28 percent remained undecided and 6 percent expressed an interest in donating only certain specific organs and tissues.[248] An earlier survey done in 1996 revealed the preferences for organ assignment: first come, first served; merit; lottery; and auction.[249] Educating the public will be an involved and protracted undertaking. As seen, a positive first step was taken by Congress when it enacted the Organ Donation and Recovery Improvement Act of 2004 and allocated significant funds for achieving this task.[250]

Instead of trying to develop new and innovative approaches to organ retrieval, it has been suggested that more emphasis be placed on promoting voluntary, altruistic donations and ensuring the access to transplants is fair and the process for assisting transplant recipients to pay for their new organs is equitable. Indeed, the suggestion is even carried further, urging public funding of transplants for the poor as well as establishing specific reimbursements policies for not only the costs of pre-transplant evaluation, food, baby-sitters, travel and housing for prospective patients but all economic assistance for those who are unable to work post-transplant.[251]

These are noble sentiments and set a broadly defined philosophical goal to total equality of opportunity. Yet these concerns are but one facet of the most central problem here: namely, developing a reliable (market) mechanism for assuring a ready supply of cadaveric organs for ready trans-plantation. Once this mechanism is set, remedial problems can be tackled. Some type of informed consensus must soon be reached in any event that develops a new mechanism for retrieving organs if, that is, the preservation of human life is to be advanced and not paralysed by social taboos. Stated otherwise, "If human lives are to be saved, the agony of hard choices cannot be avoided."[252] In the final analysis, then, a price—economic, social, legal, ethical, moral or religious—*must* be set in determining the allocative process for organ retrieval and transplantation. Market mechanisms would appear to be the most functional and objective tool for achieving this. Forced altru-ism, nurtured as such through the pursuit of lofty educational goals, does not have a practical history for dealing with the problems of this generation.

Although issues of commodification continue to haunt—directly or indirectly—all frameworks of analysis for organ and tissue transplanta-tion, the overriding issue must properly be seen as mapping the contours of permissible market activity and, thus, directly resolving the issue of whether human tissue sources or their survivors should be eligible for compensation.[253] Whether a more vigorous form of national control over the human tissue market develops will depend—ultimately—on reaching a clear resolution of the "political and legal views of the body, so that its treatment . . . will be consistent with political and legal views concerning personal autonomy and the appropriate respect to be paid to our bodies, whether living or dead."[254]

The newly revised Uniform Anatomical Gift Act is a progressive initiative designed to facilitate organ donations. Whether the states view this as the mechanism to achieve this goal is yet to be established.[255] Even if this Act is adopted widely, there still remains—as seen—a fundamental concern: namely, the need to decide who captures the value of human tissue rather than perhaps whether the tissue be sold in the first place.[256]

Much as in Shaw's *Doctor's Dilemma*, then, contemporary society must decide whether it wishes to resolve its own present transplantation dilemma by realizing a type of market mechanism in some form is necessary in order to save human lives or whether it wishes to continue playing an emotionally charged *charade* where hard economic realities are ignored in favor of comporting with perceived levels of "decency" which forbid the body to be recognized as a commodity. Perhaps the book of Deuteronomy provides a useful modern day policy—if not a construct—to embrace when it acknowledges, "I have set before you life and death, blessing and curse; therefore choose life, that you and your descendants may live."[257]

NOTES

1. See M. Meisel (1984), *Shaw and the Nineteenth Century Theatre*, p. 233; http://endeavor.med.nyu.edu/lit-med/lit-med-db/webdocs/webdescrips/shaw1595-des-.html (accessed 1 June 2006).
2. United Network for Organ Sharing, www.unos.org, (accessed 3 December 2007). On 15 November 2004, 87 310 Americans were candidates for an organ transplant. S. Calandrillo (2004), "Cash for kidneys? Utilizing incentives to end America's organ shortage," *George Mason Law Review*, **13**, pp. 69, 84, n. 69.
3. Organ Procurement and Transplantation Network, U.S. Department of Health and Human Services, www.unos.org/search.asp?site Search 2 = emergency (accessed 3 December 2007).
   In 2006, 28 293 individuals received a life saving organ transplant from 6732 living donors and 8024 from deceased donors.
4. D.L. Kaserman and A.H. Barnett (2002), *The U.S. Organ Procurement System: A Prescription for Reform*. See G. Daubert (1998), "Politics, policies and problems with organ transplantation," *Administrative Law Review*, **50**, p. 459.
5. Kaserman and Barnett, *U.S. Organ Procurement System*, Ch. 8. See H. Hansmann (1989), "The economics and ethics of markets for human organs," *Journal of Health Politics, Policy and Law*, **14**, p. 57.
6. L. Altman (2004), "The ultimate gift: 50 years of organ transplants," *New York Times*, 21 Dec., p. D6.
7. A. Atala, S. Bauer, S. Soker, J. Yoo and A. Retik (2006), "Tissue-engineered autologous bladders for patients needing cystoplasty," *Lancet*, **361**, 15–21 Apr., p. 1241.
8. Altman, "Ultimate gift." See J. Bryan and J. Clare (2001), *Organ Farm*.
9. Kaserman and Barnett, *U.S. Organ Procurement System*, p. 128.
10. Ibid., Ch. 8. See V. Perlman (2005), "The place of altruism in a raging sea of market commerce," *Journal of Law, Medicine and Ethics*, **33**, p. 163; E. Murray (1991),

"Morally obligated to make gifts of our bodies?," *Health Matrix*, **1**, p. 19. See generally M. Leachman (2004), Comment, "Regulation of the human tissue industry: a call for fast-track regulation," *Louisiana Law Review*, 65, p. 443; R. Williams (1997), "The regulation of human tissue in the United States: a regulatory and legislative analysis," *Food and Drug Law Journal*, **52**, p. 409.

11. R. Rhodes (2002), "Justice in transplant organ allocation," in R. Rhodes, M.R. Battin and A. Silvers (eds.), *Medicine and Social Justice*, Ch. 27. See also B.R. Furrow, T.L. Greaney, S.H. Johnson, T.S. Jost and R.L. Schwartz (eds.) (2004), *Bioethics: Health Care Law and Ethics*, 5th edn., Ch. 6.

12. S.J. Younger, M.W. Anderson and R. Schapiro (eds.) (2004), *Transplanting Human Tissue: Ethics, Policy and Practice*, p. 22.

13. Ibid.

14. Ibid., p. 121.

15. Ibid.

16. Ibid., p. 122.

17. Ibid.

18. Ibid., p. 123.

19. Ibid.

20. Ibid.

21. Ibid., p. 23.

22. Ibid.

23. Ibid., p. 24.

24. Ibid.

25. 42 C.F.R. §121.8 (2002).

26. Ibid.

27. Ibid.

28. Rhodes, "Justice in transplant organ allocation."

29. Ibid., p. 351.

30. Ibid.

31. Younger et al., *Transplanting Human Tissue*, Ch. 2.

32. Ibid.

33. Ibid. See R.F. Weir (ed.) (1998), *Stored Tissue Samples: Ethical, Legal and Public Policy Implications*, pp. 305, *passim*.

34. Younger et al., *Transplanting Human Tissue*.

35. Ibid., p. 16.

36. Ibid.

37. Ibid., p. 17. See L. Humphries (2005), "Decreasing latitude and increasing regulation in transplantable tissue programs," *AORN Journal*, **82**, p. 806.

38. Kaserman and Barnett, *U.S. Organ Procurement System*, Ch. 5. These regulations were limited to only certain tissues including skin, eyes, bones, tendons and ligaments or musculosketal tissues. See Interim Rule, *Federal Register*, **58**, 14 Dec. 1993, pp. 65514–21; Final Rule, *Federal Register*, **62**, 29 July 1997, p. 40429, codified at 21 C.F.R. Parts 16, 1270.

39. 21 C.F.R. Parts 1270, 1271.

40. These products include skin, eyes, musculosketal tissue, eggs and sperm, veins, blood stem cells, the membrane covering the brain, or dura matter, and more. The Center for Biologics Evaluation and Research (CBER) regulates HCT/Ps under 21 C.F.R. Part 1270. See also Humphries, "Decreasing latitude."

41. See 21 C.F.R. Parts 1270, 1271.

42. Ibid.

43. Ibid.

44. See http://www.jcrinc.com/subscribers/perspectives.asp?durki=9160&site=10&return =6065 (accessed 1 June 2006).

45. See Linda Bren (2005), "Keeping human tissue transplants safe," *FDA Consumer Magazine*, May–June, http://www.fda.gov/fdac/features/2005/305-tissue.html (accessed 1 June 2006).

46. Altman, "Ultimate gift."
47. "Organ transplants reached record in "04," *Washington Post*, 30 Mar. 2005, p. A6.
48. Ibid.
49. Ibid.
50. Ibid.
51. Altman, "Ultimate gift." But see S. Vedantam (2003), "U.S. citizens get more organs than they give: donations from foreign residents on the rise," *Washington Post*, 3 Mar., p. A3.
52. R. Pear (2003), "F.D.A. delays regulation of tissue transplants," *New York Times*, 14 May, p. A18.
53. L.R. Kass (2002), *Life, Liberty and the Defense of Dignity: The Challenge for Bioethics*, p. 177. See also Calandrillo, "Cash for kidneys?," pp. 99, *passim*; Moore v. Regents of the University of California, 793 P.2d 479 (Ca. 1990), *cert. denied*, 111 S. Ct. 1388 (1991).
54. R. Stein (2005), "Search for transplant organs becomes a web free-for-all," *Washington Post*, 23 Sept., p. A1. MatchingDonors.com and LinksForLifeCampaign.com are two online services designed to assist in meeting this goal. MatchingDonors charges $595 for unlimited access or $295 a month.
55. S. Okie (2002), "Surgeons back study of payment for organs," *Washington Post*, 30 Apr., p. A3.
56. Kass, *Life, Liberty*, p. 119.
57. Ibid. The average amount received for a kidney is $1,070. See M. Goyal, R. Metha, L. Schneiderman and A. Sefigal (2002), "Economic and health consequences of selling a kidney in India," *Journal of the American Medical Association*, **288**, p. 159; C. Davies (1991), "Live donation of human body parts: a case for negotiability," *Medico-Legal Journal*, **59**, p. 100.
58. S. Boseley (2006), "UK transplant patients go to China for organs from executed prisoners," *Guardian*, 20 Apr., p. 4 (reporting on the open advertising on Chinese transplant center websites touting the availability of Chinese organs). See C. Chan (2006), "Organ harvesting for profit in China confirmed," *Epoch Times*, 10–16 July, p. 1.
59. Calandrillo, "Cash for kidneys?," pp. 99, *passim*. See "Organ transplants: your part or mine?," *Economist*, 16 Nov. 2006, p. 60 (reporting on the success of a non-governmental organization, the Iran Association of Kidney Patients, operating—within the law—to compensate all kidney donors $1,200 and how allowances for extra compensation by patients, typically anywhere from $3,000 to $4,000, are allowed as an additional incentive for potential donors).
60. E. Friedman and A. Friedman (2006), "Payment for Donor Kidneys: Pro and Con," *Kidney International*, **69**, p. 960. (The authors propose legalizing payment of a fair market price of about $40 000 to kidney donors.)
61. Boseley, "UK transplant patients go to China." See S. Lister (2006), "Let people sell their kidneys for transplant, say doctors," *Times Online*, 17 Feb., http://www.timesonline.co.uk/article/0,,8122-2042307,00.html.
62. Kass, *Life, Liberty*, p. 180.
63. Ibid.
64. See T. Shannon (2001), "The kindness of strangers: organ transplantation in a capitalist age," *Kennedy Institute of Ethics Journal*, **11**, p. 285 (analysing the historical debate over the transplantation issue and finding a justification of its use within a Roman Catholic and cultural framework); Perlman, "Place of altruism."
65. Kass, *Life, Liberty*, p. 187.
66. R. Scott (1981), *The Body as Property*.
67. Kass, *Life, Liberty*, pp. 188–96.
68. Ibid., p. 197.
69. Scott, *Body as Property*, pp. 6, 7.
70. P. Skegg (1975), "Human corpses, medical specimens and the law of property," *Anglo-American Law Review*, **4**, p. 412.
71. Scott, *Body as Property*, pp. 6, 7.

72. Ibid., p. 11.
73. Ibid., p. 8.
74. Ibid., pp. 11, 12. See D. Maguire (1994), "Common law categories and the ownership of human tissue," *Colorado Lawyer*, **23**, p. 2337.
75. M. Powell and D. Segal (2006), "In New York, a grisly traffic in body parts," *Washington Post*, 28 Jan., p. A3. Bone, tendons, skin, bone marrow, heart valves and saphenous valves are taken routinely.
76. Ibid. See also Zeidner (2003), "Some body is with me," *Washington Post*, 21 Jan., p. F1.
77. 8A Unif. Laws Ann. §§1–9 (2003); H. Greeley (2006), "Some thoughts on academic health law," *Wake Forest Law Review*, **41**, pp. 391, 409, n. 36.
78. See note 75.
79. E. Stason (1968), "The Uniform Anatomical Gift Act," *Business Lawyer*, **23**, pp. 919, 928.
80. G. Calabresi (1991), "Do we own our babies?," *Health Matrix*, **1**, p. 5.
81. Ibid.
82. Ibid.
83. Delaware, Hawaii, Oklahoma, Nevada and New York. L. Cohen (1989), "Increasing the supply of transplant organs: the virtues of a futures market," *George Washington Law Review*, **58**, pp. 1, 7. In all, some 25 body parts and fluids have been transplanted from cadavers to humans including parts of the inner ear, various glands, nerves, tendons, cartilage, etc.
84. H. Hansman (1989), "The economics and ethics of markets for human organs," *Journal of Health, Politics, Policy and Law*, **14**, p. 57.
85. Ibid., p. 59.
86. Mississippi still allows its citizens the right to sell their body parts to hospitals—with delivery to be effectuated after death. Miss. Code Ann. §41-39-9 (1999).
87. Cohen, "Increasing the supply," p. 8.
88. M. Mehlman (1991), "Presumed consent to organ donation: a re-evaluation," *Health Matrix*, **1**, pp. 31, 33. See E. Teagarden (2005), "Human trafficking: legal issues in presumed consent laws," *North Carolina Journal of International Law and Commercial Regulation*, **30**, p. 685.
89. Mehlman, "Presumed consent," p. 23.
90. Ibid.
91. 42 U.S.C. §§273–274(c) (2000).
92. Ibid. See §273, note, §274(b)(2). Violation of the Act carries with it a fine of $50 000 or a five-year jail sentence or both. See §274(b)(2). The sale of blood, as a bodily substance, has had a ready market by hospitals and commercial blood banks for years. In 1956, 42 percent of the blood collected in New York City came from paid donors—with the New York City Memorial Hospital obtaining 60 to 70 percent of its blood from commercial sources. J. Dukeminier (1970), "Supplying organs for transplantation," *Michigan Law Review*, **68**, pp. 811, 847. Its commercial acquisition has been allowed traditionally because of the mild invasive nature by which it is obtained, the lack of risk to the donor (unlike that involved in organ donation) and its replenishable nature. Interestingly, under the National Institutes of Health Revitalization Act of 1993, it is also a criminal offense for any person to solicit or otherwise acquire human fetal tissue (from abortion or other forms of personal donation) for purposes of transplantation. 42 U.S.C. §289(g)(2) (2001).
93. Hansman, "Economics and ethics of markets," p. 59. Doubt has been expressed that intra-state sales would escape federal scrutiny. Cohen, "Increasing the supply," p. 8.
94. R. Scott (1988), "Death unto life: anencephalic infants as organ donors," *Virginia Law Review*, **74**, p. 1527.
95. 42 U.S.C. §§273–274(c) (2000).
96. 42 U.S.C. §§1320(b)-8(a)(1)(A), 1302(b)-8(a)(1)(A)(ii) (2000).
97. A. Caplan and P. Welvang (1989), "Are required request laws working? Altruism and the procurement of organs and tissues," *Clinical Transplantation*, 3, p. 170; T. Colburn (1995), "Organ donations hinge on survivor's consent," *Washington Post Health*, 4 July, p. 7.

98.   Caplan and Welvang, "Are required request laws working?," p. 174.
99.   Ibid.
100. Ibid.
101. Cohen, "Increasing the supply," p. 22.
102. Ibid.
103. See 21 C.F.R. Parts 1270, 1271.
104. Cohen, "Increasing the supply," p. 21.
105. A. Caplan (1991), "Assume nothing: the current state of cadaver organs and tissue donation in the United States," *Journal of Transplantation Coordination*, **1**, p. 78.
106. J. Katz (2006), "The re-gift of life: can charity law prevent for-profit firms from exploiting donated tissue, and non-profit tissue banks?," *DePaul Law Review*, **55**, pp. 943, 944, 946.
107. Ibid.
108. Ibid., p. 946.
109. Ibid., p. 947.
110. Ibid.
111. Ibid.
112. Ibid., p. 950.
113. Ibid.
114. Ibid.
115. Ibid.
116. 42 U.S.C.A. §273 (West Supp. 2006).
117. P. Carlson (2006), "The 2004 Organ Donation Recovery and Improvement Act: how Congress missed an opportunity to say "yes" to financial incentives for organ donation," *Journal of Contemporary Health Law and Policy*, **23**, p. 136.
118. 8A Unif. Laws Ann. 3 (Supp. 2006).
119. Ibid., §§3, 4.
120. Ibid.
121. Ibid., §§5, 9.
122. Ibid., §20.
123. Ibid., §6.
124. Ibid., §9.
125. Ibid., §§14, 21.
126. Ibid., §21.
127. Ibid., §§22, 23. See R. Stein (2007), "States revising organ law," *Washington Post*, 4 Apr., p. A1 (reporting four states have already adopted the Act, another four have approved it for governmental signature, and some 17 other states are reviewing it).
128. Scott, *Body as Property*, Ch. 5; W. Wadlington, J. Waltz and R. Dworkin (1980), *Cases and Materials on Law and Medicine*, pp. 945–62; Davies, "Live donation."
129. Scott, *Body as Property*, p. 121.
130. See Little v. Little, 574 S. W.2d 493 (Ct. App. Tex. 1979); McFall v. Shimp (No. 78-17711, Equity), C.P. Allegheny County, Pa., 26 July 1978; Strunk v. Strunk, 445 S.W.2d 145 (Ky. 1969).
131. Scott, *Body as Property*, pp. 116–20.
132. J. Robertson (1976), "Organ donations by incompetents and the substituted judgment doctrine," *Columbus Law Review*, **76**, p. 48.
133. Ibid., p. 71.
134. Ibid., p. 51.
135. Scott, *Body as Property*, pp. 120–22.
136. Ibid., p. 122. Interestingly, a father whose daughter is in need of a kidney may donate one of his kidneys—with no societal or legal retribution. Yet, if the daughter were in dire medical circumstances and in need of immediate surgery for which the father was unable to pay, by law he would be penalized and considered a criminal if he sought to sell one of his kidneys in order to defray the costs of his daughter's illness. See M. Kinsley (1989), "Take my kidney, please," *Time*, 13 Mar., p. 88.

137. Scott, *Body as Property*, p. 137.
138. Ibid., p. 183.
139. Ibid.
140. Ibid., p. 184.
141. Dukeminier, "Supplying organs," pp. 857–63.
142. See note 132, p. 50.
143. Ibid., pp. 50–51.
144. M. Morley (2003), "Increasing the supply of organs for transplantation through paired organ exchanges," Y*ale Law and Policy Review*, **21**, p. 221. See also Calandrillo, "Cash for kidneys?," pp. 75–6.
145. See note 144.
146. See http://abcnews.go.com/Health/print?id=548098 (accessed 20 June 2006). The statistical profile changes regularly. Current statistics may be referenced at http://www.organ-donation-research.info/organ-donations-statistics.html and scrolled to the organ donation statistics website. Another source is to be found at OPTN, the Organ Procurement and Transplant Network, http://www.optn.org/about/ and at UNOS, Data, at http://www.unos.org.
147. See notes 144–6.
148. Mehlman, "Presumed consent," p. 31.
149. D. Sanders and J. Dukeminier (1968), "A proposal for routine salvaging of cadaver organs," *New England Journal of Medicine*, **279**, p. 413.
150. Dukeminier, "Supplying organs," pp. 842, *passim*.
151. Mehlman, "Presumed consent," pp. 44–62, 66.
152. Ibid., p. 66.
153. Cohen, "Increasing the supply," pp. 15–21.
154. Ibid. The National Organ Transplant Task Force, in particular, inveighed against the immorality of the system.
155. K. Norrie (1985), "Human tissue transplants: legal liability in different jurisdictions," *International and Comparative Law Quarterly*, **34**, pp. 442, 460–61. The countries subscribing to escheatage in 1985 were: Austria, the then Czechoslovakia, Denmark, Finland, Greece, Hungary, Italy, Norway, Poland, Spain, Sweden, Switzerland and the then West Germany. Ibid., pp. 460–65. See T. Hoffman (2000), "Organ donors laws in the U.S. and United Kingdom," *Indiana International and Comparative Law Review*, **10**, p. 339. D. Price (2005), "The Human Tissue Act," *Modern Law Review*, **68**, p. 798; S. Ransom (2006), "Reforming the Human Tissue Acts," *Journal of Law and Medicine*, **14**, p. 167. In July 2007 the Chief Medical Officer of the UK urged the government to move to a system of presumed consent for organ donation, termed opt-out, and thereby reverse—hopefully—one of the lowest donation rates in Europe. N. Hawkes (2007), "Everyone must be an organ donor unless they opt out, says Chief Medical Officer," *Times Online*, 18 July, http://www.timesonline.co.uk/to/ life_and_style/health/article2093608.ece.
156. Cohen, "Increasing the supply," p. 15. In 1992 the District of Columbia Council passed a law allowing a medical examiner to authorize open-heart surgery for the removal of heart valves from corpses without seeking permission from their families. Additionally, some 14 states (together with the District of Columbia) allow removal of corneas from autopsied corpses without previous familial consent. S. Squires (1993), "Transplant tug-of-war: D.C. officials object to law allowing heart-valve removal from corpses," *Washington Post Health*, 23 Nov., p. 7.
157. Cohen, "Increasing the supply," p. 16.
158. Ibid., p. 17.
159. L. Cohen (1991), "The ethical value of a future market in cadaveric organs," in W. Land and J.B. Dossetor (eds.), *Organ Replacement Therapy: Ethics, Justice and Commerce*, p. 302.
160. A. Spital (1996), "Mandated choice for organ donation: time to give it a try," *Annals of International Medicine*, **125**, p. 66.
161. Ibid.
162. Ibid.

163. Ibid. See E. Naylor (1989), "The role of the family in cadaveric organs procurement," *Indiana Law Journal*, **65**, p. 167.
164. See note 160. Interestingly, depending upon the region in the United States, between 40 and 60 percent of all families contacted refused to donate the organs of a relative who had died. Okie, "Surgeons back study."
165. J. McArdle (1998), "Xenotransplantation: an opportunity to promote alternatives," *Anti-Vivisection Society Magazine*, Fall, pp. 6–9. See http://www.crt-online.org/organ.html (accessed 30 June 2006).
166. Ibid.
167. Ibid. See generally S. Statz (2006), "Finding the winning combination: how blending organ procurement systems used internationally can reduce the organ shortage," *Vanderbilt Journal of Transnational Law*, **39**, p. 1677; Ransom, "Reforming the Human Tissue Acts."
168. Cohen, "Increasing the supply," p. 1; Hansman, "Economics and ethics of markets."
169. T. Peters (1991), "Life or death: the issue of payment in cadaveric organ donation," *Journal of the American Medical Association*, **265**, p. 1302; J. Harvey (1990), "Paying organ donors," *Journal of Medical Ethics*, **16**, p. 117. Another alternative to direct compensation for organs would be a promise of free medical care and assistance given to the organ donor for either a period of years or life for any or all subsequent diseases or disabilities arising from the removal of an organ. Dukeminier, "Supplying organs," p. 848.
170. Hansman, "Economics and ethics of markets," p. 59.
171. Cohen, "Ethical value of a future market," pp. 308–309.
172. Ibid.
173. Cohen, "Increasing the supply," pp. 32–3. Presently, Brazil, China and India tolerate markets in body parts. See notes 58, 97.
174. Cohen, "Increasing the supply," p. 33.
175. See Calandrillo, "Cash for kidneys?," pp. 86–91; Goyal et al., "Economic and health consequences." But see, D. Joralemon and P. Cox (2003), "Body values: the case against compensating for transplant organs," *Hastings Center Report*, **33**, p. 27.
176. Cohen, "Increasing the supply," p. 33.
177. Ibid.
178. Ibid.
179. Ibid., p. 35.
180. Ibid.
181. Peters, "Life or death."
182. Ibid.
183. Ibid., p. 1304.
184. Ibid., p. 1303.
185. Ibid., p. 1304.
186. Ibid.
187. Okie, "Surgeons back study."
188. Joralemon and Cox, "Body values."
189. Kaserman and Barnett, *U.S. Organ Procurement System*, p. 123.
190. Ibid., p. 125.
191. Ibid.
192. Ibid., p. 160. See generally E. Thorne (1998), "When private parts are made public goods: the economics of market-inalienability," *Yale Journal on Regulation*, **15**, p. 149.
193. Kaserman and Barnett, *U.S. Organ Procurement System*, p. 124.
194. Ibid., p. 132.
195. Ibid., p. 126.
196. Ibid., p. 122.
197. Cohen, "Increasing the supply."
198. R. Arnold and S. Younger (1993), "Back to the future: obtaining organs from non-heart-beating cadavers," *Kennedy Institute of Ethics Journal*, **3**, p. 103.
199. See generally A. Caplan (1993), "The tell-tale heart: public policy and the utilization of non-heart-beating donors," *Kennedy Institute of Ethics Journal*, **3**, p. 251.

200. See Fla. Stats. §765.517 (2002); Va. State Code §32.1-295 (2002); D.C. CODE §7-1521.10a (2002).
201. D. Colburn (1993), "Changing the life-and-death rules for transplants," *Washington Post Health*, 15 June, p. 10.
202. University of Pittsburgh Medical Center Policy and Procedure Manual, reprinted in *Kennedy Institute of Ethics Journal*, **3**, (1993), App. A-1. In 1995, three years after the protocol was first approved, it was revised. Most institutions having NHBCD protocols have a version of the Pittsburgh model. See G. Van Norman (2003), "Another matter of life and death: what every anesthesiologist should know about the ethical, legal, and policy implications of the non-heart-beating cadaver organ donor," *Anesthesiology*, **98**, Mar., p. 763.
203. See note 202.
204. Ibid. The crisis in the organ transplantation market has prompted liberalizing definitions of death and the procedures for its determination—this, in an effort to prompt more efficient organ harvests. While the common law standard for death was the absence of spontaneous respiratory and cardiac functions, the Uniform Determination of Death Act extended the legal definition of death to include the cessation of brain function when a patient is maintained on artificial life support. Thirty-three states, the District of Columbia and the Virgin Islands have enacted this Act. 12A Unif. Laws Ann. 83 (Supp. 2006). See T. Engelhardt (1999), "Redefining death: the mirage of consensus," in S.J. Younger, R.M. Arnold and R. Schapiro (eds.), *The Definition of Death: Contemporary Controversies*, Ch. 19.
205. S. Younger and R. Arnold (1993), "Ethical, psychological and public policy implications of procuring organs from non-heart-beating cadaver donors," *Journal of the American Medical Association*, **269**, 2 June, pp. 2769, 2772.
206. M. DeVitta and J. Snyder (1993), "Development of the University of Pittsburgh Medical Center policy for the care of terminally ill patients who may become organ donors after death following the removal of life support," *Kennedy Institute of Ethics Journal*, **3**, p. 131.
207. Ibid., p. 132.
208. Younger and Arnold, "Ethical, psychological and public policy implications," p. 2770.
209. DeVitta and Snyder, "Development of the University of Pittsburgh Medical Center Policy."
210. Ibid.
211. Ibid.
212. Ibid.
213. See note 202.
214. Ibid.
215. See generally J. Burdick (1993), "Potential conflicts of interest generated by the use of non-heart-beating cadavers," *Kennedy Institute of Ethics Journal*, **3**, p. 199.
216. Ibid.
217. Ibid.
218. R. Steinbrook (2007), "Organ donation after cardiac death," *New England Journal of Medicine*, **357**, 19 July, p. 209.
219. Ibid.
220. Ibid., p. 210.
221. See J. Bernat, A. D'Alessandro F. Poit et al. (2006), "Report of a national conference on donation after cardiac death," *American Journal of Transplantation*, **6**, p. 281.
222. Steinbrook, "Organ donation," p. 210.
223. Ibid.
224. Ibid., p. 211.
225. Ibid.
226. Ibid.
227. J. Childress (1987), "Some moral connections between organ procurement and organ distribution," *Journal of Contemporary Health Law and Policy*, **3**, p. 85.
228. Harvey, "Paying organ donors," p. 117. Moralisms (or assimilated moral and political rights) often act in a way to prohibit organ selling. M. Radin (1987), "Market-inalienability," *Harvard Law Review*, **100**, p. 1864. Even though strong moral objections

combined with notions of self-paternalism and true paternalism may make it inefficient to sell organs and thus classify them as inalienable entitlements, this does not mean compensation to the holder of the entitlement will be denied if this entitlement is taken from him. Thus, although society forbids the sale of organs (for example, kidneys, lungs), it will still generally compensate the individual whose kidney or lung is destroyed in an automobile accident. G. Calabresi and Melamed (1972), "Property rules, liability rules and inalienability: one view of the cathedral," *Harvard Law Review*, **85**, pp. 1089, n. 4, 1112–15.

229. Cohen, "Increasing the supply," pp. 40–43.
230. Scott, *Body as Property*. See generally E. Gelfand and J. Lewis (1993), "Fetal Tissue Research: Legal Regulation of Human Fetal Transplantation," *Washington and Lee Law Review*, **50**, p. 647.
231. A. Caplan (1991), "Commentary on Cohen," *Clinical Transplantation*, **5**, pp. 467, 472. See W. Stempsey (2006), "Religion, philosophy and the commodification of human body parts," *DePaul Law Review*, **55**, p. 875.
232. Harvey, "Paying organ donors," p. 118. Some fear the slippery slope of commercializing organ sales will lead to personal discomfort, insult, degradation or loss of value because bodily integrity will have become a fungible object. Radin, "Market-inalienability," p. 1881. Others are more positivistic and view the slope as leading to a totally free market economy where everything scarce and desired is ownable and saleable (or commodified). R. Posner (1997), *Economic Analysis of Law*, pp. 29–33. For another view, see also G. Calabresi and P. Bobbitt (1978), *Tragic Choices*.
233. G.P. Smith, II (1989), *The New Biology: Law, Ethics and Biotechnology*.
234. G.P. Smith II (1985), "Triage, endgame realities," *Journal of Contemporary Health Law and Policy*, **1**, p. 23. The principle of medical success (or probability of sustaining life) is the standard approach in military or disaster (*triage*) medicine. G. Winslow (1982), *Triage and Justice*, pp. 69 ,140. Modernly, it is maintained *triage* is an empty principle because the most seriously wounded are rushed in and the merely mutilated must wait. A.R. Jonsen (1990), *The New Medicine and the Old Ethic*, p. 45.
235. See note 234. The three pivotal values that come into focus in any decisional process involving tragic choices are efficiency, honesty and equal treatment—with most societies giving precedence to the conception of equality. Calabresi and Bobbitt, *Tragic Choices*, pp. 24–5.
236. Smith, *New Biology*. See E. Pellegrino (1986), "Rationing health care: the ethics of gatekeeping," *Journal of Contemporary Health Law and Policy*, **2**, p. 23.
237. Smith, *New Biology*, Ch. 5.
238. Ibid.
239. Ibid., pp. 111, 112; Winslow, *Triage and Justice*, pp. 106, 165.
240. See note 239.
241. Ibid. See also Winslow, *Triage and Justice*, pp. 161–5 for a decision matrix for *triage* principles.
242. See note 241.
243. J. Childress (1983), "Triage in neonatal intensive care: the limitations of a metaphor," *Virginia Law Review*, **69**, p. 547.
244. Winslow, *Triage and Justice*, pp. 11–23.
245. S. Freud (1976), "Organ transplants: ethical and legal problems," in S. Gorowitz, A. Jameton, R. Macklin, J. O'Connor, E. Perrin, B. St. Clair and S. Sherwin (eds), *Moral Problems in Medicine*, p. 44.
246. G.P. Smith, II (1989), "All's well that ends well: toward a policy of assisted rational suicide or merely enlightened self-determination?," *UC Davis Law Review*, **22**, p. 275.
247. This survey was of a population of 4500 citizens from throughout the United States. See http://www.ordonorprogram.org/news_events/press_release/NotSurveyResult.html (accessed 30 June 2006).
248. Ibid.
249. See http://poll.orspub.com/export.php?format=html&email=&action=Download+the+files (accessed 30 June 2006).

250. 42 U.S.C.A. §273 (West Supp. 2006).
251. See Caplan, "Commentary on Cohen"; Joralemon & Cox, "Body values."
252. Dukeminier, "Supplying Organs".
253. J. Mahoney (2000), "The market for human tissues," *Virginia Law Review*, **86**, p. 163. See also Calandrillo, "Cash for kidneys?," pp. 98–9.
254. Younger et al., *Transplanting Human Tissue*, p. 115.
255. See Stein, "States revising organ law."
256. See Katz, "Re-gift of life," p. 950.
257. Deuteronomy 30:10.

Index

20

L2
416